Microsoft® Office Excel® 2007

ILLUSTRATED COURSE GUIDE

INTERMEDIATE

Lynn Wermers

COURSE TECHNOLOGY
CENGAGE Learning

Australia • Brazil • Japan • Korea • Mexico • Singapore • Spain • United Kingdom • United States

COURSE TECHNOLOGY
CENGAGE Learning™

Illustrated Course Guide: Microsoft® Office Excel® 2007 Intermediate
Lynn Wermers

Senior Acquisitions Editor: Marjorie Hunt

Senior Product Manager: Christina Kling Garrett

Associate Product Manager: Rebecca Padrick

Editorial Assistant: Michelle Camisa

Marketing Coordinator: Jennifer Hankin

Developmental Editor: Barbara Clemens

Content Project Manager: Daphne Barbas

Copy Editor: Gary Michael Spahl

QA Manuscript Reviewers: Nicole Ashton,
    Jeff Schwartz, John Freitas, Susan Whalen

Cover Designer: Marissa Falco

Cover Artist: Mark Hunt

Composition: GEX Publishing Services

For product information and technology assistance, contact us at
Cengage Learning Customer & Sales Support, 1-800-354-9706
For permission to use material from this text or product, submit all requests online at **www.cengage.com/permissions**
Further permissions questions can be emailed to
permissionrequest@cengage.com

ISBN-13: 978-1-4239-0535-6

ISBN-10: 1-4239-0535-0

Cengage Learning
20 Channel Center Street
Boston, MA 02210
USA

Cengage Learning is a leading provider of customized learning solutions with office locations around the globe, including Singapore, the United Kingdom, Australia, Mexico, Brazil, and Japan. Locate your local office at:
international.cengage.com/region

Cengage Learning products are represented in Canada by Nelson Education, Ltd.

Trademarks:
Some of the product names and company names used in this book have been used for identification purposes only and may be trademarks or registered trademarks of their respective manufacturers and sellers.

Microsoft and the Office logo are either registered trademarks or trademarks of Microsoft Corporation in the United States and/or other countries. Course Technology is an independent entity from Microsoft Corporation, and not affiliated with Microsoft in any manner. Microsoft product screen shot(s) reprinted with permission from Microsoft Corporation.

To learn more about Course Technology, visit **www.cengage.com/coursetechnology**

To learn more about Cengage Learning, visit **www.cengage.com.**

Purchase any of our products at your local college store or at our preferred online store **www.ichapters.com**

Printed in the United States of America
2 3 4 5 6 7 8 9 11 10 09

About The Illustrated Course Guides

Welcome to the Microsoft Office 2007 Illustrated Course Guides! The books in this series are ideally suited for a wide range of learners who need to gain skill proficiency at a particular level for Word, Excel, Access, PowerPoint or Windows Vista. The highly visual and full-color lesson material is extremely approachable for learners of all levels, and the wealth of reinforcement exercises ensures skills retention. To maximize skills retention and measure proficiency, use Illustrated Course Guides in conjunction with SAM 2007, our robust assessment and training system.

As you probably have heard by now, Microsoft completely redesigned this latest version of Office from the ground up. No more menus! No more toolbars! The software changes Microsoft made were based on years of research during which they studied users' needs and work habits. The result is a phenomenal and powerful new version of the software that will make you and your learners more productive and help you get better results faster.

Before we started working on the Illustrated Course Guides for Microsoft Office 2007, we also conducted our own research. We reached out to nearly 100 instructors like you who have used previous editions of our Microsoft Office texts. Some of you responded to one of our surveys, others of you generously spent time with us on the phone, telling us your thoughts. Seven of you agreed to serve on our Advisory Board and guided our decisions.

As a result of all the feedback you gave us, we have preserved the features that you love, and made improvements that you suggested and requested. And of course we have covered all the key features of the new software. (For more details on what's new, please read the Preface.) We are confident that the Illustrated Course Guides for Microsoft Office 2007 and all their available resources will help any type of learner master Microsoft Office 2007.

Advisory Board

We thank our Advisory Board who enthusiastically gave us their opinions and guided our every decision on content and design from beginning to end. They are:

Kristen Callahan, Mercer County Community College
Paulette Comet, Assistant Professor, Community College of Baltimore County
Barbara Comfort, J. Sargeant Reynolds Community College
Margaret Cooksey, Tallahassee Community College
Rachelle Hall, Glendale Community College
Hazel Kates, Miami Dade College
Charles Lupico, Thomas Nelson Community College

Author Acknowledgments

Lynn Wermers I would like to thank Barbara Clemens for her insightful contributions, great humor, and patience. I would also like to thank Christina Kling Garrett for her encouragement and support in guiding and managing the project.

Preface

Welcome to *Illustrated Course Guide: Microsoft Office Excel 2007 Intermediate*. If this is your first experience with the Illustrated Course Guides, you'll see that this book has a unique design: each skill is presented on two facing pages, with steps on the left and screens on the right. The layout makes it easy to digest a skill without having to read a lot of text and flip pages to see an illustration.

This book is an ideal learning tool for a wide range of learners—the "rookies" will find the clean design easy to follow and focused with only essential information presented, and the "hotshots" will appreciate being able to move quickly through the lessons to find the information they need without reading a lot of text. The design also makes this a great reference after the course is over! Note that the combined content in the Basic, Intermediate and Advanced Course Guides for Microsoft Excel 2007 content maps to the MCAS objectives, making the books an ideal preparation tool for the MCAS exam. See the illustration on the right to learn more about the pedagogical and design elements of a typical lesson.

What's New

We've made many changes and enhancements to the Microsoft Office 2007 Illustrated Course Guides. Here are some highlights of what's new:

- **New Getting Started with Microsoft® Office 2007 Unit**—This unit begins every Basic level Course Guide book and gets learners up to speed on features of Office 2007 that are common to all the applications, such as the Ribbon, the Office button, and the Quick Access toolbar.

- **Real Life Independent Challenge**—The new Real Life Independent Challenge exercises offer learners the opportunity to create projects that are meaningful to their lives, such as spreadsheets that calculate loan payments, or track personal expenses.

Each two-page spread focuses on a single skill.

Concise text introduces the basic principles in the lesson and integrates a real-world case study.

UNIT
A
Excel 2007

Editing Cell Entries

You can change, or **edit**, the contents of an active cell at any time. To do so, double-click the cell, click in the formula bar, or just start typing. Excel switches to Edit mode when you are making cell entries. Different pointers, shown in Table A-3, guide you through the editing process. You noticed some errors in the worksheet and want to make corrections. The first error is in cell A5, which contains a misspelled name.

STEPS

QUICK TIP
Pressing [Enter] also accepts the cell entry, but moves the cell pointer down one cell.

QUICK TIP
On some keyboards, you might need to press an "F Lock" key to enable the function keys.

QUICK TIP
The Undo button allows you to reverse up to 100 previous actions, one at a time.

1. **Click cell A5, then click to the right of P in the formula bar**
   As soon as you click in the formula bar, a blinking vertical line called the **insertion point** appears on the formula bar at the location where new text will be inserted. See Figure A-9. The mouse pointer changes to I when you point anywhere in the formula bar.

2. **Press [Delete], then click the Enter button ☑ on the formula bar**
   Clicking the Enter button accepts the edit, and the spelling of the employee's first name is corrected. You can also press [Enter] or [Tab] to accept an edit.

3. **Click cell B6, then press [F2]**
   Excel switches to Edit mode, and the insertion point blinks in the cell. Pressing [F2] activates the cell for editing directly in the cell instead of the formula bar. Some people prefer editing right in the cell instead of using the formula bar, but it's simply a matter of preference; the results in the worksheet are the same.

4. **Press [Backspace], type 8, then press [Enter]**
   The value in the cell changes from 35 to 38, and cell B7 becomes the active cell. Did you notice that the calculations in cells B15 and E15 also changed? That's because those cells contain formulas that include cell B6 in their calculations. If you make a mistake when editing, you can click the Cancel button ☒ on the formula bar *before* pressing [Enter] to confirm the cell entry. The Enter and Cancel buttons appear only when you're in Edit mode. If you notice the mistake *after* you have confirmed the cell entry, click the Undo button ↩ on the Quick Access toolbar.

5. **Click cell A9, press [F2], press and hold [Shift], press [Home], then release [Shift]**
   Pressing and holding [Shift] lets you select text using the keyboard. Pressing [Home] moves the cursor to the beginning of the cell; pressing [End] would move the cursor to the end or the cell.

6. **Type Maez, Javier, then press [Enter]**
   When text is selected, typing deletes it and replaces it with the new text.

7. **Double-click cell C12, press [Delete], type 4, then click ☑**
   Double-clicking a cell activates it for editing directly in the cell. Compare your screen to Figure A-10.

8. **Save your work**
   Your changes to the workbook are saved.

Recovering a lost workbook file

Sometimes while you are using Excel, you may experience a power failure or your computer may "freeze," making it impossible to continue working. If this type of interruption occurs, Excel has a built-in recovery feature that allows you to open and save files that were open at the time of the interruption. When you restart Excel after an interruption, File Recovery mode automatically starts and tries to make any necessary repairs. If you need to use a corrupted workbook, you can try and repair it manually by clicking the Office button, then clicking Open. Select the workbook file you want to repair, click the Open list arrow, then click Open and Repair.

Excel 10   Getting Started with Excel 2007

Hints as well as troubleshooting advice appear right where you need them–next to the step itself.

Clues to Use boxes provide concise information that either expands on the major lesson skill or describes an independent task that in some way relates to the major lesson skill.

Every lesson features large, full-color representations of what the screen should look like as learners complete the numbered steps.

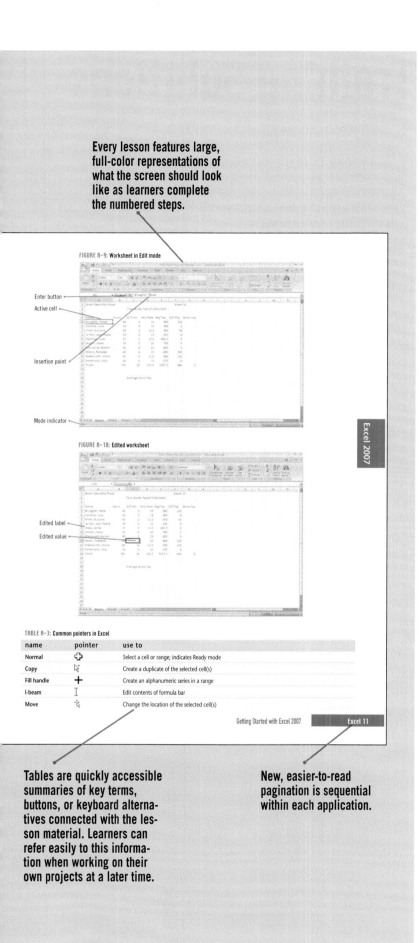

FIGURE A-9: Worksheet in Edit mode

Enter button
Active cell

Insertion point

Mode indicator

FIGURE A-10: Edited worksheet

Edited label
Edited value

TABLE A-3: Common pointers in Excel

name	pointer	use to
Normal	⊹	Select a cell or range; indicates Ready mode
Copy	⬒	Create a duplicate of the selected cell(s)
Fill handle	+	Create an alphanumeric series in a range
I-beam	I	Edit contents of formula bar
Move	⬩	Change the location of the selected cell(s)

Getting Started with Excel 2007   Excel 11

Tables are quickly accessible summaries of key terms, buttons, or keyboard alternatives connected with the lesson material. Learners can refer easily to this information when working on their own projects at a later time.

New, easier-to-read pagination is sequential within each application.

- **New Case Study**—A new case study featuring Quest Specialty Travel provides a practical scenario that learners can relate to as they learn skills and promote skills retention. This fictional company offers a wide variety of tours around the world.

- **Content Improvements**—All of the content in the every Illlustrated Course Guide has been updated to cover Office 2007 and also to address customer feedback.

Assignments

The lessons use Quest Specialty Travel, a fictional adventure travel company, as the case study. The assignments on the light purple pages at the end of each unit increase in difficulty. Data Files and case studies provide a variety of interesting and relevant business applications to help reinforce learning and retain skills. Assignments include:

- **Concepts Reviews** consist of multiple choice, matching, and screen identification questions.

- **Skills Reviews** provide additional hands-on, step-by-step reinforcement.

- **Independent Challenges** are case projects requiring critical thinking and application of the unit skills. The Independent Challenges increase in difficulty, with the first one in each unit being the easiest. Independent Challenges 2 and 3 become increasingly open-ended, requiring more independent problem solving.

- **Real Life Independent Challenges** are practical exercises in which learners create projects to help them with their every day lives.

- **Advanced Challenge Exercises** set within the Independent Challenges provide optional steps for more advanced learners.

- **Visual Workshops** are practical, self-graded capstone projects that require independent problem solving.

Assessment & Training Solutions

SAM 2007

SAM 2007 helps bridge the gap between the classroom and the real world by allowing learners to train and test on important computer skills in an active, hands-on environment.

SAM 2007's easy-to-use system includes powerful interactive exams, training, or projects on critical applications such as Word, Excel, Access, PowerPoint, Outlook, Windows, the Internet, and much more. SAM simulates the application environment, allowing learners to demonstrate their knowledge and think through the skills by performing real-world tasks.

Designed to be used with the Illustrated Course Guides, SAM 2007 includes built-in page references so learners can print helpful study guides that match the Illustrated textbooks used in class. Powerful administrative options allow instructors to schedule exams and assignments, secure tests, and run reports with almost limitless flexibility.

Online Content   Blackboard

Blackboard is the leading distance learning solution provider and class-management platform today. Course Technology has partnered with Blackboard to bring you premium online content. Instructors: Content for use with this title is available in a Blackboard Course Cartridge and may include topic reviews, case projects, review questions, test banks, practice tests, custom syllabi, and more.

Course Technology also has solutions for several other learning management systems. Please visit *www.course.com* today to see what's available for this title.

A Guided Tour of Microsoft Office 2007, Windows Vista Edition

This CD of movie tutorials helps learners get exposed to the new features of Microsoft Office 2007 quickly. Dynamic and engaging author Corinne Hoisington presents the highlights of the new features of Word, Excel, Access, and PowerPoint plus a bonus movie tutorial on Windows Vista. This CD is a great supplement to this book, offering a fun overview of the software to inspire learners and show them what is possible.

Instructor Resources

The Instructor Resources CD is Course Technology's way of putting the resources and information needed to teach and learn effectively into your hands. With an integrated array of teaching and learning tools that offer you and your learners a broad range of technology-based instructional options, we believe this CD represents the highest quality and most cutting edge resources available to instructors today. Many of these resources are available at *www.course.com*. The resources available with this book are:

- **Instructor's Manual**—Available as an electronic file, the Instructor's Manual includes detailed lecture topics with teaching tips for each unit.

- **Sample Syllabus**—Prepare and customize your course easily using this sample course outline.

- **Course Outline**—Available online, the Course outline includes suggested times for each unit as well (as time for breaks and lunch), to complete the Basic, Intermediate, or Advanced skills in one training day. You can customize it to suit your needs or provide it as a hand out.

- **PowerPoint Presentations**—Each unit has a corresponding PowerPoint presentation that you can use in lecture, distribute to your learners, or customize to suit your course.

- **Figure Files**—The figures in the text are provided on the Instructor Resources CD to help you illustrate key topics or concepts. You can create traditional overhead transparencies by printing the figure files. Or you can create electronic slide shows by using the figures in a presentation program such as PowerPoint.

- **Solutions to Exercises**—Solutions to Exercises contains every file learners are asked to create or modify in the lessons and end-of-unit material. Also provided in this section, there is a document outlining the solutions for the end-of-unit Concepts Review, Skills Review, and Independent Challenges. An Annotated Solution File and Grading Rubric accompany each file and can be used together for quick and easy grading.

- **Data Files**—To complete most of the units in this book, learners will need Data Files. You can post the Data Files on a file server for learners to copy. The Data Files are available on the Instructor Resources CD, the Review Pack, and can also be downloaded from *www.course.com*. In this edition, we have included a lesson on downloading the Data Files for this book, see page xvi.

Instruct learners to use the Data Files List included on the Review Pack and the Instructor Resources CD. This list gives instructions on copying and organizing files.

- **ExamView**—ExamView is a powerful testing software package that allows you to create and administer printed, computer (LAN-based), and Internet exams. ExamView includes hundreds of questions that correspond to the topics covered in this text, enabling learners to generate detailed study guides that include page references for further review. The computer-based and Internet testing components allow learners to take exams at their computers, and also saves you time by grading each exam automatically.

CourseCasts—Learning on the Go. Always Available...Always Relevant.

Want to keep up with the latest technology trends relevant to you? Visit our site to find a library of podcasts, CourseCasts, featuring a "CourseCast of the Week," and download them to your mp3 player at *http://coursecasts.course.com*.

Our fast-paced world is driven by technology. You know because you're an active participant—always on the go, always keeping up with technological trends, and always learning new ways to embrace technology to power your life.

Ken Baldauf, a faculty member of the Florida State University Computer Science Department, is responsible for teaching technology classes to thousands of FSU learners each year. He knows what you know; he knows what you want to learn. He's also an expert in the latest technology and will sort through and aggregate the most pertinent news and information so you can spend your time enjoying technology, rather than trying to figure it out.

Visit us at *http://coursecasts.course.com* to learn on the go!

Brief Contents

Contents

Unit H: Analyzing Table Data   **177**

Unit I: Automating Worksheet Tasks   **201**

EXCEL 2007   **Unit J: Enhancing Charts**   **225**

EXCEL 2007   **Unit N: Sharing Excel Files and Incorporating Web Information**   **321**

Read This Before You Begin

Frequently Asked Questions

What are Data Files?

A Data File is a partially completed Excel spreadsheet, or another type of file that you use to complete the steps in the units and exercises to create the final document that you submit to your instructor. Each unit opener page lists the Data Files that you need for that unit.

Where are the Data Files?

Your instructor will provide the Data Files to you or direct you to a location on a network drive from which you can download them. Alternatively, you can follow the instructions on page xvi to download the Data Files from this book's Web page.

What software was used to write and test this book?

This book was written and tested using a typical installation of Microsoft Office 2007 installed on a computer with a typical installation of Microsoft Windows Vista. The browser used for any steps that require a browser is Internet Explorer 7.

If you are using this book on Windows XP, please see the "Important Notes for Windows XP Users" on the next page. If you are using this book on Windows Vista, please see the Appendix at the end of this book.

Do I need to be connected to the Internet to complete the steps and exercises in this book?

Some of the exercises in this book assume that your computer is connected to the Internet. If you are not connected to the Internet, see your instructor for information on how to complete the exercises.

What do I do if my screen is different from the figures shown in this book?

This book was written and tested on computers with monitors set at a resolution of 1024 × 768. If your screen shows more or less information than the figures in the book, your monitor is probably set at a higher or lower resolution. If you don't see something on your screen, you might have to scroll down or up to see the object identified in the figures.

The Ribbon (the blue area at the top of the screen) in Microsoft Office 2007 adapts to different resolutions. If your monitor is set at a lower resolution than 1024 × 768, you might not see all of the buttons shown in the figures. The groups of buttons will always appear, but the entire group might be condensed into a single button that you need to click to access the buttons described in the instructions. For example, the figures and steps in this book assume that the Editing group on the Home tab in Word looks like the following:

1024 × 768 Editing Group

Editing Group on the
Home Tab of the
Ribbon at 1024 × 768

If your resolution is set to 800 × 600, the Ribbon in Word will look like the following figure, and you will need to click the Editing button to access the buttons that are visible in the Editing group.

800 × 600 Editing Group

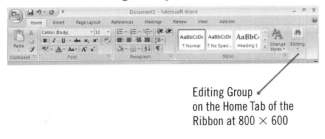

Editing Group
on the Home Tab of the
Ribbon at 800 × 600

800 × 600 Editing Group Clicked

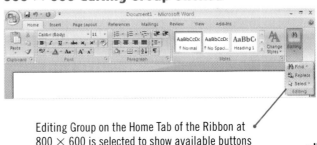

Editing Group on the Home Tab of the Ribbon at
800 × 600 is selected to show available buttons

Important Notes for Windows XP Users

The screen shots in this book show Microsoft Office 2007 running on Windows Vista. However, if you are using Microsoft Windows XP, you can still use this book because Office 2007 runs virtually the same on both platforms. There are a few differences that you will encounter if you are using Windows XP. Read this section to understand the differences.

Dialog boxes

If you are a Windows XP user, dialog boxes shown in this book will look slightly different than what you see on your screen. Dialog boxes for Windows XP have a blue title bar, instead of a gray title bar. However, beyond this difference in appearance, the options in the dialog boxes across platforms are the same. For instance, the screen shots below show the Font dialog box running on Windows XP and the Font dialog box running on Windows Vista.

FIGURE 1: Dialog box in Windows XP

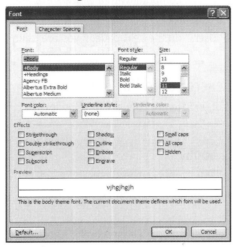

FIGURE 2: Dialog box in Windows Vista

Alternate Steps for Windows XP Users

Nearly all of the steps in this book work exactly the same for Windows XP users. However, there are a few tasks that will require you to complete slightly different steps. This section provides alternate steps for a few specific skills.

Starting a program

1. Click the **Start button** on the taskbar
2. Point to **All Programs**, point to **Microsoft Office**, then click the application you want to use

FIGURE 3: Starting a program

Saving a file for the first time

1. Click the **Office button**, then click **Save As**
2. Type a name for your file in the File name text box
3. Click the **Save in list arrow**, then navigate to the drive and folder where you store your Data Files
4. Click **Save**

FIGURE 4: Save As dialog box

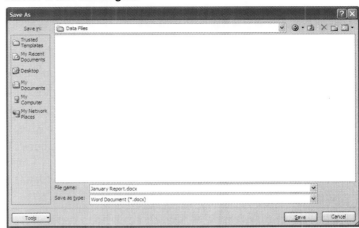

Opening a file

1. Click the **Office button**, then click **Open**
2. Click the **Look in list arrow**, then navigate to the drive and folder where you store your Data Files
3. Click the file you want to open
4. Click **Open**

FIGURE 5: Open dialog box

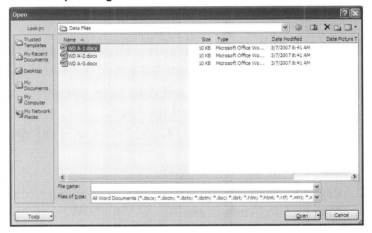

Downloading Data Files for This Book

In order to complete many of the lesson steps and exercises in this book, you are asked to open and save Data Files. A **Data File** is a partially completed file that you use as a starting point to complete the steps in the units and exercises. The benefit of using a Data File is that it saves you the time and effort needed to create a file; you can simply open a Data File, save it with a new name (so the original file remains intact), then make changes to it to complete lesson steps or an exercise. Your instructor will provide the Data Files to you or direct you to a location on a network drive from which you can download them. Alternatively, you can follow the instructions in this lesson to download the Data Files from this book's Web page.

1. **Start Internet Explorer, type www.cengage.com/coursetechnology/ in the address bar, then press [Enter]**

2. **Click in the Enter ISBN Search text box, type 9781423905356, then click Search**

3. **When the page opens for this textbook, click the About this Product link for the Student, point to Student Downloads to expand the menu, and then click the Data Files for Students link**

4. **If the File Download – Security Warning dialog box opens, click Save. (If no dialog box appears, skip this step and go to Step 6)**

5. **If the Save As dialog box opens, click the Save in list arrow at the top of the dialog box, select a folder on your USB drive or hard disk to download the file to, then click Save**

6. **Close Internet Explorer and then open Computer and display the contents of the drive and folder to which you downloaded the file**

7. **Double-click the file 9781423905356.exe in the drive or folder, then, if the Open File – Security Warning dialog box opens, click Run**

8. **In the WinZip Self-Extractor window, navigate to the drive and folder where you want to unzip the files to, then click Unzip**

9. **When the WinZip Self-Extractor displays a dialog box listing the number of files that have unzipped success-fully, click OK, click Close in the WinZip Self-Extractor dialog box, then close Computer**

The Data Files are now unzipped in the folder you specified in Step 8 and ready for you to open and use.

Managing Workbook Data

As you analyze data using Excel, you will find that your worksheets and workbooks become more complex. In this unit, you will learn several Excel features to help you manage workbook data. In addition, you will want to share workbooks with coworkers, but you need to ensure that they can view your data while preventing unwarranted changes. You will learn how to save workbooks in different formats and how to prepare workbooks for distribution. Kate Morgan, the vice president of sales at Quest Specialty Travel, asks for your help in analyzing yearly sales data from the Canadian branches. When the analysis is complete, she will distribute the workbook for branch managers to review.

OBJECTIVES

View and arrange worksheets

Protect worksheets and workbooks

Save custom views of a worksheet

Add a worksheet background

Prepare a workbook for distribution

Insert hyperlinks

Save a workbook for distribution

Group worksheets

Viewing and Arranging Worksheets

As you work with workbooks made up of multiple worksheets, you may need to compare data in the various sheets. To do this, you can view each worksheet in its own workbook window, called an **instance**, and display the windows in an arrangement that makes it easy to compare data. When you work with worksheets in separate windows, you are working with different views of the same worksheet; the data itself remains in one file. Kate asks you to compare the monthly store sales totals for the Toronto and Vancouver branches. Because the sales totals are on different worksheets, you want to arrange the worksheets side by side in separate windows.

STEPS

1. **Start Excel, open the file** EX F-1.xlsx **from the drive and folder where you store your Data Files, then save it as** Store Sales

2. **With the Toronto sheet active, click the** View tab, **then click the** New Window button **in the Window group**

    There are now two instances of the Store Sales workbook on the task bar: Store Sales.xlsx:1 and Store Sales.xlsx:2. The Store Sales.xlsx:2 window is active—you can see its button selected on the taskbar, and the filename in the title bar has :2 after it.

3. **Click the** Vancouver sheet tab, **click the** Switch Windows button **in the Window group, then click** Store Sales.xlsx:1

    The Store Sales.xlsx:1 instance is active. The Toronto sheet is active in the Store Sales.xlsx:1 workbook and the Vancouver sheet is active in the Store Sales.xlsx:2 workbook.

4. **Click the** Arrange All button **in the Window group**

    The Arrange Windows dialog box, shown in Figure F-1, provides configurations for displaying the worksheets. You want to view the workbooks vertically.

5. **Click the** Vertical option button **to select it, then click** OK

    The windows are arranged vertically, as shown in Figure F-2. You can activate a workbook by clicking one of its cells. You can also view only one of the workbooks by hiding the one you do not wish to see.

6. **Scroll horizontally to view the data in the Store Sales.xlsx:1 workbook, click anywhere in the Store Sales.xlsx:2 workbook, scroll horizontally to view the data in the Store Sales.xlsx:2 workbook, then click the** Hide button **in the Window group**

    When you hide the second instance, only the Store Sales.xlsx:1 workbook is visible.

7. **Click the** Unhide button **in the Window group; click** Store Sales.xlsx:2, **if necessary, in the Unhide dialog box; then click** OK

    The Store Sales.xlsx:2 book appears.

8. **Close the Store Sales.xlsx:2 instance, then maximize the Toronto worksheet in the Store Sales.xlsx workbook**

    Closing the Store Sales.xlsx:2 instance leaves only the first instance open, which is now named Store Sales.xlsx in the title bar.

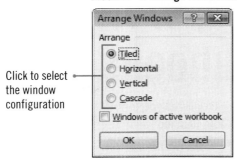

FIGURE F-1: Arrange Windows dialog box

Click to select the window configuration

FIGURE F-2: Windows displayed vertically

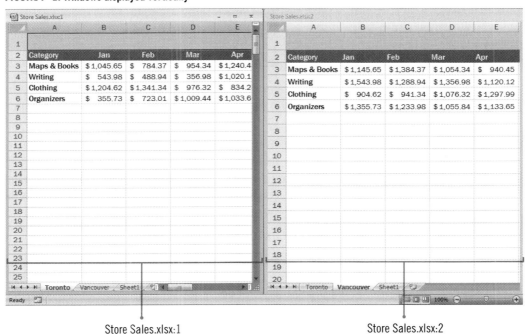

Store Sales.xlsx:1

Store Sales.xlsx:2

Splitting the worksheet into multiple panes

Excel lets you split the worksheet area into vertical and/or horizontal panes, so that you can click inside any one pane and scroll to locate information in that pane while the other panes remain in place, as shown in Figure F-3. To split a worksheet area into multiple panes, drag a split box (the small box at the top of the vertical scroll bar or at the right end of the horizontal scroll bar) in the direction you want the split to appear. To remove the split, move the pointer over the split until the pointer changes to a double-headed arrow, then double-click.

FIGURE F-3: Worksheet split into two horizontal and two vertical panes

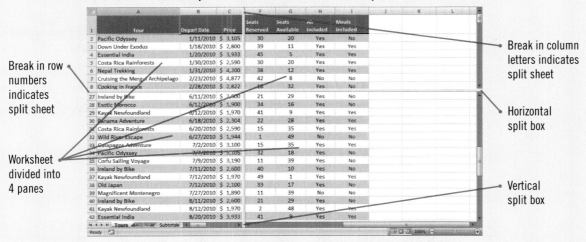

Break in row numbers indicates split sheet

Worksheet divided into 4 panes

Break in column letters indicates split sheet

Horizontal split box

Vertical split box

Excel 2007

Protecting Worksheets and Workbooks

To protect sensitive information, Excel allows you to **lock** selected cells so that other people are able to view the data (values, numbers, labels, formulas, etc.) in those cells, but not change it. Excel locks all cells by default, but this protection does not take effect until you activate the Excel protection feature. A common worksheet protection strategy is to unlock cells in which data will be changed, sometimes referred to as the **data entry area**, and to lock cells in which the data should not be changed. Then, when you protect the worksheet, the unlocked areas can still be changed. ▰▰▰▰▰ Because the Toronto sales figures for January through March have been confirmed as final, Kate asks you to protect that area of the worksheet so the figures cannot be altered.

STEPS

1. **On the Toronto sheet, select the range E3:M6, click the Home tab, click the Format button in the Cells group, click Format Cells, then in the Format Cells dialog box click the Protection tab**

   The Locked check box in the Protection tab is already checked, as shown in Figure F-4. This check box is selected by default, meaning that all the cells in a new workbook start out locked. However, cell locking is not applied unless the protection feature is also activated. The protection feature is inactive by default. Because the April through December sales figures have not yet been confirmed as final and may need to be changed, you do not want those cells to be locked when the protection feature is activated.

QUICK TIP

To hide any formulas that you don't want to be visible, select the cells that contain formulas that you want to hide, then click the Hidden check box on the Protection tab to select it. The formula will be hidden after the worksheet is protected.

2. **Click the Locked check box to deselect it, then click OK**

   The data remains unlocked until you set the protection in the next step.

3. **Click the Review tab, then click the Protect Sheet button in the Changes group**

   The Protect Sheet dialog box opens, as shown in Figure F-5. In the "Allow users of this worksheet to" list, you can select the actions that you want your worksheet users to be able to perform. The default options protect the worksheet while allowing users to select locked or unlocked cells only. You choose not to use a password.

4. **Verify that Protect worksheet and contents of locked cells is checked and that Select locked cells and Select unlocked cells are checked, then click OK**

   You are ready to test the new worksheet protection.

5. **In cell B3, type 1 to confirm that locked cells cannot be changed, then click OK**

   When you attempt to change a locked cell, a dialog box, shown in Figure F-6, reminds you of the protected cell's read-only status. **Read-only format** means that users can view but not change the data.

6. **Click cell F3, type 1, and notice that Excel allows you to begin the entry, press [Esc] to cancel the entry, then save the workbook**

   Because you unlocked the cells in columns E through M before you protected the worksheet, you can make changes to these cells. You decide to protect the workbook, but you want users to open the workbook without typing a password first.

7. **Click the Protect Workbook button in the Changes group, in the Protect Structure and Windows dialog box make sure the Structure check box is selected, click the Windows check box to select it, then click OK**

   You are ready to test the new workbook protection.

8. **Right-click the Toronto sheet tab**

   The Insert, Delete, Rename, Move or Copy, Tab Color, Hide, and Unhide menu options are not available. You decide to remove the workbook and worksheet protections.

9. **Click the Unprotect Workbook button in the Changes group, then click the Unprotect Sheet button to remove the worksheet protection**

FIGURE F-4: **Protection tab in Format Cells dialog box**

Click to remove
check mark

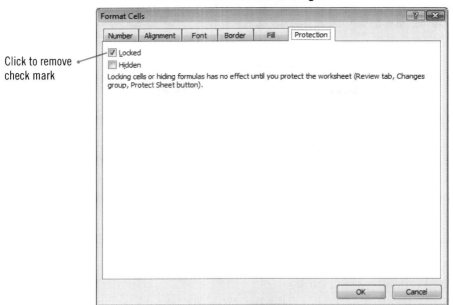

FIGURE F-5: **Protect Sheet dialog box**

Prevents locked
cells from
changes

Allows users to select
worksheet cells

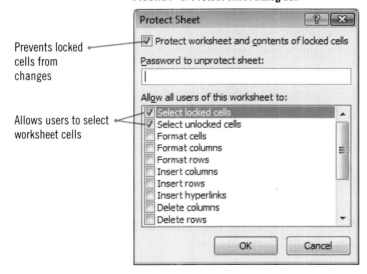

FIGURE F-6: **Reminder of protected cell's read-only status**

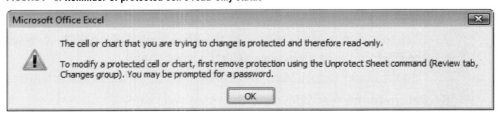

Freezing rows and columns

As the rows and columns of a worksheet fill up with data, you might need to scroll through the worksheet to add, delete, modify, and view information. You can temporarily freeze columns and rows so you can keep labeling information in view as you scroll. **Panes** are the columns and rows that **freeze**, or remain in place, while you

scroll through your worksheet. To freeze panes you need to click the View tab, click the Freeze Panes button in the Window group then click Freeze Panes. Excel freezes the columns to the left and the rows above the selected cell. You can also select Freeze Top Row or Freeze First Column to freeze the top row or left worksheet column.

Saving Custom Views of a Worksheet

A **view** is a set of display and/or print settings that you can name and save, then access at a later time. By using the Excel Custom Views feature, you can create several different views of a worksheet without having to create separate sheets. For example, if you often hide columns in a worksheet, you can create two views, one that displays all of the columns and another with the columns hidden. You set the worksheet display first, then name the view. ▰▰▰▰▰ Because Kate wants to generate a sales report from the final sales data for January through March, she asks you to save the first-quarter sales data as a custom view. You begin by creating a view showing all of the worksheet data.

STEPS

1. **With the Toronto sheet active, click the View tab, then click the Custom Views button in the Workbook Views group**

   The Custom Views dialog box opens. Any previously defined views for the active worksheet appear in the Views box. No views are defined for the Toronto worksheet. You decide to add a named view that shows all the worksheet columns.

2. **Click Add**

   The Add View dialog box opens, as shown in Figure F-7. Here, you enter a name for the view and decide whether to include print settings and hidden rows, columns, and filter settings. You want to include the selected options.

3. **In the Name box, type Year Sales, then click OK**

   You have created a view called Year Sales that shows all the worksheet columns. You want to set up another view that will hide the April through December columns.

4. **Select columns E through M, right-click the selected area, then click Hide on the shortcut menu**

   You are ready to create a custom view of the January through March sales data.

5. **Click cell A1, click the Custom Views button in the Workbook Views group, click Add, in the Name box type First Quarter, then click OK**

   You are ready to test the two custom views.

6. **Click the Custom Views button in the Workbook Views group, click Year Sales in the Views list, then click Show**

   The Year Sales custom view displays all of the months' sales data. Now you are ready to test the First Quarter custom view.

7. **Click the Custom Views button in the Workbook Views group, then with First Quarter in the Custom Views dialog box selected, click Show**

   Only the January through March sales figures appear on the screen, as shown in Figure F-8.

8. **Return to the Year Sales view, then save your work**

FIGURE F-7: Add View dialog box

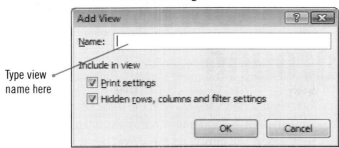

Type view name here

Break in column letters indicates hidden columns

FIGURE F-8: First Quarter view

	A	B	C	D	N
1	QST Toronto				
2	Category	Jan	Feb	Mar	
3	Maps & Books	$1,045.65	$ 784.37	$ 954.34	
4	Writing	$ 543.98	$ 488.94	$ 356.98	
5	Clothing	$1,204.62	$1,341.34	$ 976.32	
6	Organizers	$ 355.73	$ 723.01	$1,009.44	
7					

January – March sales figures

Using Page Break Preview

The vertical and horizontal dashed lines in the Normal view of worksheets represent page breaks. Excel automatically inserts a page break when your worksheet data doesn't fit on one page. These page breaks are **dynamic**, which means they adjust automatically when you insert or delete rows and columns and when you change column widths or row heights. Everything to the left of the first vertical dashed line and above the first horizontal dashed line is printed on the first page. You can manually add or remove page breaks by clicking the Page Layout tab, clicking the Breaks button in the Page Setup group, then clicking the appropriate command. You can also view and change page breaks manually by clicking the View tab, then clicking the Page Break Preview button in the Workbook Views group, or by clicking the Page Break Preview button on the status bar, then clicking OK. You can drag the blue page break lines to the desired location, as shown in Figure F-9. If you drag a page break to the right to include more data on a page, Excel shrinks the type to fit the data on that page. To exit Page Break Preview, click the Normal button in the Workbook Views group.

FIGURE F-9: Page Break Preview window

	A	B	C	D	E	F	G	H	I	J	K	L	M
1	QST Toronto												
2	Category	Jan	Feb	Mar	Apr	May	Jun	Jul	Aug	Sep	Oct	Nov	Dec
3	Maps & Books	$1,045.65	$ 784.37	$ 954.34	$1,240.45	$ 567.76	$1,240.76	$1,240.43	$1,240.34	$ 675.54	$1,240.54	$1,240.34	$1,240.34
4	Writing	$ 543.98	$ 488.94	$ 356.98	$1,020.12	$ 378.23	$ 392.41	$ 934.62	$ 145.89	$ 345.98	$ 435.78	$ 359.76	$ 289.88
5	Clothing	$1,204.62	$1,341.34	$ 976.32	$ 834.23	$1,022.35	$ 634.22	$1,309.22	$ 749.33	$1,209.04	$ 1,383.11	$ 1,456.21	$1,341.47
6	Organizers	$ 355.73	$ 723.01	$1,009.44	$1,033.65	$ 998.98	$1,003.48	$1,006.23	$ 942.56	$1,097.99	$ 865.11	$ 898.99	$1,012.75

Drag blue page break lines to change page breaks

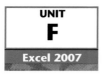

UNIT
F
Excel 2007

Adding a Worksheet Background

In addition to using a theme's font colors and fills, you can make your Excel data more attractive to view by adding a picture to the worksheet background. Companies often use their logo as a worksheet background. A worksheet background will display on the screen but will not print with the worksheet. If you want to add a worksheet background that appears on printouts, you can add a **watermark**, a translucent background design that prints behind your data. To add a watermark, you add the image to the worksheet header or footer. Kate asks you to add the Quest logo to the printed background of the Toronto worksheet. You will begin by adding the logo as a worksheet background.

STEPS

1. **With the Toronto sheet active, click the** Page Layout tab, **then click the** Background button **in the Page Setup group**

   The Sheet Background dialog box opens.

2. **Navigate to the drive and folder where you store your Data Files, click** Logo.gif, **then click** Insert

   The Quest logo is tiled behind the worksheet data. It appears twice because the graphic is **tiled**, or repeated, to fill the background.

3. **Preview the Toronto worksheet, then click the** Close Print Preview button

   Because the logo is only for display purposes, it will not print with the worksheet, so is not visible in Print Preview. You want the logo to print with the worksheet, so you decide to remove the background and add the logo to the worksheet header.

4. **Click the** Delete Background button **in the Page Setup group, click the** Insert tab, **then click the** Header & Footer button **in the Text group**

   The Design tab of the Header & Footer Tools appears, as shown in Figure F-10. The Header & Footer group buttons add preformatted headers and footers to a worksheet. The Header & Footer Elements buttons allow you to add page numbers, the date, the time, pictures, and names to the header or footer. The Navigation group buttons move the insertion point from the header to the footer and back. The Options group buttons specify special circumstances for the worksheet's headers and footers. You want to add a picture to the header.

5. **With the insertion point in the center section of the header, click the** Picture button **in the Header & Footer Elements group, navigate to the drive and folder where you store your Data Files, click** Logo.gif, **then click** Insert

   A code representing a picture, &[Picture], appears in the center of the header.

6. **Click cell A1, then click the** Normal button 🔲 **on the Status Bar**

   You want to scale the worksheet data to print on one page.

7. **Click the** Page Layout tab, **click the** Width list arrow **in the Scale to Fit group, click** 1 page, **click the** Height list arrow **in the Scale to Fit group, click** 1 page, **then preview the worksheet**

   Your worksheet should look like Figure F-11.

8. **Click the** Close Print Preview button, **then save the workbook**

Managing Workbook Data

FIGURE F-10: Design tab of the Header & Footer tools

Click these buttons to customize the header and footer

Header & Footer Tools Design tab

Some cells may temporarily display ######### while header is added

FIGURE F-11: Preview of Toronto worksheet with logo in the background

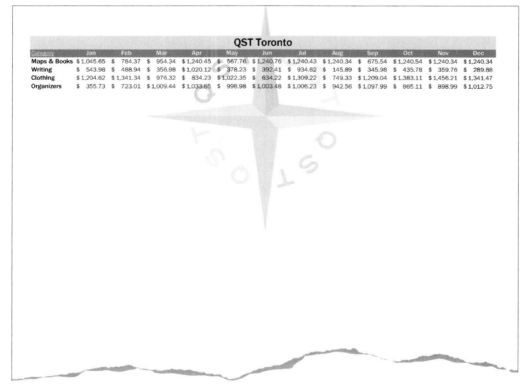

Preparing a Workbook for Distribution

If you are collaborating with others and want to share a workbook with them, you might want to remove sensitive information, such as headers, footers, or hidden elements, before distributing the file. You can use the Document Inspector feature to find and remove hidden data and personal information in your workbooks. On the other hand, you might want to add helpful information, called **properties**, to a file to help others identify, understand, and locate it, such as keywords, the author's name, a title, the status, and comments. **Keywords** are terms users can search for that will help them locate your workbook. Properties are a form of **metadata**, information that describe data and are used in Microsoft Windows document searches. You enter properties in the Document Properties Panel. In addition, to insure that others do not make unauthorized changes to your workbook, you can mark a file as final, which changes it to a read-only file, which others can open but not alter. To protect the workbook and prepare it for distribution to the sales managers, Kate asks you to remove sensitive information, add document properties, and mark the workbook as final.

STEPS

1. **Click the Office button, point to Prepare, then click Inspect Document**
   The Document Inspector dialog box opens, as shown in Figure F-12. It lists items that you can have Excel evaluate for personal information. All the components are selected by default.

2. **Click Inspect**
   After inspecting your document, the inspector displays the inspection results. Areas with personal information have a ! in front of them. Headers and footers are also flagged. You want to keep the file's header and footer and remove personal information.

> **QUICK TIP**
> You can view a file's summary information by clicking the Document Properties list arrow in the Document Properties Panel, then clicking Advanced Properties.

3. **Click Remove All next to Document Properties and Personal Information, then click Close**
   You decide to add keywords to help the sales managers find the worksheet using the search words Toronto or Vancouver.

4. **Click, point to Prepare, then click Properties**
   The Document Properties Panel appears at the top of the worksheet, as shown in Figure F-13. You decide to add a title, status, keywords, and comments.

> **QUICK TIP**
> If you have Windows Rights Management Services (RMS) client software installed, you can use the Information Rights Management (IRM) feature to specify access permissions. Click the Office button, point to Prepare, point to Restrict Permission, then select permission options.

5. **In the Title text box type Store Sales, in the Keywords text box type Toronto Vancouver store sales, in the Status text box type DRAFT, then in the Comments text box type The first-quarter figures are final., then click the Close button on the Document Properties Panel**
   You are ready to mark the workbook as final.

6. **Click, point to Prepare, click Mark as Final, click OK, then click OK again**
   The workbook is saved as a read-only file. [Read-Only] appears in the title bar.

7. **Click cell B3, then type 1 to confirm that the cell cannot be changed**
   Marking a workbook as final prevents accidental changes to the workbook. However, it is not a strong form of workbook protection because a workbook recipient can remove this Final status and edit the document. You decide to remove the read-only status from the workbook so that it is again editable.

8. **Click, point to Prepare, then click Mark as Final**
   The title bar no longer displays [Read-Only] after the workbook title, indicating that you can now edit the workbook.

FIGURE F-12: Document Inspector dialog box

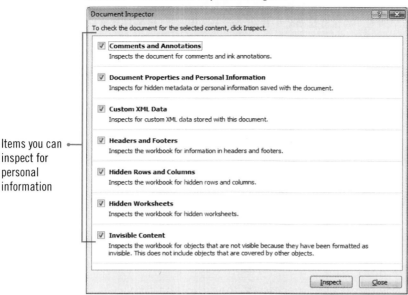

Items you can inspect for personal information

FIGURE F-13: Document Properties Panel

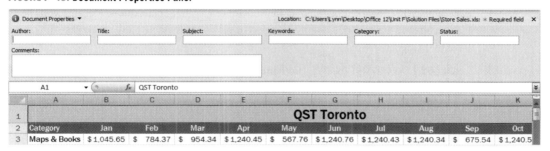

Adding a digital signature to a workbook

You can digitally sign a workbook to establish its validity and prevent it from being changed. You must obtain a valid certificate from a certificate authority to authenticate the workbook. To add a signature line in a workbook, click the Insert tab, click the Signature Line button in the Text group, then click OK. In the Signature Setup dialog box, enter information about the signer of the worksheet and then click OK. To add a signature, double-click the signature line, click OK, if prompted with a Get a Digital ID dialog box, click the Create your own digital ID option button, save your file if prompted, in the Sign dialog box click Select Image next to the sign box, browse to the location where your signature is saved, click Sign, then click OK. To add the certificate authenticating the workbook, click the Office button , point to Prepare, click Add a Digital Signature, then click OK. In the Sign dialog box click Sign, then click OK. The workbook will be saved as read-only and it will not be able to be changed by other users.

Sharing a workbook

You can make an Excel file a **shared workbook** so that several users can open and modify it at the same time. Click the Review tab, click the Share Workbook button in the Changes group, then on the Editing tab of the Share Workbook dialog box click "Allow changes by more than one user at the same time. This also allows workbook merging." If you get an error that the workbook cannot be shared because privacy is enabled, click the Office button, click Excel Options, click the Trust Center category on the left side of the dialog box, click Trust Center Settings, click Privacy Options in the list on the left, click the "Remove personal information from file properties on save" check box to deselect it, then click OK twice. When you share workbooks, it is often helpful to **track** modifications, or identify who made which changes. You can track all changes to a workbook by clicking the Track Changes button in the Changes group, and then clicking Highlight Changes. To resolve the tracked changes in a workbook, click the Track Changes button, then click Accept/Reject Changes. The changes are displayed one by one. You can accept the change or, if you disagree with any of the changes, you can reject them.

Inserting Hyperlinks

As you manage the content and appearance of your workbooks, you may want the workbook user to view information in another location. It might be nonessential information or data that is too detailed to place in the workbook itself. In these cases, you can create a hyperlink. A **hyperlink** is an object (a filename, word, phrase, or graphic) in a worksheet that, when you click it, displays, or "jumps to," another location, called the **target**. The target can also be a worksheet, another document, or a site on the World Wide Web. For example, in a worksheet that lists customer invoices, at each customer's name, you might create a hyperlink to an Excel file containing payment terms for each customer. 🖥️ Kate wants managers who view the Store Sales workbook to be able to view the item totals for each sales category in the Toronto sheet. She asks you to create a hyperlink at the Category heading so that users can click the hyperlink to view the items for each category.

STEPS

1. **Click cell A2 on the Toronto worksheet**

QUICK TIP

To remove a hyper-link or change its tar-get, right-click it, then click Remove Hyperlink or Edit Hyperlink.

2. **Click the Insert tab if necessary, then click the Hyperlink button in the Links group**
   The Insert Hyperlink dialog box opens, as shown in Figure F-14. The icons under "Link to" on the left side of the dialog box let you specify the type of location you want the link to jump to: an existing file or Web page, a place in the same document, a new document, or an e-mail address. Because you want the link to dis-play an already-existing document, the selected first icon, Existing File or Web Page, is correct, so you won't have to change it.

3. **Click the Look in list arrow, navigate to the location where you store your Data Files if necessary, then click Toronto Sales.xlsx in the file list**
   The filename you selected and its path appear in the Address text box. This is the document users will see when they click the hyperlink. You can also specify the ScreenTip that users see when they hold the pointer over the hyperlink.

4. **Click ScreenTip, type Items in each category, click OK, then click OK again**
   Cell A2 now contains underlined red text, indicating that it is a hyperlink. The color of a hyperlink depends on the worksheet theme colors. You need to change the text color of the hyperlink text so it is visible on the dark background. After you create a hyperlink, you should check it to make sure that it jumps to the correct destination.

QUICK TIP

If you link to a Web page, you must be connected to the Internet to test the link.

5. **Click the Home tab, click the Font Color list arrow ▲▾ in the Font group, click the White, Background 1 color (first color in the Theme Colors), move the pointer over the Category text, view the ScreenTip, then click once**
   After you click, the Toronto Sales workbook opens, displaying the Sales sheet, as shown in Figure F-15.

6. **Close the Toronto Sales workbook, then save the Store Sales workbook**

Returning to your document

After you click a hyperlink and view the destination document, you will often want to return to your original document that contains the hyperlink. To do this, you can add the Back button to the Quick Access Toolbar. However, the Back button does not appear in the Quick Access toolbar by default; you need to customize the toolbar. (If you are using a computer in a lab, check with your system administrator to see if you have permission to do this.) To cus-tomize the Quick Access toolbar, click the Office button, click Excel Options, click Customize in the Excel Options dialog box, click the "Choose Commands from" list arrow, select All Commands, click the Back button, click Add>>, then click OK.

FIGURE F-14: **Insert Hyperlink dialog box**

Locations a hyperlink can jump to

Click here to browse to hyperlink target

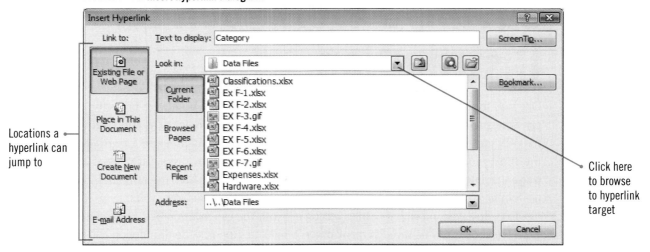

FIGURE F-15: **Target document**

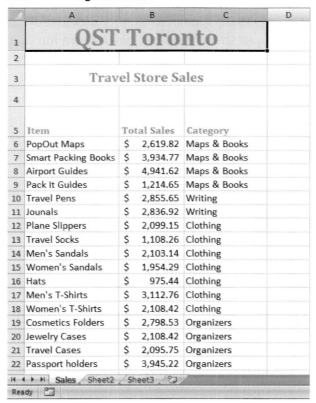

Using research tools

You can access resources online and locally on your computer using the Research task pane. To open the Research task pane, click the Review tab, then click the Research button in the Proofing group. You can click the Thesaurus button in the Proofing group for help with synonyms. You can click the Translate button in the Proofing group to translate your text into a selected language. The Search for text box in the Research pane allows you to specify a research topic. The Research pane has a drop-down list of the resources available to search for your topic.

UNIT
F
Excel 2007

Saving a Workbook for Distribution

One way to share Excel data is to place, or **publish**, the data on a network or on the Web so that others can access it using their Web browsers. To publish an Excel document to an **intranet** (a company's internal Web site) or the Web, you can save it in an **HTML (Hypertext Markup Language)** format, which is the coding format used for all Web documents. You can also save your Excel file as a **single file Web page** that integrates all of the worksheets and graphical elements from the workbook into a single file. This file format is called MHTML. In addition to distributing files on the Web, you may need to distribute your files to people working with an earlier version of Excel. You can save your files as Excel 97-2003 workbooks. Excel workbooks can be saved in many other formats to support wide distribution and to make them load faster. The most popular formats are listed in Table F-1. Kate asks you to create a workbook version that managers running an earlier version of Excel can open and modify. She also asks you to save the Store Sales workbook in MHT format so she can publish it on the Quest intranet for their sales managers to view.

STEPS

> **QUICK TIP**
>
> You can check your files for unsupported features before saving them by clicking the Office button, pointing to Prepare, then clicking Run Compatibility Checker.

1. **Click the Office button , point to Save As, click Excel 97-2003 Workbook, in the Save As dialog box, navigate to the drive and folder where you store your Data Files, then click Save**
   The Compatibility Checker appears on the screen, alerting you to the features that will be lost by saving in the earlier format. Some Excel 2007 features are not available in earlier versions of Excel.

2. **Click Continue, close the workbook, then reopen the Store Sales.xls workbook**
   [Compatibility Mode] appears in the title bar, as shown in Figure F-16. Compatibility mode prevents you from including Excel features in your workbook that are not supported in Excel 97-2003 workbooks. To exit compatibility mode, you need to save your file in one of the Excel 2007 formats and reopen the file.

3. **Click , point to Save As, click Excel Workbook, if necessary navigate to the drive and folder where you store your Data Files, click Save, then click Yes when you are asked if you want to replace the existing file**
   [Compatibility Mode] remains displayed in the title bar. You decide to close the file and reopen it to exit compatibility mode.

4. **Close the workbook, then reopen the Store Sales.xlsx workbook**
   The title bar no longer displays [Compatibility mode]. You decide to save the file for Web distribution.

> **QUICK TIP**
>
> To ensure that your workbook displays the same way on different computer platforms and screen settings, you can publish it in PDF format. You need to download an Add-in to save files in this format. The PDF format preserves all of the workbook's formatting so that it appears on the Web exactly as it was created.

5. **Click , click Save As, in the Save As dialog box, navigate to the drive and folder where you store your Data Files, change the filename to sales, then click the Save as type list arrow and click Single File Web Page (*.mht, *.mhtml)**
   The Save as type list box indicates that the workbook is to be saved as a Single File Web Page, which is in mhtml or mht format. To avoid problems when publishing your pages to a Web server, it is best to use lowercase characters, omit special characters and spaces, and limit your filename to eight characters with an additional three-character extension.

6. **Click Save, then click Yes**
   The dialog box indicated that some features may not be retained in the Web page file. Excel saves the workbook as an MHT file in the folder location you specified in the Save As dialog box. The MHT file is open on your screen, as shown in Figure F-17. It's a good idea to open an mht file in your browser to see how it will look to viewers.

7. **Close the sales.mht file in Excel, open Windows Explorer, open the sales.mht file, click the Vancouver sheet tab, then close your browser window**

Managing Workbook Data

FIGURE F-16: Workbook in compatibility mode

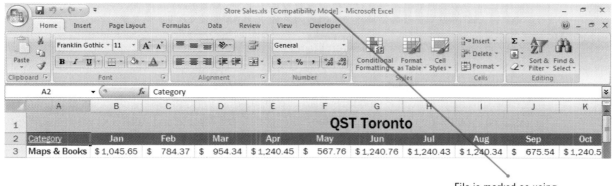

File is marked as using
compatibility mode

FIGURE F-17: Workbook saved as a single file web page

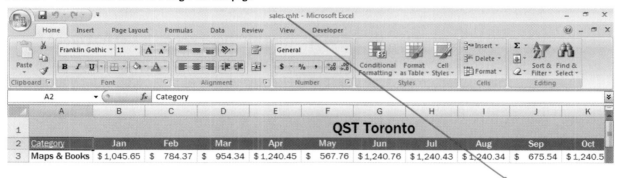

Web file with new name

TABLE F-1: Workbook formats

type of file	file extension(s)	Used for
Macro-enabled workbook	xlsm	Files that contain macros
Excel 97-2003 workbook	xls	Working with people using older versions of Excel
Single file Web page	mht, mhtml	Web sites with multiple pages and graphics
Web page	htm, html	Simple single-page Web sites
Excel template	xltx	Excel files that will be reused with small changes
Excel macro-enabled template	xltm	Excel files that will be used again and contain macros
Portable document format	pdf	Files with formatting that needs to be preserved
XML paper specification	xps	Files with formatting that needs to be preserved and files that need to be shared

Understanding Excel file formats

The default file format for Excel 2007 files is the Office Open XML format, which supports all Excel features. This format stores Excel files in small XML components which are zipped for compression. This default format has different types of files with their own extensions that are also often called formats themselves. The most often used format, xlsx , does not support macros. Macros, programmed instructions that perform tasks, can be a security risk. If your worksheet contains macros, you need to save it with an extension of xlsm so the macros will function in the workbook. If you use a workbook's text and formats repeatedly, you may want to save it as a template with the extension xltx. If your template contains macros, you need to save it with the xltm extension.

Grouping Worksheets

You can group worksheets to work on them as a collection so that data entered into one worksheet is automatically entered into all of the selected worksheets. This is useful for data that is common to every sheet of a workbook, such as headers and footers, or for column headings that will apply to all monthly worksheets in a yearly summary. Grouping worksheets can also be used to print multiple worksheets at one time. Kate asks you to add the text Quest to the footer of both the Toronto and Vancouver worksheets. You will also add one-inch margins to the left and right sides of both worksheets.

STEPS

1. **Open the Store Sales.xlsx file from the drive and folder where you store your Data Files**

2. **With the Toronto sheet active, press and hold [Shift], click the Vancouver sheet, then release [Shift]**

   Both sheet tabs are selected, and the title bar now contains [Group], indicating that the worksheets are grouped together, so any changes you make to the Toronto sheet will also be made to the Vancouver sheet.

3. **Click the Insert tab, then click the Header & Footer button in the Text group**

4. **On the Header & Footer Tools Design tab, click the Go to Footer button in the Navigation group, type Quest in the center section of the footer, enter your name in the left section of the footer, click cell A1, then click the Normal button ⊞ on the Status Bar**

   You decide to check the footers in Print Preview.

5. **With the worksheets still grouped, click the Office button 🔘, point to Print, click Print Preview, then click the Next Page button in the Preview group**

   Because the worksheets are grouped, both pages contain the footer with Quest and your name. The worksheets would look better with a wider top margin.

6. **Click the Close Print Preview button, click the Page Layout tab, click the Margins button in the Page Setup group, click Custom Margins, in the Top text box type 1, then click OK**

7. **Preview and print the worksheets**

   The Toronto worksheet is shown in Figure F-18; the Vancouver worksheet is shown in Figure F-19. You decide to ungroup the worksheets.

8. **Right-click the Toronto worksheet sheet tab, then click Ungroup Sheets**

9. **Save the workbook, then close it and exit Excel**

Creating a workspace

If you work with several workbooks at a time, you can group them so that you can open them in one step by creating a **workspace**, a file with an .xlw extension. Then, instead of opening each workbook individually, you can open the workspace. To create a workspace, open the workbooks you wish to group, then position and size them as you would like them to appear. Click the View tab, click the Save Workspace button in the Window group, type a name for the workspace file, navigate to the location where you want to store it, then click Save. Remember, however, that the workspace file does not contain the workbooks themselves, so you still have to save any changes you make to the original workbook files. If you work at another computer, you need to have the workspace file and all of the workbooks that are part of the workspace.

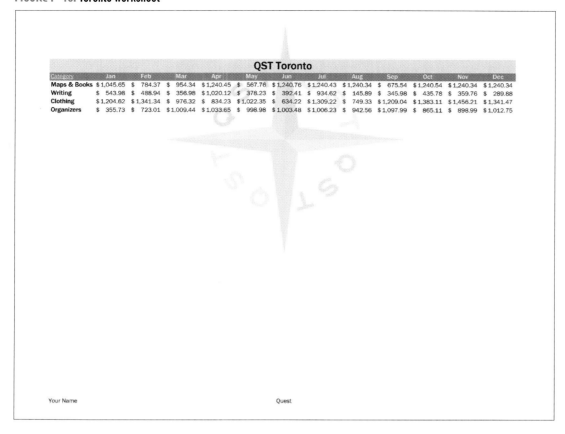

QST Toronto

Category	Jan	Feb	Mar	Apr	May	Jun	Jul	Aug	Sep	Oct	Nov	Dec
Maps & Books	$1,045.65	$ 784.37	$ 954.34	$1,240.45	$ 567.76	$1,240.76	$1,240.43	$1,240.34	$ 675.54	$1,240.54	$1,240.34	$1,240.34
Writing	$ 543.98	$ 488.94	$ 356.98	$1,020.12	$ 378.23	$ 392.41	$ 934.62	$ 145.89	$ 345.98	$ 435.78	$ 359.76	$ 289.88
Clothing	$1,204.62	$1,341.34	$ 976.32	$ 834.23	$1,022.35	$ 634.22	$1,309.22	$ 749.33	$1,209.04	$1,383.11	$1,456.21	$1,341.47
Organizers	$ 355.73	$ 723.01	$1,009.44	$1,033.65	$ 998.98	$1,003.48	$1,006.23	$ 942.56	$1,097.99	$ 865.11	$ 898.99	$1,012.75

Your Name

Quest

FIGURE F-19: Vancouver worksheet

QST Vancouver

Category	Jan	Feb	Mar	Apr	May	Jun	Jul	Aug	Sep	Oct	Nov	Dec
Maps & Books	$1,145.65	$1,384.37	$1,054.34	$ 940.45	$1,567.76	$1,040.76	$ 940.43	$1,140.34	$1,275.54	$ 940.54	$1,040.34	$1,040.34
Writing	$1,543.98	$1,288.94	$1,356.98	$1,120.12	$1,311.22	$1,392.41	$1,134.62	$1,145.89	$1,194.86	$ 835.78	$ 859.76	$ 889.88
Clothing	$ 904.62	$ 941.34	$1,076.32	$1,297.99	$ 922.35	$1,234.22	$1,509.22	$1,049.33	$1,009.04	$1,283.11	$1,126.21	$1,141.47
Organizers	$1,355.73	$1,233.98	$1,055.84	$1,133.65	$1,298.98	$1,303.48	$1,106.23	$ 842.56	$1,197.99	$ 965.11	$ 988.99	$1,112.75

Your Name

Quest

Practice

If you have a SAM user profile, you may have access to hands-on instruction, practice, and assessment of the skills covered in this unit. Log in to your SAM account (http://sam2007.course.com/) to launch any assigned training activities or exams that relate to the skills covered in this unit.

▼ CONCEPTS REVIEW

FIGURE F-20

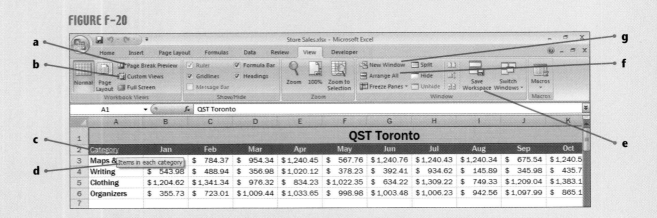

1. **Which element do you click to organize windows in a specific configuration?**
2. **Which element points to a ScreenTip for a hyperlink?**
3. **Which element points to a hyperlink?**
4. **Which element do you click to open the active worksheet in a new window?**
5. **Which element do you click to name and save a set of display and/or print settings?**
6. **Which element do you click to group workbooks so that they open together as a unit?**
7. **Which element do you click to view and change the way worksheet data is distributed on printed pages?**

Match each term with the statement that best describes it.

8. **Data entry area**
9. **Hyperlink**
10. **Watermark**
11. **HTML**
12. **Dynamic page breaks**

a. Web page format
b. Portion of a worksheet that can be changed
c. Translucent background design on a printed worksheet
d. An object that when clicked displays another worksheet or a Web page
e. Adjusted automatically when rows and columns are inserted or deleted

Select the best answer from the list of choices.

13. **You can establish the validity of a workbook by adding a _____.**
    a. Keyword
    b. Custom Views
    c. Digital signature
    d. Template
14. **You can group several workbooks in a _____ so they can be opened together rather than individually.**
    a. Workgroup
    b. Consolidated workbook
    c. Workspace
    d. Work unit

15. Which of the following formats means that users can view but not change data in a workbook?

   a. Macro   **c.** Read-only

   b. PDF   **d.** Template

16. You can group noncontiguous worksheets by pressing and holding _____ while clicking the sheet tabs that you want to group.

   a. [Ctrl]   **c.** [Alt]

   b. [Spacebar]   **d.** [F6]

▼ SKILLS REVIEW

1. View and arrange worksheets.

  a. Start Excel, open the file EX F-2.xlsx from the drive and folder where you store your Data Files, then save it as **Chicago Budget**.

  b. Activate the 2010 sheet if necessary, then open the 2011 sheet in a new window.

  c. Activate the 2010 sheet in the Chicago Budget.xlsx:1 workbook. Activate the 2011 sheet in the Chicago Budget.xlsx:2 workbook.

  d. View the Chicago Budget.xlsx:1 and Chicago Budget.xlsx:2 workbooks tiled horizontally. View the workbooks in a vertical arrangement.

  e. Hide the Chicago Budget.xlsx:2 instance, then unhide the instance. Close the Chicago Budget.xlsx:2 instance and maximize the Chicago Budget.xlsx workbook.

  f. Split the 2010 sheet into two horizontal panes. (*Hint*: Drag the Horizontal split box.) Remove the split by double-clicking it, then save your work.

2. Protect worksheets and workbooks.

  a. On the 2010 sheet, unlock the expense data in the range C9:F17.

  b. Protect the sheet without using a password.

  c. To make sure the other cells are locked, attempt to make an entry in cell D4. You should see the error message displayed in Figure F-21.

  d. Change the first-quarter mortgage expense to 4500.

FIGURE F-21

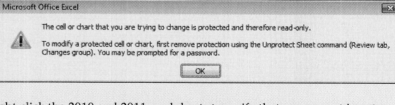

  e. Protect the workbook's structure and windows without applying a password. Right-click the 2010 and 2011 worksheets to verify that you cannot insert, delete, rename, move, copy, hide, or unhide the sheets, or change their tab color.

  f. Unprotect the workbook. Unprotect the 2010 worksheet.

  g. Save the workbook.

3. Save custom views of a worksheet

  a. Using the 2010 sheet, create a view of the entire worksheet called **Entire 2010 Budget**.

  b. Hide rows 8 through 19, then make a new view called **Income** showing only the income data.

  c. Use the Custom Views dialog box to display all of the data on the 2010 worksheet.

  d. Use the Custom Views dialog box to display only the income data on the 2010 worksheet.

  e. Use the Custom Views dialog box to return to the Entire 2010 Budget view.

  f. Save the workbook.

4. Add a worksheet background.

  a. Use EX F-3.gif as a worksheet background for the 2010 sheet.

  b. Delete the background image on the 2010 sheet.

  c. Add EX F-3.gif to the 2010 header.

  d. Preview the 2010 worksheet to verify that the background will print, then exit Print Preview and save the workbook.

  e. Add your name to the center section of the 2010 worksheet footer, then print the worksheet.

5. Prepare a workbook for distribution.

- **a.** Inspect the workbook and remove any document properties, personal information, and header and footer information.
- **b.** Use the Document Properties Panel to add a title of Quarterly Budget and the keywords café and Chicago.(*Hint*: Separate the keywords with a space.) If you are using your own computer, add your name in the Author text box.
- **c.** Mark the workbook as final and verify that [Read-Only] is in the title bar.
- **d.** Remove the final status of the workbook.
- **e.** Save the workbook.

6. Insert hyperlinks.

- **a.** On the 2010 worksheet, make cell A8 a hyperlink to the file **Expenses.xlsx** in your Data Files folder.
- **b.** Test the link, then print Sheet 1 of the Expenses workbook.
- **c.** Return to the Chicago Budget workbook, edit the hyperlink in cell A8, adding a ScreenTip that reads **Expense Details**, then verify that the ScreenTip appears.
- **d.** On the 2011 worksheet, enter the text **Based on 2010 budget** in cell A21.
- **e.** Make the text in cell A21 a hyperlink to cell A1 in the 2010 worksheet. (*Hint*: Use the Place in This Document button and note the cell reference in the Type the cell reference text box.)
- **f.** Test the hyperlink.
- **g.** Remove the hyperlink in cell A8 of the 2010 worksheet.
- **h.** Save the workbook.

7. Save a workbook for distribution.

- **a.** Save the Chicago Budget workbook as a single file Web page with the name chicago.mht. Close the chicago.mht file in Excel, then open the chicago.mht file in your Web browser. Close your browser window and reopen the Chicago Budget.xlsx file.
- **b.** If you have the PDF Add-in installed on your computer, save the Chicago Budget workbook as a PDF file.
- **c.** Save the Chicago Budget workbook as an Excel 97-2003 workbook and review the results of the Compatibility Checker.
- **d.** Close the Chicago Budget.xls file and reopen the Chicago Budget.xlsx file.
- **e.** Save the file as a macro-enabled template in the drive and folder where you store your Data Files. (*Hint*: Select the type Excel Macro-Enabled template xltm in the Save as type list.)
- **f.** Close the template file, then reopen the Chicago Budget.xlsx file.

8. Grouping worksheets.

- **a.** Group the 2010 and 2011 worksheets.
- **b.** Add your name to the center footer section of the worksheets.
- **c.** Save the workbook, then preview both sheets.
- **d.** Print both sheets, compare your sheets to Figure F-22, then ungroup the sheets.
- **e.** Close all open files and exit Excel.

FIGURE F-22

	A	B	C	D	E	F	G	H
1	Chicago 2010 Quarterly Café Budget							
2	Income	Description	1st QTR	2nd QTR	3rd QTR	4th QTR	TOTAL	% OF TOTAL
3		Coffee	$ 8,500	$ 8,700	$ 7,500	$ 8,100	$ 32,800	34.02%
4		Tea	$ 7,500	$ 6,800	$ 5,700	$ 6,800	$ 26,800	27.80%
5		Pastries	$ 9,100	$ 9,100	$ 8,700	$ 9,900	$ 36,800	38.17%
6		TOTAL	$ 25,100	$ 24,600	$ 21,900	$ 24,800	$ 96,400	100.00%
7								
8	Expenses							
9		Mortgage	$ 4,500	$ 4,300	$ 4,300	$ 4,300	$ 17,400	32.67%
10		Payroll	$ 5,500	$ 5,500	$ 5,500	$ 5,800	$ 22,300	41.87%
11		Pastries	$ 1,150	$ 1,150	$ 1,180	$ 1,150	$ 4,630	8.69%
12		Utilities	$ 580	$ 580	$ 580	$ 580	$ 2,320	4.36%
13		Phone	$ 490	$ 490	$ 490	$ 450	$ 1,920	3.60%
14		Coffee	$ 580	$ 580	$ 590	$ 580	$ 2,330	4.37%
15		Tea	$ 370	$ 370	$ 330	$ 370	$ 1,440	2.70%
16		Advertising	$ 230	$ 230	$ 230	$ 230	$ 920	1.73%
17		TOTAL	$ 13,400	$ 13,200	$ 13,200	$ 13,460	$ 53,260	100.00%
18								
19	Cash Flow		$ 11,700	$ 11,400	$ 8,700	$ 11,340	$ 43,140	
20								

	A	B	C	D	E	F	G	H
1	Chicago 2011 Quarterly Café Budget							
2	Income	Description	1st QTR	2nd QTR	3rd QTR	4th QTR	TOTAL	% OF TOTAL
3		Coffee	$ 8,800	$ 8,500	$ 7,500	$ 8,100	$ 32,900	33.64%
4		Tea	$ 7,700	$ 6,900	$ 5,700	$ 6,800	$ 27,100	27.71%
5		Pastries	$ 9,900	$ 9,300	$ 8,700	$ 9,900	$ 37,800	38.65%
6		TOTAL	$ 26,400	$ 24,700	$ 21,900	$ 24,800	$ 97,800	100.00%
7								
8	Expenses							
9		Mortgage	$ 4,300	$ 4,300	$ 4,300	$ 4,300	$ 4,300	31.85%
10		Payroll	$ 5,600	$ 5,600	$ 5,600	$ 5,600	$ 5,600	41.48%
11		Pastries	$ 1,250	$ 1,250	$ 1,250	$ 1,250	$ 1,250	9.26%
12		Utilities	$ 590	$ 590	$ 590	$ 590	$ 590	4.37%
13		Phone	$ 500	$ 500	$ 500	$ 500	$ 500	3.70%
14		Coffee	$ 590	$ 590	$ 590	$ 590	$ 590	4.37%
15		Tea	$ 390	$ 390	$ 390	$ 390	$ 390	2.89%
16		Advertising	$ 280	$ 280	$ 280	$ 280	$ 280	2.07%
17		TOTAL	$ 13,500	$ 13,500	$ 13,500	$ 13,500	$ 13,500	100.00%
18								
19	Cash Flow		$ 12,900	$ 11,200	$ 8,400	$ 11,300	$ 84,300	
20								
21	Based on 2010 Budget							
22								

▼ INDEPENDENT CHALLENGE 1

You manage Old City Photo, a photo supply company located in Montreal, Canada. You are organizing your first-quarter sales in an Excel worksheet. Because the sheet for the month of January includes the same type of information you need for February and March, you decide to enter the headings for all of the first-quarter months at the same time. You use a separate worksheet for each month and create data for three months.

a. Start Excel, create a new workbook, then save it as **Photo Sales.xlsx** in the drive and folder where you store your Data Files.

b. Name the first sheet January, name the second sheet February, and name the third sheet March.

c. Group the worksheets.

d. With the worksheets grouped, use Table F-2 as a guide to enter the row and column labels that need to appear on each of the three sheets. Add the headings in rows one and two. Center the first row across columns A and B. Enter the labels with the data in the range B3:B9 and the Total label in cell A10.

e. Enter the formula to sum the Amount column in cell B10. Ungroup the worksheets and enter your own data for each of the sales categories in the January, February, and March sheets.

f. Display each worksheet in its own window, then arrange the three sheets vertically.

g. Hide the window displaying the March sheet. Unhide the March sheet window.

h. Split the March window into two panes, the upper pane displaying rows one through five and the lower pane displaying rows six through ten. Scroll through the data in each pane, then remove the split.

i. Close the windows displaying Photo Sales.xlsx:2 and Photo Sales.xlsx:3, then maximize the Photo Sales.xlsx workbook.

j. Add the keywords **photo supplies** to your workbook, using the Document Properties Panel.

k. Group the worksheets again.

l. Add headers that include your name in the left section to all three worksheets.

m. With the worksheets still grouped, format the worksheets appropriately.

n. Ungroup the worksheets, then mark the workbook status as final.

o. Save the workbook, preview and print the three worksheets, then exit Excel.

TABLE F-2

Old City Photo
Amount in $ (Canada)
Cameras
Color Processing
B & W Processing
Film
Digital Media
Frames
Darkroom Supplies
TOTAL

▼ INDEPENDENT CHALLENGE 2

As the payroll manager at Media Communications, an advertising firm, you decide to organize the weekly timecard data using Excel worksheets. You use a separate worksheet for each week and track the hours for employees with different job classifications. A hyperlink in the worksheet provides pay rates for each classification and custom views limit the information that is displayed.

a. Start Excel, open the file EX F-4.xlsx from the drive and folder where you store your Data Files, then save it as **Timesheets**.

b. Compare the data in the workbook by arranging the Week 1, Week 2, and Week 3 sheets horizontally.

c. Maximize the Week 1 window. Unlock the hours data in the Week 1 sheet and protect the worksheet. Verify that the employee names, numbers, and classifications cannot be changed. Verify that the total hours data can be changed, but do not change the data.

d. Unprotect the Week 1 sheet and create a custom view called **Complete Worksheet** that displays all of the worksheet data.

e. Hide column E and create a custom view of the data in the range A1:D22. Give the view a name of **Employee Classifications**. Display each view, then return to the Complete Worksheet view.

▼ INDEPENDENT CHALLENGE 2 (CONTINUED)

f. Add a page break between columns D and E so that the Total Hours data prints on a second page. Preview the worksheet, then remove the page break. (*Hint*: Use the Breaks button on the Page Layout tab.)

g. Add a hyperlink to the Classification heading in cell D1 that links to the file Classifications.xlsx. Add a ScreenTip that reads Pay rates, then test the hyperlink. Compare your screen to Figure F-23.

h. Save the workbook as an Excel 97-2003 workbook, reviewing the Compatibility Checker information. Close the Timesheets.xls file, then reopen the Timesheets.xlsx workbook.

i. Group the three worksheets and add your name to the center section of the footer.

j. Save the workbook, then preview the grouped worksheets.

k. Ungroup the worksheets and add two-inch top and left margins to the Week 1 worksheet.

l. Hide the Week 2 and Week 3 worksheets.

m. Inspect the file and remove all document properties, personal information, headers, footers, and hidden worksheets.

n. Add the keyword hours to the workbook, save the workbook, then mark it as final.

FIGURE F-23

	A	B
1	**Media Communications**	
2	Classifications	Pay Rate
3	Associate	$37
4	Sr. Associate	$45
5	Assistant	$22
6	Sr. Assistant	$30
7		

Advanced Challenge Exercise

■ Remove the final status from the workbook.

■ If you have Windows Rights Management Services client software installed on your computer, restrict the permissions to the workbook by granting only yourself permission to change the workbook.

■ If you have a valid certificate authority, add a digital signature to the workbook.

■ Delete the hours data in the worksheet and save the workbook as an Excel Template.

o. Add your name to the center footer section, save the workbook, print the Week 1 worksheet, close the workbook and exit Excel.

▼ INDEPENDENT CHALLENGE 3

One of your responsibilities as the office manager at your technology training company is to order paper supplies for the office. You decide to create a spreadsheet to track these orders, placing each month's orders on its own sheet. You create custom views that will focus on the categories of supplies. A hyperlink will provide the supplier's contact information.

a. Start Excel, open the file EX F-5.xlsx from the drive and folder where you store your Data Files, then save it as **Supplies**.

b. Arrange the sheets for the three months horizontally to compare supply expenses, then close the extra workbook windows and maximize the remaining window.

c. Create a custom view of the entire January worksheet named **All Supplies**. Hide the paper, pens, and miscellaneous supply data and create a custom view displaying only the hardware supplies. Call the view **Hardware**.

d. Display the All Supplies view, group the worksheets, and create totals for the total costs in cell D28 on each month's sheet.

e. With the sheets grouped, add the sheet name to the center section of each sheet's header and your name to the center section of each sheet's footer.

f. Use the compatibility checker to view the unsupported features in earlier Excel formats.

g. Add a hyperlink in cell A1 of the January sheet that opens the file Hardware.xlsx. Add a ScreenTip of **Hardware Supplier**. Test the link, viewing the ScreenTip, then return to the Supplies workbook.

h. Create a workspace that includes the workbooks Supplies.xlsx and Hardware.xlsx in the tiled layout. Name the workspace **Office Supplies**. (*Hint*: Save Workspace is a button on the View tab in the Window group.)

i. Hide the Hardware.xlsx workbook.

j. Unhide the Hardware.xlsx workbook.

▼ INDEPENDENT CHALLENGE 3 (CONTINUED)

k. Close the Hardware.xlsx file and maximize the Supplies.xlsx worksheet.

l. Save the Supplies workbook as a macro-enabled workbook.

m. Print the January worksheet, close the workbook, and exit Excel.

▼ REAL LIFE INDEPENDENT CHALLENGE

Excel can be a useful tool in planning vacations. Whether you are planning a trip soon or in the distant future, you can use Excel to organize your travel budget. Use the table below as a guide in organizing your travel expenses. After your data is entered, you create custom views of the data, add a hyperlink and keywords, and save the file in an earlier version of Excel.

a. Start Excel, create a new workbook, then save it as **Travel Budget** in the drive and folder where you store your Data Files.

b. Enter your travel budget data using the relevant items from the Table F-3.

c. Add a hyperlink to your accommodations label that links to a Web page with information about the hotel, campground, B & B, or inn that you will stay at on your trip.

d. Create a custom view called **Entire Budget** that displays all of the budget information. Create a custom view named **Transportation** that displays only the transportation data. Check each view, then display the entire budget.

e. Add appropriate keywords to the workbook.

f. Add a footer that includes your name on the left side of the printout.

g. Unlock the price information in the worksheet. Protect the worksheet without using a password.

h. Save the workbook, then print the worksheet.

i. Save the workbook in Excel 97-2003 format.

j. Close the Travel Budget.xls file.

Advanced Challenge Exercise

- Open the Travel Budget.xlsx file and unprotect the worksheet.
- Enable the workbook to be changed by multiple people simultaneously.
- Set up the shared workbook so that all future changes will be tracked.
- Change the data for two of your dollar amounts.
- Review the tracked changes and accept the first change and reject the second change
- Save the workbook.

k. Exit Excel.

TABLE F-3

	Amount
Transportation	
Air	
Auto	
Train	
Cab	
Bus	
Accommodations	
Hotel	
Campground fees	
Bed & Breakfast	
Inn	
Meals	
Food	
Beverage	
Miscellaneous	
Admissions fees	
Souvenirs	

Excel 2007

▼ VISUAL WORKSHOP

Start Excel, open the file EX F-6.xlsx from the drive and folder where you store your Data Files, then save it as **Summer Rentals**. Create the worksheet shown in Figure F-24. Enter your name in the footer, then print the worksheet. The text in cell A18 is a hyperlink to the Price Information workbook; the worksheet background is the Data File EX F-7.gif, and the picture in the header is the file EX F-7.gif.

FIGURE F-24

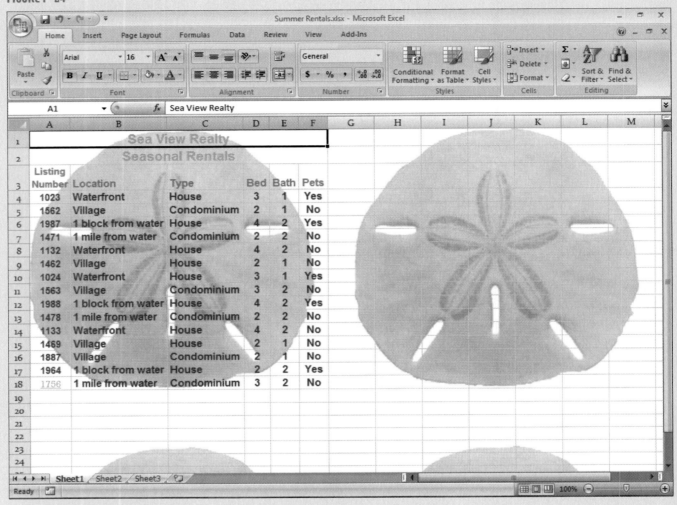

Using Tables

Files You Will Need:

EX G-1.xlsx
EX G-2.xlsx
EX G-3.xlsx
EX G-4.xlsx
EX G-5.xlsx

In addition to using Excel spreadsheet features, you can analyze and manipulate data in a table structure. An Excel **table** is an organized collection of rows and columns of similarly structured data in a worksheet. For example, a table might contain customer, sales, or inventory information. When you designate a particular range of worksheet data as a table, its formatting is extended when you add data and all table formulas are updated to include the new data. Without a table, you would have to manually adjust formatting and formulas every time data is added to a range. In this unit, you'll learn how to plan and create a table; add, change, find, and delete information in a table; and then sort, perform table calculations, and print a table. Quest uses tables to analyze tour data. The vice president of sales, Kate Morgan, asks you to help her build and manage a table of 2010 tour information.

OBJECTIVES

Plan a table
Create a table
Add table data
Find and replace table data
Delete table data
Sort table data
Use formulas in a table
Print a table

Planning a Table

When planning a table, consider what information you want your table to contain and how you want to work with the data, now and in the future. As you plan a table, you should understand its most important components. A table is organized into rows called records. A **record** contains data about an object, person, or other type of table item. Records are composed of fields. **Fields** are columns in the table; each field describes a characteristic of the record, such as a customer's last name or street address. Each field has a **field name**, which is a column label, such as "Address," that describes its contents. Tables usually have a **header row** as the first row that contains the field names. To plan your table, use the steps below. See Table G-1 for additional planning guidelines. 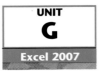 Kate asks you to compile a table of the 2010 tours. Before entering the tour data into an Excel worksheet, you plan the table contents.

DETAILS

As you plan your table, use the following guidelines:

*   **Identify the purpose of the table**
    Determine the kind of information the table should contain. You want to use the tours table to quickly find all departure dates of a particular tour. You also want to display the tours in order of departure date.

*   **Plan the structure of the table**
    Determine the fields that are necessary to achieve the table's purpose. You have worked with the sales department to determine the type of information that they need to obtain about each tour. Figure G-1 shows a layout sketch for the table. Each row will contain one tour record. The columns represent fields that contain pieces of descriptive information you will enter for each tour, such as the name, departure date, and duration.

*   **Document the table design**
    In addition to your table sketch, you should make a list of the field names that documents the type of data and any special number formatting required for each field. Field names should be as short as possible while still accurately describing the column info. When naming fields it is important to use text rather than numbers because numbers may be interpreted as parts of formulas. Your field names should be unique and not easily confused with cell addresses, such as the name D2. Your Tours table will contain eight field names, each one corresponding to the major characteristics of the 2010 tours. Table G-2 shows the documentation of the field names in your table.

TABLE G-1: Guidelines for planning a table

worksheet structure guidelines	row and column content guidelines
Tables can be created from any contiguous range of cells on your worksheet	Plan and design your table so that all rows have similar items in the same column
A table should not have any blank rows or columns	Do not insert extra spaces at the beginning of a cell because this can affect sorting and searching
Data in your table can be used independently of data outside of the table on the worksheet	Instead of blank rows or columns between your labels and your data, use formatting to make column labels stand out from the data
Data can be organized on a worksheet using multiple tables to define sets of related data	Use the same format for all cells below the field name in a column

Tour	Depart Date	Number of Days	Seat Capacity	Seats Reserved	Price	Air Included	Meals Included

Header row will contain
field names

Each tour will be
placed in a table row

Excel 2007

TABLE G-2: Table documentation

field name	type of data	description of data
Tour	Text	Name of tour
Depart Date	Date	Date tour departs
Number of Days	Number with 0 decimal places	Duration of the tour
Seat Capacity	Number with 0 decimal places	Maximum number of people the tour can accommodate
Seats Reserved	Number with 0 decimal places	Number of reservations for the tour
Price	Accounting with 0 decimal places and $ symbol	Tour price (This price is not guaranteed until a 30% deposit is received)
Air Included	Text	Yes: Airfare is included in the price No: Airfare is not included in the price
Meals Included	Text	Yes: Breakfast and dinner included in the price No: Meals are not included in the price

Creating a Table

Once you have planned the table structure, the sequence of fields, and appropriate data types, you are ready to create the table in Excel. After you create a table, a Table Tools Design tab appears, containing a gallery of table styles. **Table styles** allow you to easily add formatting to your table by using preset formatting combinations that define fill color, borders, and type style and color. ▓▓▓▓▓ Kate asks you to build a table with the 2010 tour data. You begin by entering the field names. Then you enter the tour data that corresponds to each field name, create the table, and format the data using a table style.

STEPS

1. **Start Excel, open the file** EX G-1.xlsx **from the drive and folder where you store your Data Files, then save it as** 2010 Tours

TROUBLE
Don't worry if your field names are wider than the cells; you will fix this later.

2. **Beginning in cell A1 of the Practice sheet, enter each field name in a separate column, as shown in Figure G-2**
   Field names are usually entered in the first row of the table.

3. **Enter the information from Figure G-3 in the rows immediately below the field names, leaving no blank rows**
   The data appears in columns organized by field name.

4. **Select the range A1:H4, click the** Format **button in the Cells group, click** AutoFit Column Width, **then click cell** A1
   Resizing the column widths this way is faster than double-clicking the column divider lines.

5. **With cell A1 selected, click the** Insert tab, **then click the** Table **button in the Tables group, in the Create Table dialog box verify that your table data is in the range** $A$1:$H$4 **and make sure** My table has headers **is checked, then click** OK
   Filter list arrows, which let you display portions of your data, appear next to each column header. When you create a table, Excel automatically applies a default table style. The Table Tools Design tab appears and the Table Styles group displays a gallery of table formatting options. You decide to use a different table style from the gallery.

6. **Click the** Table Styles More button ▾, **scroll to view all of the table styles, then move the mouse pointer over several styles without clicking**
   As you point to each table style, Live Preview shows you what your table will look like with the style applied. However, you only see a preview of each style; you need to click a style to apply it.

7. **Click the** Table Style Medium 7 **to apply it to your table, then click cell** A1
   Compare your table to Figure G-4.

Coordinating table styles with your document

The Table Styles gallery on the Table Tools Design tab has three style categories: Light, Medium, and Dark. Each category has numerous design types; for example, in some of the designs, the header row and total row are darker and the rows alternate colors. The available table designs use the current workbook theme colors so the table coordinates with your existing workbook content. If you select a different workbook theme and color scheme in the Themes group on the Page Layout tab, the Table Styles gallery uses those colors. You can modify gallery styles further by using the options in the Table Style Options group on the Table Tools Design tab; for example, if you select Header Row, the table styles in the gallery will all display distinctive header rows.

FIGURE G-2: Field names entered in row 1

	A	B	C	D	E	F	G	H	I
1	Tour	Depart Date	Number of Days	Seat Capacity	Seats Reserved	Price	Air Included	Meals Included	
2									

FIGURE G-3: Three records entered in the worksheet

	A	B	C	D	E	F	G	H	I
1	Tour	Depart Date	Number of Days	Seat Capacity	Seats Reserved	Price	Air Included	Meals Included	
2	Pacific Odyssey	1/11/2010	14	50	50	3105	Yes	No	
3	Old Japan	1/12/2010	21	47	41	2100	Yes	No	
4	Down Under Exodus	1/18/2010	10	30	28	2800	Yes	Yes	
5									

FIGURE G-4: Formatted table with three records

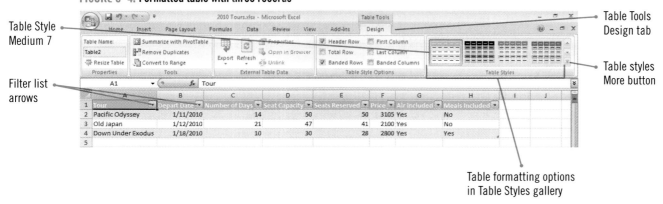

Table Style Medium 7

Filter list arrows

Table Tools Design tab

Table styles More button

Table formatting options in Table Styles gallery

Excel 2007

Changing table style options

You can modify a table's appearance by using the check boxes in the Table Styles Options group on the Table Tools Design tab. For example, you can turn on or turn off the following options: **banding**, which creates different formatting for adjacent rows and columns; special formatting for first and last columns; Total Row, which calculates totals for each column; and Header Row, which displays or hides the header row. Use these options to modify a table's appearance either before or after applying a Table Style. For example, if your table has banded rows, you can select the Banded Columns check box to change the table to display with banded columns. Also, you may want to deselect the Header Row check box to hide a table's header row if a table will be included in a presentation. Figure G-5 shows the available table style options.

You can also create your own table style by clicking the Table Styles More button, then at the bottom of the Table Styles Gallery, clicking New Table Style. In the New Table Quick Style dialog box, name the style in the Name text box, click a table element, then

format selected table elements by clicking Format. You can also set a custom style as the default style for your tables by checking the Set as default table quick style for this document check box. You can click Clear at the bottom of the Table Styles gallery if you want to clear a table style.

FIGURE G-5: Table Styles Options

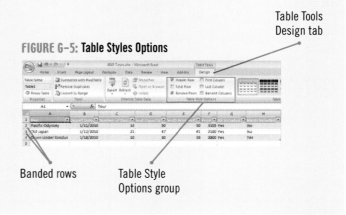

Table Tools Design tab

Banded rows

Table Style Options group

Adding Table Data

You can add records to a table by typing data directly below the last row of the table. After you press [Enter], the new row is added to the table and the table formatting is extended to the new data. When the active cell is the last cell of a table, you can add a new row by pressing [Tab]. You can add rows in any table location. If you decide you need additional data fields, you can add new columns to a table. Another way to expand a table is to drag the sizing handle in a table's lower-right corner; drag down to add rows and drag to the right to add columns. ⬛⬛⬛ After entering all of the 2010 tour data, Kate decides to offer two additional tours. She also wants the table to display the number of available seats for each tour and whether visas are required for the destination.

STEPS

1. **Activate the 2010 Tours sheet**
   The sheet contains the 2010 tour data.

QUICK TIP

You can select a table column by clicking the top edge of the field name. Be careful not to click a column letter or row number, however, because this selects the entire worksheet column or row. You can select the table data by clicking the upper-left corner of the first table cell. Clicking a second time will include the table header in the selection.

2. **Click cell A65 in the table, enter the data for the new Costa Rica Rainforest tour, as shown in Figure G-6, then press [Enter]**
   The new Costa Rica tour is part of the table. You want to enter a record about a new January tour above row 6.

3. **Click the inside left edge of cell A6 to select the table row data, click the Insert list arrow in the Cells group, then click Insert Table Rows Above**
   Clicking the left edge of the first cell in a table row selects the entire table row. A new blank row 6 is available to enter the new record.

4. **Click cell A6, then enter the Nepal Trekking record, as shown in Figure G-7**
   The new Nepal tour is part of the table. You want to add a new field that displays the number of available seats for each tour.

5. **Click cell I1, enter the field name Seats Available, then press [Enter]**
   The new field becomes part of the table and the header formatting extends to the new field. The AutoCorrect menu allows you to undo or stop the automatic table expansion, but in this case, you decide to leave this feature on. You want to add another new field to the table to display tours that require visas, but this time you will add the new field by resizing the table.

QUICK TIP

You can also resize a table by clicking the Table Tools Design tab, clicking the Resize Table button in the Properties group, selecting the new data range for the table, then clicking OK.

6. **Scroll down until cell I66 is visible, drag the sizing handle in the table's lower-right corner one column to the right to add column J to the table, as shown in Figure G-8.**
   The table range is now A1:J66 and the new field name is Column1.

7. **Click cell J1, enter Visa Required, then press [Enter]**

8. **Click the Insert tab, click the Header & Footer button in the Text group, enter your name in the center header text box, click cell A1, click the Normal button ⊞ in the status bar, then save the workbook**

FIGURE G-6: New record in row 65

61	Galapagos Adventure	12/20/2010	14	15	1	$ 3,100	Yes	Yes
62	Pacific Odyssey	12/21/2010	14	50	10	$ 3,105	Yes	No
63	Essential India	12/30/2010	18	51	15	$ 3,933	Yes	Yes
64	Old Japan	12/31/2010	21	47	4	$ 2,100	Yes	No
65	Costa Rica Rainforests	1/30/2010	7	20	0	$ 2,590	Yes	Yes
66								

New record
in row 65

FIGURE G-7: New record in row 6

	A	B	C	D	E	F	G	H
1	Tour	Depart Date	Number of Days	Seat Capacity	Seats Reserved	Price	Air Included	Meals Included
2	Pacific Odyssey	1/11/2010	14	50	50	$ 3,105	Yes	No
3	Old Japan	1/12/2010	21	47	41	$ 2,100	Yes	No
4	Down Under Exodus	1/18/2010	10	30	28	$ 2,800	Yes	Yes
5	Essential India	1/20/2010	18	51	40	$ 3,933	Yes	Yes
6	Nepal Trekking	1/31/2010	14	18	0	$ 4,200	Yes	Yes
7	Amazing Amazon	2/23/2010	14	43	38	$ 2,877	No	No
8	Cooking in France	2/28/2010	7	18	15	$ 2,822	Yes	No
9	Pearls of the Orient	3/12/2010	14	50	15	$ 3,400	Yes	No
10	Silk Road Travels	3/18/2010	18	25	19	$ 2,190	Yes	Yes

New record
in row 6

FIGURE G-8: Resizing a table using the resizing handles

60	Panama Adventure	12/18/2010	10	50	21	$ 2,304	Yes	Yes
61	Galapagos Adventure	12/20/2010	14	15	1	$ 3,100	Yes	Yes
62	Galapagos Adventure	12/20/2010	14	15	1	$ 3,100	Yes	Yes
63	Pacific Odyssey	12/21/2010	14	50	10	$ 3,105	Yes	No
64	Essential India	12/30/2010	18	51	15	$ 3,933	Yes	Yes
65	Old Japan	12/31/2010	21	47	4	$ 2,100	Yes	No
66	Costa Rica Rainforests	1/30/2010	7	20	0	$ 2,590	Yes	Yes
67								
68								
69								

Drag sizing handle
to add column J

Finding and Replacing Table Data

From time to time, you need to locate specific records in your table. You can use the Excel Find feature to search your table for a particular record. You can also use the Replace feature to locate and replace existing entries or portions of entries with information you specify. If you don't know the exact spelling of the text you are searching for, you can use wildcards to help locate the records. **Wildcards** are special symbols that substitute for unknown characters. ▓▓▓▓ In response to feedback from the sales representatives about customers' lack of familiarity of Istria, Kate wants to replace "Istria" with "Croatia" in all of the tour names. She also wants to know how many Pacific Odyssey tours are scheduled for the year. You begin by searching for records with the text "Pacific Odyssey".

STEPS

1. **Click cell A1 if necessary, click the Home tab, click the Find & Select button in the Editing group, then click Find**

   The Find and Replace dialog box opens, as shown in Figure G-9. In this dialog box, you enter criteria that specify the records you want to find in the Find what text box. You want to search for records whose Tour field contains the label "Pacific Odyssey".

2. **Type Pacific Odyssey in the Find what text box, then click Find Next**

   A2 is the active cell because it is the first instance of Pacific Odyssey in the table.

3. **Click Find Next and examine the record for each found Pacific Odyssey tour until no more matching cells are found in the table and the active cell is A2 again, then click Close**

   There are four Pacific Odyssey tours.

4. **Return to cell A1, click the Find & Select button in the Editing group, then click Replace**

   The Find and Replace dialog box opens with the Replace tab selected and the insertion point in the Replace with text box, as shown in Figure G-10. You will search for entries containing "Istria" and replace them with "Croatia". You are not sure of the spelling of Istria, so you will use the * wildcard to help you locate the records containing the correct tour name.

   QUICK TIP

   You can also use the question mark (?) wildcard to represent any single character. For example, using "to?" as your search text would only find 3-letter words beginning with "to", such as "top" and "tot"; it would not find "tone" or "topography".

5. **Delete any text in the Find what text box, type Is* in the Find what text box, click the Replace with text box, then type Croatia**

   The asterisk (*) wildcard stands for one or more characters, meaning that the search text Is* will find words such as "Is", "Isn't", and "Islington". Because you notice that there are other table entries containing the text "is" with a lowercase "i" (in the Visa Required column heading), you need to make sure that only capitalized instances of the letter I are replaced.

6. **Click Options >>, click the Match case check box to select it, click Options <<, then click Find Next**

   Excel moves the cell pointer to the first occurrence of "Istria".

7. **Click Replace All, click OK, then click Close**

   The dialog box closes. Excel made two replacements, in cells A22 and A51. The Visa Required field heading remains unchanged because the "is" in "Visa" is lowercase.

8. **Save the workbook**

FIGURE G-9: Find and Replace dialog box

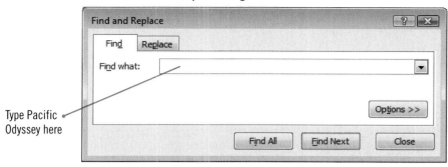

Type Pacific
Odyssey here

FIGURE G-10: The Replace tab in the Find and Replace dialog box

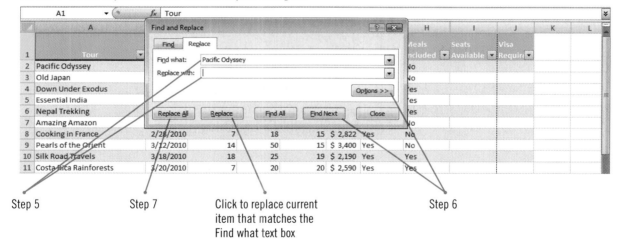

Step 5   Step 7   Click to replace current   Step 6
                                item that matches the
                                Find what text box

Using Find and Select features

You can also use the Find feature to navigate to a specific place in a workbook by clicking the Find & Select button in the Editing group, clicking Go To, typing a cell address, then clicking OK. Clicking the Find & Select button also allows you to find comments and conditional formatting in a worksheet by clicking Go to Special. You can use the Go to Special dialog box to select cells that contain different types of formulas, objects, or data validation. Some Go to Special commands also appear on the Find & Select menu. Using this menu, you can also change the mouse pointer shape to the Select Objects pointer ⬚ so you can quickly select drawing objects when necessary. To return to the standard Excel pointer, press [Esc].

Deleting Table Data

In order to keep a table up to date, you need to be able to periodically remove records. You may even need to remove fields if the information stored in a field becomes unnecessary. You can delete table data using the Delete button or by dragging the sizing handle at the table's lower right corner. You can also easily delete duplicate records from a table. ▰▰▰▰ Kate is canceling the Old Japan tour that departs on 1/12/2010 and asks you to delete the record from the table. You will also remove any duplicate records from the table. Because the visa requirements are difficult to keep up with, Kate asks you to delete the field with visa information.

STEPS

1. **Click the left edge of cell A3 to select the table row data, click the Delete button list arrow in the Cells group, then click Delete Table Rows**

   The Old Japan tour is deleted and the Down Under Exodus tour moves up to row 3, as shown in Figure G-11. You can also delete a table row or a column using the Resize Table button in the Properties group of the Table Tools Design tab, or by right-clicking the row or column, pointing to Delete on the shortcut menu, then clicking Table Columns or Table Rows. You decide to check the table for duplicate records.

2. **Click the Table Tools Design tab, then click the Remove Duplicates button in the Tools group**

   The Remove Duplicates dialog box opens, as shown in Figure G-12. You need to select the columns that the program should use to evaluate duplicates. Because you don't want to delete tours with the same destination but different departure dates, you will look for duplicate data in all of the columns.

3. **Make sure that "My data has headers" is checked and that all the columns headers are checked, then click OK**

   Two duplicate records are found and removed, leaving 63 rows in the table, including the header row. You want to remove the last column, which contains space for visa information.

4. **Click OK, scroll down until cell J63 is visible, drag the sizing handle of the table's lower-right corner one column to the left to remove column J from the table**

   The table range is now A1:I63 and the Visa Required field no longer appears in the table.

5. **Delete the contents of cell J1, return to cell A1, then save the workbook**

FIGURE G-11: Table with row deleted

	A	B	C	D	E	F	G	H	I	J
1	Tour	Depart Date	Number of Days	Seat Capacity	Seats Reserved	Price	Air Included	Meals Included	Seats Available	Visa Require
2	Pacific Odyssey	1/11/2010	14	50	50	$ 3,105	Yes	No		
3	Down Under Exodus	1/18/2010	10	30	28	$ 2,800	Yes	Yes		
4	Essential India	1/20/2010	18	51	40	$ 3,933	Yes	Yes		
5	Nepal Trekking	1/31/2010	14	18	0	$ 4,200	Yes	Yes		
6	Amazing Amazon	2/23/2010	14	43	38	$ 2,877	No	No		
7	Cooking in France	2/28/2010	7	18	15	$ 2,822	Yes	No		
8	Pearls of the Orient	3/12/2010	14	50	15	$ 3,400	Yes	No		
9	Silk Road Travels	3/18/2010	18	25	19	$ 2,190	Yes	Yes		
10	Costa Rica Rainforests	3/20/2010	7	20	20	$ 2,590	Yes	Yes		
11	Green Adventures in Ecuador	3/23/2010	18	25	22	$ 2,450	No	No		
12	African National Parks	4/7/2010	30	12	10	$ 4,870	Yes	Yes		
13	Experience Cambodia	4/10/2010	12	40	21	$ 2,908	Yes	No		
14	Old Japan	4/14/2010	21	47	30	$ 2,100	Yes	No		
15	Down Under Exodus	4/18/2010	10	30	20	$ 2,800	Yes	Yes		
16	Essential India	4/20/2010	18	51	31	$ 3,933	Yes	Yes		
17	Amazing Amazon	4/23/2010	14	43	30	$ 2,877	No	No		
18	Catalonia Adventure	5/9/2010	14	51	30	$ 3,100	Yes	No		
19	Treasures of Ethiopia	5/18/2010	10	41	15	$ 3,200	Yes	Yes		
20	Monasteries of Bulgaria	5/20/2010	7	19	11	$ 2,103	Yes	Yes		
21	Cooking in Croatia	5/23/2010	7	12	10	$ 2,110	No	No		
22	Magnificent Montenegro	5/27/2010	10	48	4	$ 1,890	No	No		
23	Catalonia Adventure	6/9/2010	14	51	15	$ 3,100	Yes	No		
24	Nepal Trekking	6/9/2010	14	18	18	$ 4,200	Yes	Yes		
25	Corfu Sailing Voyage	6/10/2010	21	12	10	$ 3,190	Yes	No		
26	Ireland by Bike	6/11/2010	10	15	10	$ 2,600	Yes	No		

Practice | **2010 Tours** | Sheet2

Ready   Average: 8612.8   Count: 8   Sum: 43064   100%

Row is deleted and
tours move up one row

Excel 2007

FIGURE G-12: Remove Duplicates dialog box

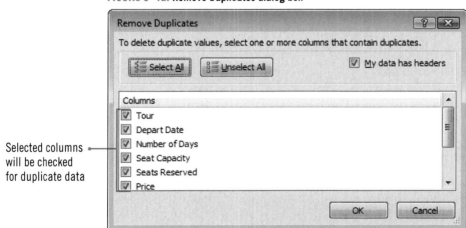

Selected columns
will be checked
for duplicate data

Sorting Table Data

Usually, you enter table records in the order in which you receive information, rather than in alphabetical or numerical order. When you add records to a table, you usually enter them at the end of the table. You can change the order of the records any time using the Excel **sort** feature. You can sort a table in ascending or descending order on one field using the filter list arrows next to the field name. In **ascending order**, the lowest value (the beginning of the alphabet or the earliest date) appears at the top of the table. In a field containing labels and numbers, numbers appear first in the sorted list. In **descending order**, the highest value (the end of the alphabet or the latest date) appears at the top of the table. In a field containing labels and numbers, labels appear first. Table G-3 provides examples of ascending and descending sorts. Because the data is structured as a table, Excel changes the order of the records while keeping each record, or row of information, together. ░░░ Kate wants the tour data sorted by departure date, displaying tours that depart the soonest at the top of the table.

STEPS

QUICK TIP

Before you sort records, consider making a backup copy of your table or create a field that numbers the records so you can return them to their original order, if necessary.

1. **Click the** Depart Date filter list arrow, **then click** Sort Oldest to Newest

   Excel rearranges the records in ascending order by depart date, as shown in Figure G-13. The Depart Date filter list arrow has an upward pointing arrow indicating the ascending sort in the field. You can also sort the table on one field using the Sort & Filter button.

QUICK TIP

You can also add a multilevel sort by clicking the Data tab and then clicking the Sort button in the Sort & Filter group.

2. **Click the** Home tab, **click any cell in the Price column, click the** Sort & Filter button **in the Editing group, then click** Sort Largest to Smallest

   Excel sorts the table, placing those records with the higher price at the top. The Price filter list arrow now has a downward pointing arrow next to the filter list arrow, indicating the descending sort order. You can also rearrange the table data using a **multilevel sort**. This type of sort rearranges the table data using different levels. If you use two sort levels, the data is sorted by the first field and the second field is sorted within each grouping of the first field. Since you have many groups of tours with different departure dates, you want to use a multilevel sort to arrange the table data by tours and then by departure dates within each tour.

3. **Click the** Sort & Filter button **in the Editing group, then click** Custom Sort

   The Sort dialog box opens, as shown in Figure G-14.

QUICK TIP

You can include capitalization as a sort criterion by clicking Options in the Sort dialog box, then selecting the Case sensitive box. When you choose this option, lowercase entries precede uppercase entries.

4. **Click the** Sort by list arrow, **click** Tour, **click the** Order list arrow, **click** A to Z, **click** Add Level, **click the** Then by list arrow, **click** Depart Date, **click the second** Order list arrow, **click** Oldest to Newest **if necessary, then click** OK

   Figure G-15 shows the table sorted alphabetically in ascending order (A-Z) by Tour and, within each tour, in ascending order by the Depart Date.

5. **Save the workbook**

Sorting a table using conditional formatting

If conditional formats have been applied to a table, you can sort the table using conditional formatting to arrange the rows. For example, if cells are conditionally formatted with color, you can sort a field on Cell Color, using the color with the order of On Top or On Bottom in the Sort dialog box.

TABLE G-3: Sort order options and examples

option	alphabetic	numeric	date	alphanumeric
Ascending	A, B, C	7, 8, 9	1/1, 2/1, 3/1	12A, 99B, DX8, QT7
Descending	C, B, A	9, 8, 7	3/1, 2/1, 1/1	QT7, DX8, 99B, 12A

FIGURE G-13: Table sorted by depature date

Up arrow indicates ascending sort in the field

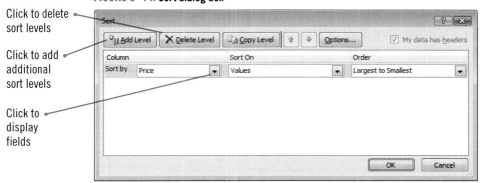

	A	B	C	D	E	F	G	H	I
1	Tour	Depart Date	Number of Days	Seat Capacity	Seats Reserved	Price	Air Included	Meals Included	Seats Available
2	Pacific Odyssey	1/11/2010	14	50	50	$ 3,105	Yes	No	
3	Down Under Exodus	1/18/2010	10	30	28	$ 2,800	Yes	Yes	
4	Essential India	1/20/2010	18	51	40	$ 3,933	Yes	Yes	
5	Costa Rica Rainforests	1/30/2010	7	20	0	$ 2,590	Yes	Yes	
6	Nepal Trekking	1/31/2010	14	18	0	$ 4,200	Yes	Yes	
7	Amazing Amazon	2/23/2010	14	43	38	$ 2,877	No	No	
8	Cooking in France	2/28/2010	7	18	15	$ 2,822	Yes	No	
9	Pearls of the Orient	3/12/2010	14	50	15	$ 3,400	Yes	No	
10	Silk Road Travels	3/18/2010	18	25	19	$ 2,190	Yes	Yes	
11	Costa Rica Rainforests	3/20/2010	7	20	20	$ 2,590	Yes	Yes	
12	Green Adventures in Ecuador	3/23/2010	18	25	22	$ 2,450	No	No	
13	African National Parks	4/7/2010	30	12	10	$ 4,870	Yes	Yes	
14	Experience Cambodia	4/10/2010	12	40	21	$ 2,908	Yes	No	
15	Old Japan	4/14/2010	21	47	30	$ 2,100	Yes	No	
16	Down Under Exodus	4/18/2010	10	30	20	$ 2,800	Yes	Yes	
17	Essential India	4/20/2010	18	51	31	$ 3,933	Yes	Yes	
18	Amazing Amazon	4/23/2010	14	43	30	$ 2,877	No	No	
19	Catalonia Adventure	5/9/2010	14	51	30	$ 3,100	Yes	No	
20	Treasures of Ethiopia	5/18/2010	10	41	15	$ 3,200	Yes	Yes	
21	Monasteries of Bulgaria	5/20/2010	7	19	11	$ 2,103	Yes	Yes	
22	Cooking in Croatia	5/23/2010	7	12	10	$ 2,110	No	No	
23	Magnificent Montenegro	5/27/2010	10	48	4	$ 1,890	No	No	
24	Catalonia Adventure	6/9/2010	14	51	15	$ 3,100	Yes	No	
25	Nepal Trekking	6/9/2010	14	18	18	$ 4,200	Yes	Yes	

FIGURE G-14: Sort dialog box

Click to delete sort levels

Click to add additional sort levels

Click to display fields

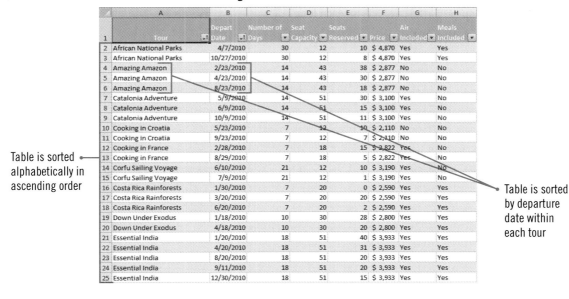

FIGURE G-15: Table sorted using two levels

	A	B	C	D	E	F	G	H
1	Tour	Depart Date	Number of Days	Seat Capacity	Seats Reserved	Price	Air Included	Meals Included
2	African National Parks	4/7/2010	30	12	10	$ 4,870	Yes	Yes
3	African National Parks	10/27/2010	30	12	8	$ 4,870	Yes	Yes
4	Amazing Amazon	2/23/2010	14	43	38	$ 2,877	No	No
5	Amazing Amazon	4/23/2010	14	43	30	$ 2,877	No	No
6	Amazing Amazon	8/23/2010	14	43	18	$ 2,877	No	No
7	Catalonia Adventure	5/9/2010	14	51	30	$ 3,100	Yes	No
8	Catalonia Adventure	6/9/2010	14	51	15	$ 3,100	Yes	No
9	Catalonia Adventure	10/9/2010	14	51	11	$ 3,100	Yes	No
10	Cooking in Croatia	5/23/2010	7	12	10	$ 2,110	No	No
11	Cooking in Croatia	9/23/2010	7	12	7	$ 2,110	No	No
12	Cooking in France	2/28/2010	7	18	15	$ 2,822	Yes	No
13	Cooking in France	8/29/2010	7	18	5	$ 2,822	Yes	No
14	Corfu Sailing Voyage	6/10/2010	21	12	10	$ 3,190	Yes	No
15	Corfu Sailing Voyage	7/9/2010	21	12	1	$ 3,190	Yes	No
16	Costa Rica Rainforests	1/30/2010	7	20	0	$ 2,590	Yes	Yes
17	Costa Rica Rainforests	3/20/2010	7	20	20	$ 2,590	Yes	Yes
18	Costa Rica Rainforests	6/20/2010	7	20	2	$ 2,590	Yes	Yes
19	Down Under Exodus	1/18/2010	10	30	28	$ 2,800	Yes	Yes
20	Down Under Exodus	4/18/2010	10	30	20	$ 2,800	Yes	Yes
21	Essential India	1/20/2010	18	51	40	$ 3,933	Yes	Yes
22	Essential India	4/20/2010	18	51	31	$ 3,933	Yes	Yes
23	Essential India	8/20/2010	18	51	20	$ 3,933	Yes	Yes
24	Essential India	9/11/2010	18	51	20	$ 3,933	Yes	Yes
25	Essential India	12/30/2010	18	51	15	$ 3,933	Yes	Yes

Table is sorted alphabetically in ascending order

Table is sorted by departure date within each tour

Specifying a custom sort order

You can identify a custom sort order for the field selected in the Sort by box. Click the Order list arrow in the Sort dialog box, click Custom List, then click the desired custom order. Commonly used custom sort orders are days of the week (Sun, Mon, Tues, Wed, etc.) and months (Jan, Feb, Mar, etc.); alphabetic sorts do not sort these items properly.

UNIT
G
Excel 2007

Using Formulas in a Table

Many tables are large, making it difficult to know from viewing them the "story" the table tells. The Excel table calculation features help you summarize table data so you can see important trends. After you enter a single formula into a table cell, the **calculated columns** feature fills in the remaining cells with the formula's results. The column continues to fill with the formula results as you enter rows in the table. This makes it easy to update your formulas because you only need to edit the formula once, and the change will fill in to the other column cells. The **structured reference** feature allows your formulas to refer to table columns by names that are automatically generated when you create the table. These names automatically adjust as you add or delete table fields. An example of a table reference is =[Sales]–[Costs], where Sales and Costs are field names in the table. Tables also have a specific area at the bottom called the **table total row** for calculations using the data in the table columns. The cells in this row contain a dropdown list of functions that can be used for the column calculation. The table total row adapts to any changes in the table size. Kate wants you to use a formula to calculate the number of available seats for each tour. You will also add summary information to the end of the table.

STEPS

1. **Click cell I2, then type =[**
   A list of the table field names is displayed, as shown in Figure G-16. Structured referencing allows you to use the names that Excel created when you defined your table to reference fields in a formula. You can choose a field by clicking it and pressing [TAB] or by double-clicking the field name.
2. **Click [Seat Capacity], press [Tab], then type]**
   Excel begins the formula, placing [Seat Capacity] in the cell in blue and framing the Seat Capacity data in a blue border.
3. **Type -[, double-click [Seats Reserved], then type]**
   Excel places [Seats Reserved] in the cell in green and outlines the Seats Reserved data in a green border.
4. **Press [Enter]**
   The formula result, 2, is displayed in cell I2. The table column also fills with the formula displaying the number of available seats for each tour.
5. **Click the AutoCorrect Options list arrow**
   Because the calculated columns option saves time, you decide to leave the feature on. You want to display the total number of available seats on all of the tours.
6. **Click any cell inside the table, click the Table Tools Design tab, then click the Total Row check box in the Table Style Options group to select it**
   A total row appears at the bottom of the table and the sum of the available seats, 1035, is displayed in cell I64. You can select other formulas in the total row.
7. **Click cell C64, then click the cell list arrow on the right side of the cell**
   The list of available functions appears, as shown in Figure G-17. You want to find the average tour length.
8. **Click Average, then save your workbook**
   The average tour length, 13 days, appears in cell C64.

QUICK TIP

You can undo the calculated column results by clicking Undo Calculated Column in the AutoCorrect Options list. You can turn off the Calculated Columns feature by clicking Stop Automatically Creating Calculated Columns in the AutoCorrect Options list.

FIGURE G-16: Table field names

	A	B	C	D	E	F	G	H	I	J
1	Tour	Depart Date	Number of Days	Seat Capacity	Seats Reserved	Price	Air Included	Meals Included	Seats Available	
2	African National Parks	4/7/2010	30	12	10	$ 4,870	Yes	Yes	=[	
3	African National Parks	10/27/2010	30	12	8	$ 4,870	Yes	Yes		
4	Amazing Amazon	2/23/2010	14	43	38	$ 2,877	No	No		
5	Amazing Amazon	4/23/2010	14	43	30	$ 2,877	No	No		
6	Amazing Amazon	8/23/2010	14	43	18	$ 2,877	No	No		
7	Catalonia Adventure	5/9/2010	14	51	30	$ 3,100	Yes	No		
8	Catalonia Adventure	6/9/2010	14	51	15	$ 3,100	Yes	No		
9	Catalonia Adventure	10/9/2010	14	51	11	$ 3,100	Yes	No		
10	Cooking in Croatia	5/23/2010	7	12	10	$ 2,110	No	No		
11	Cooking in Croatia	9/23/2010	7	12	7	$ 2,110	No	No		
12	Cooking in France	2/28/2010	7	18	15	$ 2,822	Yes	No		

Dropdown list:
- Tour
- Depart Date
- Number of Days
- Seat Capacity
- Seats Reserved
- Price
- Air Included
- Meals Included
- Seats Available

Table field names

FIGURE G-17: Functions in the Total Row

	Tour	Depart Date	Number of Days	Seat Capacity	Seats Reserved	Price	Air Included	Meals Included	Seats Available	J
51	Pacific Odyssey	7/7/2010	14	50	35	$ 3,105	Yes	No	15	
52	Pacific Odyssey	9/14/2010	14	50	20	$ 3,105	Yes	No	30	
53	Pacific Odyssey	12/21/2010	14	50	10	$ 3,105	Yes	No	40	
54	Panama Adventure	6/18/2010	10	50	29	$ 2,304	Yes	Yes	21	
55	Panama Adventure	12/18/2010	10	50	21	$ 2,304	Yes	Yes	29	
56	Pearls of the Orient	3/12/2010	14	50	15	$ 3,400	Yes	No	35	
57	Pearls of the Orient	9/12/2010	14	50	11	$ 3,400	Yes	No	39	
58	Silk Road Travels	3/18/2010	18	25	19	$ 2,190	Yes	Yes	6	
59	Silk Road Travels	9/18/2010	18	25	9	$ 2,190	Yes	Yes	16	
60	Treasures of Ethiopia	5/18/2010	10	41	15	$ 3,200	Yes	Yes	26	
61	Treasures of Ethiopia	11/18/2010	10	41	12	$ 3,200	Yes	Yes	29	
62	Wild River Escape	6/27/2010	10	21	21	$ 1,944	No	No	0	
63	Wild River Escape	8/27/2010	10	21	11	$ 1,944	No	No	10	
64	Total								1035	
65										
66										
67										
68										
69										
70										
71										
72										

Dropdown list:
- None
- Average
- Count
- Count Numbers
- Max
- Min
- Sum
- StdDev
- Var
- More Functions...

Functions available in the Total Row

Using structured references

Structured references make it easier to work with formulas that use table data. You can reference all of the table, columns in the table, or specific data. What makes structured references helpful to use in formulas is that they automatically adjust as data ranges change in a table, so you don't need to edit formulas. When you create a table from worksheet data, Excel creates a default table name such as Table1. This references all of the table data but not the header row or any total rows. To refer to a table such as Table1 with its header row, you need to use the reference =Table1[#All]. Excel also names each column of a table which can be referenced in formulas. For example, in Table 1, the formula =Table1[Sales] references the data in the Sales field.

Printing a Table

You can determine the way a table will print using the Page Layout tab. Because tables often have more rows than can fit on a page, you can define the first row of the table (containing the field names) as the **print title**, which prints at the top of every page. You can also scale the table to print more or fewer rows on each page. Most tables do not have any descriptive information above the field names on the work-sheet, so to augment the field name information, you can use headers and footers to add identifying text, such as the table title or the report date. ▰▰▰▰▰ Kate asks you for a printout of the tour information. You begin by previewing the table.

STEPS

1. **Click the Office button ⊙, point to Print, then click Print Preview**
   The status bar reads Preview: Page 1 of 3. All of the field names in the table fit across the width of the page.

2. **In the Print Preview window, click the Next Page button in the Preview group to view the second page, then click Next Page again to view the third page**
   The third page contains only one record and the total row, so you will scale the table to print on two pages.

QUICK TIP

You can hide or print headings and grid-lines using the check boxes in the Sheet Options group on the Page Layout tab. You might want to hide a worksheet's headings if it will be displayed in a presentation.

3. **Click the Close Print Preview button, click the Page Layout tab, click the Width list arrow in the Scale to Fit group, click 1 page, click the Height list arrow, then click 2 pages**
   You decide to preview the table again to view the changes in scale.

4. **Click the Office button, point to Print, click Print Preview, then click the Next Page button in the Preview group**
   The records are scaled to fit on two pages. The status bar reads Preview: Page 2 of 2. Because the records on page 2 appear without column headings, you want to set up the first row of the table, which contains the field names, as a repeating print title.

5. **Click the Close Print Preview button, click the Print Titles button in the Page Setup group, click inside the Rows to repeat at top text box under Print titles, click any cell in row 1 on the table, then compare your Page Setup dialog box to Figure G-18**
   When you select row 1 as a print title, Excel automatically inserts an absolute reference to the row that will repeat at the top of each page.

6. **Click Print Preview, click the Next Page button to view the second page, then click the Close Print Preview button**
   Setting up a print title to repeat row 1 causes the field names to appear at the top of each printed page. The printout would be more informative with a header to identify the table information.

QUICK TIP

You can also add headers and footers by clicking the Page Layout View in the status bar.

7. **Click the Insert tab, click the Header & Footer button in the Text group, click the left header section text box, then type 2010 Tours**

8. **Select the left header section information, click the Home tab, click the Increase Font Size button A˄ in the Font group twice to change the font size to 14, click the Bold button B in the Font group, click any cell in the table, then click the Normal button ▦ in the status bar**

9. **Save the table, preview then print it, close the workbook, then exit Excel**
   Compare your printed table with Figure G-19.

FIGURE G-18: Page Setup dialog box

Print title is set to row 1

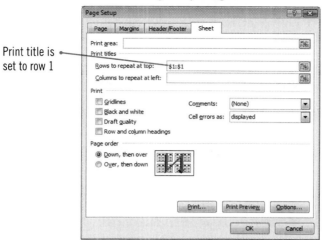

FIGURE G-19: Completed table

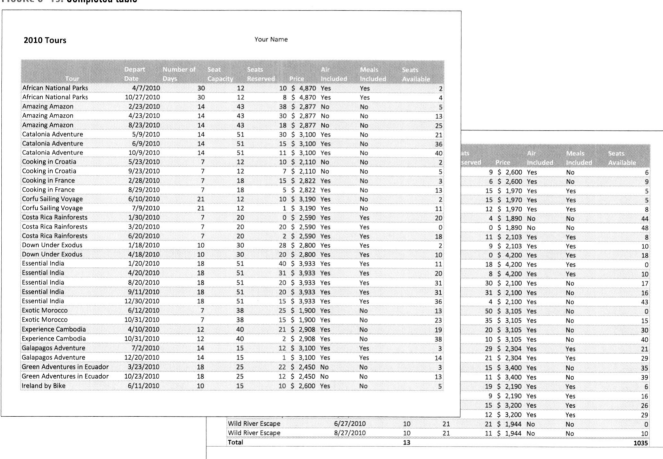

Tour	Depart Date	Number of Days	Seat Capacity	Seats Reserved	Price	Air Included	Meals Included	Seats Available
African National Parks	4/7/2010	30	12	10	$ 4,870	Yes	Yes	2
African National Parks	10/27/2010	30	12	8	$ 4,870	Yes	Yes	4
Amazing Amazon	2/23/2010	14	43	38	$ 2,877	No	No	5
Amazing Amazon	4/23/2010	14	43	30	$ 2,877	No	No	13
Amazing Amazon	8/23/2010	14	43	18	$ 2,877	No	No	25
Catalonia Adventure	5/9/2010	14	51	30	$ 3,100	Yes	No	21
Catalonia Adventure	6/9/2010	14	51	15	$ 3,100	Yes	No	36
Catalonia Adventure	10/9/2010	14	51	11	$ 3,100	Yes	No	40
Cooking in Croatia	5/23/2010	7	12	10	$ 2,110	No	No	2
Cooking in Croatia	9/23/2010	7	12	7	$ 2,110	No	No	5
Cooking in France	2/28/2010	7	18	15	$ 2,822	Yes	No	3
Cooking in France	8/29/2010	7	18	5	$ 2,822	Yes	No	13
Corfu Sailing Voyage	6/10/2010	21	12	10	$ 3,190	Yes	No	2
Corfu Sailing Voyage	7/9/2010	21	12	1	$ 3,190	Yes	No	11
Costa Rica Rainforests	1/30/2010	7	20	0	$ 2,590	Yes	Yes	20
Costa Rica Rainforests	3/20/2010	7	20	20	$ 2,590	Yes	Yes	0
Costa Rica Rainforests	6/20/2010	7	20	2	$ 2,590	Yes	Yes	18
Down Under Exodus	1/18/2010	10	30	28	$ 2,800	Yes	Yes	2
Down Under Exodus	4/18/2010	10	30	20	$ 2,800	Yes	Yes	10
Essential India	1/20/2010	18	51	40	$ 3,933	Yes	Yes	11
Essential India	4/20/2010	18	51	31	$ 3,933	Yes	Yes	20
Essential India	8/20/2010	18	51	20	$ 3,933	Yes	Yes	31
Essential India	9/11/2010	18	51	20	$ 3,933	Yes	Yes	31
Essential India	12/30/2010	18	51	15	$ 3,933	Yes	Yes	36
Exotic Morocco	6/12/2010	7	38	25	$ 1,900	Yes	No	13
Exotic Morocco	10/31/2010	7	38	15	$ 1,900	Yes	No	23
Experience Cambodia	4/10/2010	12	40	21	$ 2,908	Yes	No	19
Experience Cambodia	10/31/2010	12	40	2	$ 2,908	Yes	No	38
Galapagos Adventure	7/2/2010	14	15	12	$ 3,100	Yes	Yes	3
Galapagos Adventure	12/20/2010	14	15	1	$ 3,100	Yes	Yes	14
Green Adventures in Ecuador	3/23/2010	18	25	22	$ 2,450	No	No	3
Green Adventures in Ecuador	10/23/2010	18	25	12	$ 2,450	No	No	13
Ireland by Bike	6/11/2010	10	15	10	$ 2,600	Yes	No	5

2010 Tours   Your Name

Setting a print area

Sometimes you will want to print only part of a worksheet. To do this, select any worksheet range, click the Office button, click Print, in the Print dialog box choose Selection under Print what, then click OK. If you want to print a selected area repeatedly, it's best to define a **print area**, which prints when you use the Quick Print feature. To set a print area, click the Page Layout tab, click the Print Area button in the Page Setup group, then click Set Print Area. You can extend the print area by selecting a range, clicking the Print Area button, then clicking Add to Print Area. If you want to print the table rather than a print area, click the Ignore print areas check box in the Print what section of the Print dialog box. To clear a print area, click the Print Area button, then click Clear Print Area.

Practice

▼ CONCEPTS REVIEW

FIGURE G-20

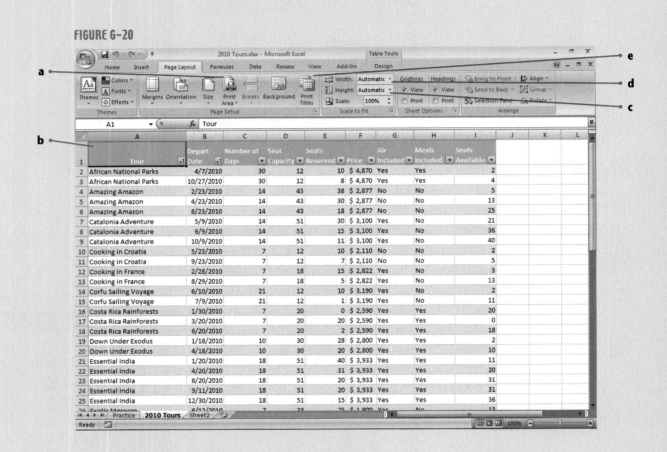

1. Which element points to a field that has been sorted in ascending order?
2. Which element do you click to adjust the number of rows printed on a page?
3. Which element do you click to adjust the number of fields printed on a page?
4. Which element do you click to print field names at the top of every page?
5. Which element do you click to set a range in a table that will print using Quick Print?

Match each term with the statement that best describes it.

6. **Header row**
7. **Record**
8. **Table**
9. **Field**
10. **Sort**

a. Organized collection of related information in Excel
b. Arrange records in a particular sequence
c. Column in an Excel table
d. First row of a table containing field names
e. Row in an Excel table

Select the best answer from the list of choices.

11. **Which of the following Excel sorting options do you use to sort a table of employee names in order from Z to A?**
    a. Absolute
    b. Ascending
    c. Alphabetic
    d. Descending

12. **Which of the following series appears in descending order?**
    a. 4, 5, 6, A, B, C
    b. 8, 6, 4, C, B, A
    c. 8, 7, 6, 5, 6, 7
    d. C, B, A, 6, 5, 4

13. **You can easily add formatting to a table by using:**
    a. Table styles.
    b. Print titles.
    c. Print areas.
    d. Calculated columns.

14. **When printing a table on multiple pages, you can define a print title to:**
    a. Include appropriate fields in the printout.
    b. Include the sheet name in table reports.
    c. Include field names at the top of each printed page.
    d. Exclude from the printout all rows under the first row.

▼ SKILLS REVIEW

1. **Create a table.**
   a. Start Excel, open the file EX G-2.xlsx from the drive and folder where you store your data files, then save it as **Employees**.
   b. Using the Practice sheet, enter the field names in the first row and the first two records in rows two and three, as shown in Table G-4. Create a table using the data you entered.

   TABLE G-4

Last Name	First Name	Years Employed	Position	Full/Part Time	Training Completed
Leone	Sally	5	Book Sales	F	Y
Mello	Donato	3	Video Sales	P	N

   c. Create a table with a header row using the data on the Staff sheet. Adjust the column widths, if necessary, to display the field names.
   d. Apply a table style of Light 12 to the table and adjust the columns widths if necessary.
   e. Enter your name in the center section of the worksheet footer, then save the workbook.

2. **Add table data.**
   a. Add a new record in row seven for **Hank Worthen**, a five-year employee in book sales. Hank works full time and has completed training. Adjust the height of the new row to match the other table rows.
   b. Insert a row above Jay Kherian's record and add a new record for **Stacy Atkins**. Stacy works full time, has worked at the company for two years in video sales, and has not completed training.
   c. Insert a new data field in cell G1 with a label **Weeks Vacation**. Adjust the column width and wrap the label in the cell to display the field name with Weeks above Vacation.
   d. Add a new column to the table by dragging the table's sizing handle and give the new field a label of **Employee #**.
   e. Save the file.

3. **Find and replace table data.**
   a. Return to cell A1.
   b. Open the Find and Replace dialog box and if necessary uncheck the Match Case option. Find the first record that contains the text **Book Sales**.
   c. Find the second record that contains the text **Book Sales**.
   d. Replace all Video text in the table with **Movie**.
   e. Save the file.

4. **Delete table data.**

   a. Go to cell A1.

   b. Delete the record for **Sally Leone**.

   c. Use the Remove Duplicates button to confirm that the table does not have any duplicate records.

   d. Delete the **Employee** # column from the table, then delete its column header.

   e. Save the file.

5. **Sort table data.**

   a. Sort the table by years employed in largest to smallest order.

   b. Sort the table by last name in A to Z order.

   c. Sort the table first by Full/Part Time in A to Z order and then by last name in A to Z order.

   d. Check the table to make sure the records appear in the correct order.

   e. Save the file.

6. **Use formulas in a table.**

   a. In cell G2, enter the formula that calculates an employee's vacation time; base the formula on the company policy that employees working at the company less than three years have two weeks of vacation. At three years of employment and longer, an employee has three weeks of vacation time. Use the table's field names where appropriate. (*Hint:* The formula is: **=IF([Years Employed]<3,2,3)**)

   b. Check the table to make sure the formula filled into the cells in column G and that the correct vacation time is calculated for all cells in the column. **FIGURE G-21**

   c. Add a Total Row and verify the accuracy of the total number of vacation weeks.

   d. Change the function in the Total Row to display the average number of vacation weeks.

   e. Compare your table to Figure G-21, then save the workbook.

	A	B	C	D	E	F	G
	A1	▾	fx	Last Name			
	A	B	C	D	E	F	G
1	Last Name	First Name	Years Employed	Position	Full/Part Time	Training Completed	Weeks Vacation
2	Atkins	Stacy	2	Movie Sales	F	N	2
3	Guan	Joyce	1	Book Sales	F	N	2
4	Kherian	Jay	1	Book Sales	F	Y	2
5	Worthen	Hank	5	Book Sales	F	Y	3
6	Mello	Donato	3	Movie Sales	P	N	3
7	Rabin	Mimi	1	Movie Sales	P	Y	2
8	Total						2.333333333
9							

7. **Print a table.**

   a. Add a header that reads **Employees** in the center section, then format the header in bold with a font size of 16.

   b. Add column A as a print title that repeats at the left of each printed page.

   c. Preview your table to check that the last names appear on both pages.

   d. Change the page orientation to landscape, save the workbook, then print the Staff sheet.

   e. Close the workbook, then exit Excel.

▼ INDEPENDENT CHALLENGE 1

You are the marketing director for a national sporting goods store. Your assistants have created an Excel worksheet with customer data including the results of an advertising survey. You will create a table using the customer data and analyze the survey results to help focus the company's advertising expenses in the most successful areas.

   a. Start Excel, open the file EX G-3.xlsx from the drive and folder where you store your Data Files, then save it as **Customers**.

   b. Create a table from the worksheet data and apply Table Style Light 20. Widen the columns as necessary to display the table data.

▼ INDEPENDENT CHALLENGE 1 (CONTINUED)

c. Use the data below to add the two records shown in Table G-5 to the table:

TABLE G-5

Last Name	First Name	Street Address	City	State	Zip	Area Code	Ad Source	Comments
Ross	Cathy	92 Arrow St.	Seattle	WA	98101	206	Yellow Pages	found ad informative
Janis	Steve	402 9th St.	Seattle	WA	98001	206	Newspaper	found in restaurant section

d. Find, then delete the record for Mary Ryder.

e. Click cell A1 and replace all instances of TV with WWIN TV, making sure the case is properly matched. Compare your table to Figure G-22.

f. Remove duplicate records where all fields are identical.

g. Sort the list by Last Name in A to Z order.

h. Sort the list again by Area Code in Smallest to Largest order.

i. Sort the table first by State in A to Z order, then within the state, by Zip in Smallest to Largest order.

FIGURE G-22

	Last Name	First Name	Street Address	City	State	Zip	Area Code	Ad Source	Comments
2	Kim	Kathy	19 North St.	San Francisco	CA	94177	415	Newspaper	favorite with friends
3	Jacobs	Martha	Hamilton Park St.	San Francisco	CA	94107	415	Newspaper	no comments
4	Majors	Kathy	1 Spring St.	San Luis	CA	94018	510	Radio	loved ad voice
5	Wong	Sandy	2120 Central St.	San Francisco	CA	93772	415	Newspaper	graphics caught eye
6	Hesh	Gayle	1192 Dome St.	San Diego	CA	93303	619	Newspaper	great ads
7	Chavez	Jane	11 Northern St.	San Diego	CA	92208	619	WWIN TV	interesting ad
8	Chelly	Yvonne	900 Sola St.	San Diego	CA	92106	619	Newspaper	likes description of products
9	Smith	Carolyn	921 Lopez St.	San Diego	CA	92104	619	Newspaper	likes ad prose
10	Owen	Scott	72 Yankee St.	Brookfield	CT	06830	203	Newspaper	no comments
11	Wallace	Salvatore	100 Westside St.	Chicago	IL	60620	312	Newspaper	likes graphics
12	Roberts	Bob	56 Water St.	Chicago	IL	60618	771	Newspaper	likes ad graphic
13	Miller	Hope	111 Stratton St.	Chicago	IL	60614	773	Newspaper	likes ad in local newspaper
14	Duran	Maria	Galvin St.	Chicago	IL	60614	773	Subway	no comments
15	Roberts	Bob	56 Water St.	Chicago	IL	60614	312	Newspaper	liked photo
16	Graham	Shelley	989 26th St.	Chicago	IL	60611	773	Yellow Pages	great store description
17	Kim	Janie	9 First St.	San Francisco	CA	94177	415	Newspaper	great ads
18	Kim	Janie	9 First St.	San Francisco	CA	94177	415	Newspaper	great ads
19	Williams	Tasha	1 Spring St.	Reading	MA	03882	413	Newspaper	likes font we use
20	Julio	Manuel	544 Cameo St.	Belmont	MA	02483	617	Newspaper	no comments
21	Masters	Latrice	88 Las Puntas Rd.	Boston	MA	02205	617	Yellow Pages	likes clear store location
22	Kooper	Peter	671 Main St.	Cambridge	MA	02138	617	WWIN TV	no comments
23	Kelly	Shawn	22 Kendall St.	Cambridge	MA	02138	617	Yellow Pages	found under "cafés"
24	Rodriguez	Virginia	123 Main St.	Boston	MA	02007	617	Radio	loves radio personality
25	Frei	Carol	123 Elm St.	Salem	MA	01970	978	Newspaper	no comments
26	Stevens	Crystal	14 Waterford St.	Salem	MA	01970	508	Radio	does not like radio personality
27	Ichikawa	Pam	232 Shore Rd.	Boston	MA	01801	617	Newspaper	told friends
28	Paxton	Gail	100 Main St.	Woburn	MA	01801	508	Newspaper	no comments
29	Spencer	Robin	293 Serenity Dr.	Concord	MA	01742	508	Radio	loved radio personality
30	Lopez	Luis	1212 City St.	Kansas City	MO	64105	816	WWIN TV	liked characters
31	Nelson	Michael	229 Rally Rd.	Kansas City	MO	64105	816	Yellow Pages	found under "Compact Discs"
32	Lee	Ginny	3 Way St.	Kansas City	MO	64102	816	Radio	intrigued by announcer

j. Scale the table width to 1 page and the height to 2 pages.

k. Enter your name in the center section of the worksheet footer.

l. Add a centered header that reads **Customer Survey Data** in bold with a font size of 16.

m. Add print titles to repeat the first row at the top of printed pages.

n. Save the workbook, preview it, then print the table on two pages.

Advanced Challenge Exercise

- Create a print area that prints only the first six columns of the table.
- Print the print area.
- Clear the print area

o. Save the workbook, close the workbook, then exit Excel.

▼ INDEPENDENT CHALLENGE 2

You own Around the World, a travel bookstore located in New Zealand. The store sells travel-related items such as maps, travel books, journals, and DVDs of travel destinations. Your customers are primarily tour guides who purchase items in quantities of ten or more for their tour customers. You decide to plan and build a table of sales information with eight records using the items sold.

a. Prepare a plan for a table that states your goal, outlines the data you need, and identifies the table elements.

b. Sketch a sample table on a piece of paper, indicating how the table should be built. Create a table documenting the table design including the field names, type of data, and description of the data.

▼ INDEPENDENT CHALLENGE 2 (CONTINUED)

c. Start Excel, create a new workbook, then save it as **Store Items** in the drive and folder where you store your Data Files. Enter the field names from Table G-6 in the designated cells.

d. Enter eight data records using your own data.

e. Create a table using the data in the range A1:E9. Adjust the column widths as necessary.

f. Apply the Table Style Light 4 to the table.

g. Add the following fields to the table: **Subtotal** in cell F1, and **Total** in cell G1.

h. Add the label **Tax** in cell H1 and click the first option in the AutoCorrect Options to undo the table AutoExpansion. Enter **.125** in cell I1 (the 12.5% Goods and Services tax).

i. Enter formulas to calculate the subtotal (Quantity*Cost) in cell F2 and the total (including tax) in cell G2. Check that the formulas were filled down both of the columns. (*Hint:* Remember to use an absolute reference to the tax rate cell.)

j. Format the Cost, Subtotal, and Total columns using the Accounting number format with two decimal places and the symbol $ English (New Zealand). Adjust the column widths as necessary.

k. Add a new record to your table in row 10. Add another record above row 4.

l. Sort the table in ascending order by Item.

m. Enter your name in the worksheet footer, then save the workbook.

n. Preview the worksheet, use the Scale to Fit width option to scale the worksheet to print on one page.

o. Print the worksheet, close the workbook, then exit Excel.

TABLE G-6

Cell	Field name
A1	Customer Last
B1	Customer First
C1	Item
D1	Quantity
E1	Cost

▼ INDEPENDENT CHALLENGE 3

You are the project manager at a local advertising firm. You are managing your accounts using an Excel worksheet and have decided that a table will provide additional features to help you keep track of the accounts. You will use the table sorting features and table formulas to analyze your account data.

a. Start Excel, open the file EX G-4.xlsx from the drive and folder where you store your Data Files, then save it as **Accounts**.

b. Create a table with the worksheet data and apply Table Style Light 3.

c. Sort the table on the Budget field using the Smallest to Largest order. Compare your table to Figure G-23.

d. Sort the table using two fields, by Contact in A to Z order, then by Budget in Smallest to Largest order.

e. Add the new field label **Balance** in cell G1 and adjust the column width as necessary. Format the Budget, Expenses, and Balance columns using the Accounting format with no decimal places.

FIGURE G-23

	A	B	C	D	E	F	G
1	Project	Deadline	Code	Budget	Expenses	Contact	
2	Kelly	2/1/2010	AA1	100000	30000	Connie Blake	
3	Vincent	1/15/2010	C43	100000	150000	Jane Smith	
4	Jaffrey	3/15/2010	A3A	200000	210000	Kate Jeung	
5	Karim	4/30/2010	C43	200000	170000	Connie Blake	
6	Landry	11/15/2010	V53	200000	210000	Jane Smith	
7	Kaplan	9/30/2010	V51	300000	320000	Jane Smith	
8	Graham	7/10/2010	V13	390000	400000	Charlie Katter	
9	Lannou	10/10/2010	C21	450000	400000	Connie Blake	
10	Mason	6/1/2010	AA5	500000	430210	Jane Smith	
11	Melon	12/15/2010	B12	810000	700000	Nelly Atli	
12							

f. Enter a formula in cell G2 that uses structured references to table fields to calculate the balance on an account as the Budget minus the Expenses.

g. Add a new record for a project named **Franklin** with a deadline of **2/15/2010**, a code of **AB2**, a budget of **200000**, expenses of **150000**, and a contact of **Connie Blake**.

h. Verify that the formula accurately calculated the balance for the new record.

i. Replace all of the Jane Smith data with **Jane Jacobson** and adjust the column width as necessary.

j. Enter your name in the center section of the worksheet footer, add a center section header of **Accounts** using formatting of your choice, then save the workbook.

▼ INDEPENDENT CHALLENGE 3 (CONTINUED)

Advanced Challenge Exercise

- Sort the table on the Balance field using the smallest to largest order.
- Use conditional formatting to format the cells of the table containing negative balances with a dark green text on a green fill.
- Sort the table using the order of no cell color on top.
- Format the table to emphasize the Balance column and turn off the banded rows. (*Hint*: Use the Table Style Options on the Table Tools Design tab.)
- Compare your table with Figure G-24.

FIGURE G-24

	A	B	C	D	E	F	G	H
1	Project	Deadline	Code	Budget	Expenses	Contact	Balance	
2	Karim	4/30/2010	C43	$ 200,000	$ 170,000	Connie Blake	$ 30,000	
3	Lannou	10/10/2010	C21	$ 450,000	$ 400,000	Connie Blake	$ 50,000	
4	Franklin	2/15/2010	AB2	$ 200,000	$ 150,000	Connie Blake	$ 50,000	
5	Mason	6/1/2010	AA5	$ 500,000	$ 430,210	Jane Jacobson	$ 69,790	
6	Kelly	2/1/2010	AA1	$ 100,000	$ 30,000	Connie Blake	$ 70,000	
7	Melon	12/15/2010	B12	$ 810,000	$ 700,000	Nelly Atli	$ 110,000	
8	Vincent	1/15/2010	C43	$ 100,000	$ 150,000	Jane Jacobson	$ (50,000)	
9	Kaplan	9/30/2010	V51	$ 300,000	$ 320,000	Jane Jacobson	$ (20,000)	
10	Graham	7/10/2010	V13	$ 390,000	$ 400,000	Charlie Katter	$ (10,000)	
11	Landry	11/15/2010	V53	$ 200,000	$ 210,000	Jane Jacobson	$ (10,000)	
12	Jaffrey	3/15/2010	A3A	$ 200,000	$ 210,000	Kate Jeung	$ (10,000)	
13								
14								

k. Save the workbook, print the table, close the workbook, then exit Excel.

▼ REAL LIFE INDEPENDENT CHALLENGE

You have decided to organize your recording collection using a table in Excel. This will enable you to easily find songs in your music library. You will add records as you purchase new music and delete records if you discard a recording.

a. Use the fields Title, Artist, Genre, and Format and prepare a diagram of your table structure.

b. Document the table design by detailing the type of data that will be in each field and a description of the data. For example, in the Format field you may have mp3, aac, wma, or other formats.

c. Start Excel, create a new workbook, then save it as **Music Titles** in the drive and folder where you store your Data Files.

d. Enter the field names into the worksheet, enter the records for seven of your music recordings, then save the workbook.

e. Create a table that contains your music information. Resize the columns as necessary.

f. Choose a Table Style and apply it to your table.

g. Add a new field with a label of Comments. Enter information in the new table column describing the setting in which you listen to the title, such as driving, exercising, entertaining, or relaxing.

h. Sort the records by the Format field using A to Z order.

i. Add a record to the table for the next recording you will purchase.

j. Add a Total row to your table and verify that the Count function accurately calculated the number of your recordings.

k. Enter your name in the worksheet footer, then save the workbook.

l. Print the table, close the workbook, then exit Excel.

▼ VISUAL WORKSHOP

Start Excel, open the file EX G-5.xlsx from the drive and folder where you store your Data Files, then save it as **Products**. Sort the data as shown in Figure G-25. The table is formatted using Table Style Light 3. Add a header with the file name that is centered and formatted in bold with a size of 18. Enter your name in the worksheet footer. Save the workbook, preview and print the table, close the workbook, then exit Excel.

FIGURE G–25

Products.xlsx

Order Number	Order date	Amount	Shipping	Sales Rep
1134	4/30/2010	$ 200,000	Air	Edward Callegy
1465	11/15/2010	$ 210,000	Air	Edward Callegy
7733	3/15/2010	$ 230,000	Air	Edward Callegy
2889	2/15/2010	$ 300,000	Air	Edward Callegy
1532	10/10/2010	$ 450,000	Air	Edward Callegy
9345	1/15/2010	$ 100,000	Ground	Gary Clarkson
5623	2/1/2010	$ 130,000	Air	Gary Clarkson
1112	9/30/2010	$ 300,000	Ground	Gary Clarkson
2156	6/1/2010	$ 500,000	Ground	Gary Clarkson
2134	7/10/2010	$ 390,000	Ground	Ned Blair
2144	12/15/2010	$ 810,000	Ground	Ned Blair

Analyzing Table Data

Files You Will Need:

EX H-1.xlsx
EX H-2.xlsx
EX H-3.xlsx
EX H-4.xlsx
EX H-5.xlsx
EX H-6.xlsx

Excel data tables let you manipulate and analyze data in many ways. One way is to filter a table so that it displays only the rows that meet certain criteria. In this unit, you will display selected records using the filter feature, create a custom filter, and filter a table using an Advanced Filter. In addition, you will learn to insert automatic subtotals, use lookup functions to locate table entries, and apply database functions to summarize table data that meet specific criteria. You'll also learn how to restrict entries in a column by using data validation. The vice president of sales, Kate Morgan, asks you to extract information from a table of the 2010 scheduled tours to help the sales representatives with customer inquiries. She also asks you to prepare summaries of the tour sales for a presentation at the international sales meeting.

OBJECTIVES

Filter a table

Create a custom filter

Filter a table with Advanced Filter

Extract table data

Look up values in a table

Summarize table data

Validate table data

Create subtotals

Filtering a Table

When you create a table, arrows automatically appear next to each column header. These arrows are called **filter list arrows**, or **list arrows**, and you can use them to **filter** a table to display only the records that meet criteria you specify, temporarily hiding records that do not meet those criteria. For example, you can use the filter list arrow next to the Tour field header to display only records that contain Nepal Trekking in the Tour field. Once you filter data, you can copy, chart, and print the displayed records. You can easily clear a filter to redisplay all the records.  Kate asks you to display only the records for the Pacific Odyssey tours. She also asks for information about the tours that sell the most seats and the tours that depart in March.

STEPS

1. **Start Excel, open the file EX H-1.xlsx from the drive and folder where you save your Data Files, then save it as Tours**

2. **Click the Tour list arrow**

   Sort options appear at the top of the menu, advanced filtering options appear in the middle, and at the bottom is a list of the tour data from column A, as shown in Figure H-1. Because you want to display data for only the Pacific Odyssey tours, your **search criterion** (the text you are searching for) is Pacific Odyssey. You can select one of the Tour data options in the menu, which acts as your search criterion.

   > **QUICK TIP**
   > You can also filter or sort a table by the color of the cells if conditional formatting has been applied.

3. **In the list of tours for the Tour field, click Select All to clear the checks from the tours, scroll down the list of tours, click the Pacific Odyssey check box, then click OK**

   Only those records containing Pacific Odyssey in the Tour field appear, as shown in Figure H-2. The row numbers for the matching records change to blue, and the list arrow for the filtered field has a filter icon. Both indicate that there is a filter in effect and that some of the records are temporarily hidden.

4. **Move the pointer over the Tour list arrow**

   The ScreenTip (Tour: Equals "Pacific Odyssey") describes the filter for the field, meaning that only the Pacific Odyssey records appear. You decide to remove the filter to redisplay all of the table data.

5. **Click the Tour list arrow, then click Clear Filter From "Tour"**

   You have cleared the Pacific Odyssey filter, and all the records reappear. You want to display the most popular tours, those that are in the top five percent of seats reserved.

6. **Click the Seats Reserved list arrow, point to Number Filters, click Top 10, select 10 in the middle box, type 5, click the Items list arrow, click Percent, then click OK**

   Excel displays the records for the top five percent in the number of Seats Reserved field, as shown in Figure H-3. You decide to clear the filter to redisplay all the records.

   > **TROUBLE**
   > If the Clear command is not available, check to be sure the active cell is inside the table.

7. **Click the Home tab, click the Sort & Filter button in the Editing group, then click Clear**

   You have cleared the filter and all the records reappear. You want to find all of the tours that depart in March.

8. **Click the Depart Date list arrow, point to Date Filters, point to All Dates in the Period, then click March**

   Excel displays the records for the four tours that leave in March. You decide to clear the filter and display all of the records.

   > **QUICK TIP**
   > You can also clear a filter by clicking the Clear button in the Sort & Filter group on the Data tab.

9. **Click Sort & Filter button in the Editing group, click Clear, then save the workbook**

FIGURE H-1: Worksheet showing filter options

Tour filter list arrow

Sort Options

Advanced filtering options

List of tours

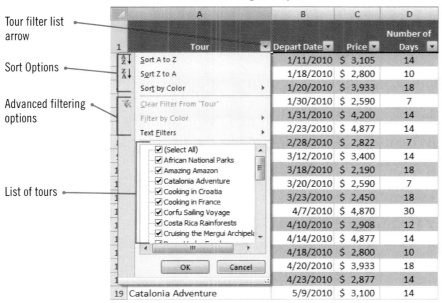

	A	B	C	D
1	Tour	Depart Date	Price	Number of Days
		1/11/2010	$ 3,105	14
		1/18/2010	$ 2,800	10
		1/20/2010	$ 3,933	18
		1/30/2010	$ 2,590	7
		1/31/2010	$ 4,200	14
		2/23/2010	$ 4,877	14
		2/28/2010	$ 2,822	7
		3/12/2010	$ 3,400	14
		3/18/2010	$ 2,190	18
		3/20/2010	$ 2,590	7
		3/23/2010	$ 2,450	18
		4/7/2010	$ 4,870	30
		4/10/2010	$ 2,908	12
		4/14/2010	$ 4,877	14
		4/18/2010	$ 2,800	10
		4/20/2010	$ 3,933	18
		4/23/2010	$ 2,877	14
19	Catalonia Adventure	5/9/2010	$ 3,100	14

Sort A to Z
Sort Z to A
Sort by Color
Clear Filter From "Tour"
Filter by Color
Text Filters

☑ (Select All)
☑ African National Parks
☑ Amazing Amazon
☑ Catalonia Adventure
☑ Cooking in Croatia
☑ Cooking in France
☑ Corfu Sailing Voyage
☑ Costa Rica Rainforests
☑ Cruising the Mergui Archipela

OK   Cancel

FIGURE H-2: Table filtered to show Pacific Odyssey tours

	A	B	C	D	E	F	G	H	I
1	Tour	Depart Date	Price	Number of Days	Seat Capacity	Seats Reserved	Seats Available	Air Included	Meals Included
2	Pacific Odyssey	1/11/2010	$ 3,105	14	50	30	20	Yes	No
34	Pacific Odyssey	7/7/2010	$ 3,105	14	50	32	18	Yes	No
48	Pacific Odyssey	9/14/2010	$ 3,105	14	50	26	24	Yes	No
61	Pacific Odyssey	12/21/2010	$ 3,105	14	50	50	0	Yes	No
64									

Matching row numbers are blue and sequence indicates that not all rows appear

Filter displays only Pacific Odyssey tours

Filter icon

FIGURE H-3: Table filtered with top 5% of Seats Reserved

	A	B	C	D	E	F	G	H	I
1	Tour	Depart Date	Price	Number of Days	Seat Capacity	Seats Reserved	Seats Available	Air Included	Meals Included
18	Amazing Amazon	4/23/2010	$ 2,877	14	50	48	2	No	No
37	Kayak Newfoundland	7/12/2010	$ 1,970	7	50	49	1	Yes	Yes
45	Cooking in France	8/29/2010	$ 2,822	7	50	48	2	Yes	No
61	Pacific Odyssey	12/21/2010	$ 3,105	14	50	50	0	Yes	No
64									

Table filtered with top 5% in this field

Creating a Custom Filter

So far, you have filtered rows based on an entry in a single column. You can perform more complex filters by using options in the Custom Filter dialog box. For example, your criteria can contain comparison operators such as "greater than" or "less than" that let you display values above or below a certain amount. You can also use **logical conditions** like And and Or to narrow a search even further. You can have Excel display records that meet a criterion in a field *and* another criterion in that same field. This is often used to find records between two values. For example, by specifying an And logical condition, you can display records for customers with incomes between $40,000 *and* $70,000. You can also have Excel display records that meet either criterion in a field by specifying an Or condition. The Or condition is used to find records that satisfy either of two values. For example, in a table of book data you can use the Or condition to find records that contain either Beginning *or* Introduction in the title name. ▓▓▓▓▓ Kate wants to locate water tours for customers who like boating adventures. She also wants to find tours that depart between February 15, 2010 and April 15, 2010. She asks you to create custom filters to find the tours satisfying these criteria.

STEPS

1. **Click the Tour list arrow, point to Text Filters, then click Contains**
   The Custom AutoFilter dialog box opens. You enter your criteria in the text boxes. The left text box on the first line currently displays "contains." You want to display tours that contain the word sailing in their names.

2. **Type sailing in the right text box on the first line**
   You want to see entries that contain either sailing or cruising.

3. **Click the Or option button to select it, click the left text box list arrow on the second line, select contains, then type cruising in the right text box on the second line**
   Your completed Custom AutoFilter dialog box should match Figure H-4.

4. **Click OK**
   The dialog box closes, and only those records having sailing or cruising in the Tour field appear in the worksheet. You want to find all tours that depart between February 15, 2010 and April 15, 2010.

5. **Click the Tour list arrow, click Clear Filter From "Tour", click the Depart Date list arrow, point to Date Filters, then click Custom Filter**
   The Custom AutoFilter dialog box opens. The word "equals" appears in the left text box on the first line. You want to find the departure dates that are between February 15, 2010 and April 15, 2010 (that is, after February 15th *and* before April 15th).

6. **Click the left text box list arrow on the first line, click is after, then type 2/15/2010 in the right text box on the first line**
   The And condition is selected, which is correct.

7. **Click the left text box list arrow on the second line, select is before, type 4/15/2010 in the right text box on the second line, then click OK**
   The records displayed have departing dates between February 15, 2010 and April 15, 2010. Compare your records to those shown in Figure H-5.

8. **Add your name to the center section of the footer, scale the page width to one page, then preview and print the filtered table**
   The worksheet prints using the existing landscape orientation, on one page with your name in the footer.

9. **Click the Depart Date list arrow, then click Clear Filter From "Depart Date"**
   You have cleared the filter, and all the tour records reappear.

FIGURE H-4: Custom AutoFilter dialog box

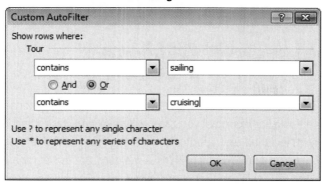

FIGURE H-5: Results of custom filter

	A	B	C	D	E	F	G	H	I
1	Tour	Depart Date	Price	Number of Days	Seat Capacity	Seats Reserved	Seats Available	Air Included	Meals Included
7	Cruising the Mergui Archipelago	2/23/2010	$ 4,877	14	50	42	8	No	No
8	Cooking in France	2/28/2010	$ 2,822	7	50	18	32	Yes	No
9	Pearls of the Orient	3/12/2010	$ 3,400	14	50	22	28	Yes	No
10	Silk Road Travels	3/18/2010	$ 2,190	18	50	44	6	Yes	Yes
11	Costa Rica Rainforests	3/20/2010	$ 2,590	7	50	32	18	Yes	Yes
12	Green Adventures in Ecuador	3/23/2010	$ 2,450	18	50	45	5	No	No
13	African National Parks	4/7/2010	$ 4,870	30	50	18	32	Yes	Yes
14	Experience Cambodia	4/10/2010	$ 2,908	12	50	29	21	Yes	No
15	Cruising the Mergui Archipelago	4/14/2010	$ 4,877	14	50	20	30	No	No
64									

Depature dates are
between 2/15 and 4/15

Using more than one rule when conditionally formatting data

You can apply conditional formatting to table cells in the same way that you can format a range of worksheet data. You can add multiple rules by clicking the Home tab, clicking the Conditional Formatting button in the Styles group, then clicking New Rule for each additional rule that you want to apply. You can also add rules using the Conditional Formatting Rules Manager, which displays all of the rules for a data range. To use the Rules Manager, click the Home tab, click the Conditional Formatting button in the Styles group, click Manage Rules, then click New Rule for each rule that you want to apply to the data range.

Filtering a Table with Advanced Filter

The Advanced Filter command lets you search for data that matches criteria in more than one column, using And and Or conditions. For example, you can use Advanced Filter to find Tours that leave before a certain date *and* have meals included. To use advanced filtering, you must create a criteria range. A **criteria range** is a cell range containing one row of labels (usually a copy of the column labels) and at least one additional row underneath the row of labels that contains the criteria you want to match. Placing the criteria in the same row indicates that the records you are searching for must match both criteria; that is, it specifies an **And condition**. Placing the criteria in the different rows indicates that the records you are searching for must match only one of the criterion; that is, it specifies an **Or condition**. ⬛⬛⬛ Kate wants to identify tours that depart after 6/1/2010 and that cost less than $2000. She asks you to use the Advanced Filter to retrieve these records. You begin by defining the criteria range.

STEPS

1. **Select table rows 1 through 6, click the Insert list arrow in the Cells group, click Insert Sheet Rows; click cell A1, type Criteria Range, then click the Enter button ☑ on the Formula bar**

   Six blank rows are added above the table. Excel does not require the label Criteria Range, but it is useful in organizing the worksheet. It is also helpful to see the column labels.

2. **Select the range A7:I7, click the Copy button 🖻 in the Clipboard group, click cell A2, click the Paste button in the Clipboard group, then press [Esc]**

   Next, you want to list records for only those tours that depart after June 1, 2010 and that cost under $2000.

3. **Click cell B3, type >6/1/2010, click cell C3, type <2000, then click ☑**

   You have entered the criteria in the cells directly beneath the Criteria Range labels, as shown in Figure H-6.

4. **Click any cell in the table, click the Data tab, then click the Advanced button in the Sort & Filter group**

   The Advanced Filter dialog box opens, with the table range already entered. The default setting under Action is to filter the table in its current location ("in-place") rather than copy it to another location.

TROUBLE
If your filtered records don't match Figure H-7, make sure there are no spaces between the > symbol and the 6 in cell B3 and the < symbol and the 2 in cell C3.

5. **Click the Criteria range text box, select range A2:I3 in the worksheet, then click OK**

   You have specified the criteria range and performed the filter. The filtered table contains eight records that match both criteria—the departure date is after 6/1/2010 and the price is less than $2000, as shown in Figure H-7. You'll filter this table even further in the next lesson.

FIGURE H-6: Criteria in the same row

	Tour	Depart Date	Price	Number of Days	Seat Capacity	Seats Reserved	Seats Available	Air Included	Meals Included
1	Criteria Range								
2	Tour	Depart Date	Price	Number of Days	Seat Capacity	Seats Reserved	Seats Available	Air Included	Meals Included
3		>6/1/2010	<2000						
4									
5									
6									
7	Tour	Depart Date	Price	Number of Days	Seat Capacity	Seats Reserved	Seats Available	Air Included	Meals Included
8	Pacific Odyssey	1/11/2010	$ 3,105	14	50	30	20	Yes	No
9	Down Under Exodus	1/18/2010	$ 2,800	10	50	39	11	Yes	Yes

Filtered records will match these criteria

FIGURE H-7: Filtered table

	Tour	Depart Date	Price	Number of Days	Seat Capacity	Seats Reserved	Seats Available	Air Included	Meals Included
1	Criteria Range								
2	Tour	Depart Date	Price	Number of Days	Seat Capacity	Seats Reserved	Seats Available	Air Included	Meals Included
3		>6/1/2010	<2000						
4									
5									
6									
7	Tour	Depart Date	Price	Number of Days	Seat Capacity	Seats Reserved	Seats Available	Air Included	Meals Included
34	Exotic Morocco	6/12/2010	$ 1,900	7	50	34	16	Yes	No
35	Kayak Newfoundland	6/12/2010	$ 1,970	7	50	41	9	Yes	Yes
38	Wild River Escape	6/27/2010	$ 1,944	10	50	1	49	No	No
43	Kayak Newfoundland	7/12/2010	$ 1,970	7	50	49	1	Yes	Yes
45	Magnificent Montenegro	7/27/2010	$ 1,890	10	50	11	39	No	No
47	Kayak Newfoundland	8/12/2010	$ 1,970	7	50	2	48	Yes	Yes
50	Wild River Escape	8/27/2010	$ 1,944	10	50	18	32	No	No
62	Exotic Morocco	10/31/2010	$ 1,900	7	50	18	32	Yes	No
70									

Dates are after 6/1/2010

Prices are less than $2,000

Using advanced conditional formatting options

You can emphasize top or bottom ranked values in a field using conditional formatting. To highlight the top or bottom values in a field, select the field data, click the Conditional Formatting button on the Home tab, point to Top/Bottom Rules, select a Top or Bottom rule, if necessary enter the percentage or number of cells in the selected range that you want to format, select the format for the cells that meet the top or bottom criteria, then click OK. You can also format your worksheet or table data using icon sets and color scales based on the cell values. A **color scale** uses a set of two, three, or four fill colors to convey relative values. For example, red could fill cells to indicate they have higher values and green could signify lower values. To add a color scale, select a data range, click the Home tab, click the Conditional Formatting button in the Styles group, then point to Color Scales. On the submenu, you can select preformatted color sets or click More Rules to create your own color sets. **Icon sets** let you visually communicate relative cell values by adding icons to cells based on the values they contain. An upward-pointing green arrow might represent the highest values, and downward-pointing red arrows could represent lower values. To add an icon set to a data range, select a data range, click the Conditional Formatting button in the Styles group, then point to Icon Sets. You can customize the values that are used as thresholds for color scales and icon sets by clicking the Conditional Formatting button in the Styles group, clicking Manage Rules, clicking the rule in the Conditional Formatting Rules Manager dialog box, then clicking Edit Rule.

Extracting Table Data

Whenever you take the time to specify a complicated set of search criteria, it's a good idea to extract the matching records, rather than filtering it in-place. When you **extract** data, you place a copy of a filtered table in a range that you specify in the Advanced Filter dialog box. This way, you won't accidentally clear the filter or lose track of the records you spent time compiling. To extract data, you use an advanced filter and enter the criteria beneath the copied field names, as you did in the previous lesson.  Kate needs to filter the table one step further to reflect only the Exotic Morocco or Kayak Newfoundland tours in the current filtered table. She asks you to complete this filter by specifying an Or condition, which you will do by entering two sets of criteria in two separate rows. You decide to save the filtered records by extracting them to a different location in the worksheet.

STEPS

1. **In cell A3, enter Exotic Morocco, then in cell A4, enter Kayak Newfoundland**

   The new sets of criteria need to appear in two separate rows, so you need to copy the previous filter criteria to the second row.

2. **Copy the criteria in B3:C3 to B4:C4**

   The criteria are shown in Figure H-8. When you perform the advanced filter this time, you indicate that you want to copy the filtered table to a range beginning in cell A75, so that Kate can easily refer to the data, even if you perform more filters later.

3. **Click the Data tab if necessary, then click Advanced in the Sort & Filter group**

4. **Under Action, click the Copy to another location option button to select it, click the Copy to text box, then type A75**

   The last time you filtered the table, the criteria range included only rows 2 and 3, and now you have criteria in row 4.

TROUBLE
Make sure the criteria range in the Advanced Filter dialog box includes the field names and the number of rows underneath the names that contain criteria. If you leave a blank row in the criteria range, Excel filters nothing and shows all records.

5. **Edit the contents of the Criteria range text box to show the range $A$2:$I$4, click OK, then if necessary scroll down until row 75 is visible**

   The matching records appear in the range beginning in cell A75, as shown in Figure H-9. The original table, starting in cell A7, contains the records filtered in the previous lesson.

6. **Select the range A75:I80, click the Office button ⊚, click Print, under Print what click the Selection option button, click Preview, then click Print**

   The selected area prints.

7. **Press [Ctrl][Home], then click the Clear button in the Sort & Filter group**

   The original table is displayed starting in cell A7, and the extracted table remains in A75:I80.

8. **Save the workbook**

FIGURE H-8: Criteria in separate rows

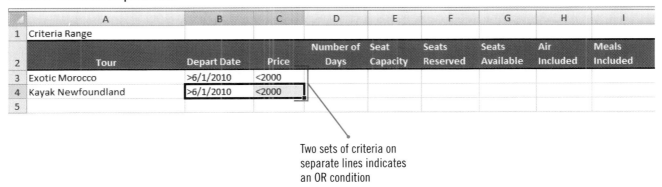

	A	B	C	D	E	F	G	H	I
1	Criteria Range								
2	Tour	Depart Date	Price	Number of Days	Seat Capacity	Seats Reserved	Seats Available	Air Included	Meals Included
3	Exotic Morocco	>6/1/2010	<2000						
4	Kayak Newfoundland	>6/1/2010	<2000						
5									

Two sets of criteria on
separate lines indicates
an OR condition

FIGURE H-9: Extracted data records

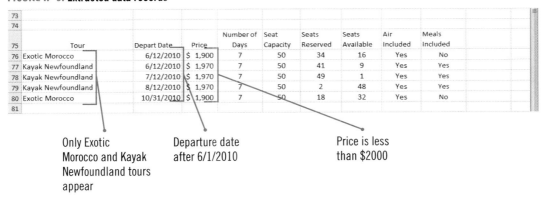

	Tour	Depart Date	Price	Number of Days	Seat Capacity	Seats Reserved	Seats Available	Air Included	Meals Included
73									
74									
75	Tour	Depart Date	Price	Number of Days	Seat Capacity	Seats Reserved	Seats Available	Air Included	Meals Included
76	Exotic Morocco	6/12/2010	$ 1,900	7	50	34	16	Yes	No
77	Kayak Newfoundland	6/12/2010	$ 1,970	7	50	41	9	Yes	Yes
78	Kayak Newfoundland	7/12/2010	$ 1,970	7	50	49	1	Yes	Yes
79	Kayak Newfoundland	8/12/2010	$ 1,970	7	50	2	48	Yes	Yes
80	Exotic Morocco	10/31/2010	$ 1,900	7	50	18	32	Yes	No
81									

Only Exotic
Morocco and Kayak
Newfoundland tours
appear

Departure date
after 6/1/2010

Price is less
than $2000

Understanding the criteria range and the copy-to location

When you define the criteria range and the copy-to location in the Advanced Filter dialog box, Excel automatically creates the names Criteria and Extract for these ranges in the worksheet. The criteria range includes the field names and any criteria rows underneath them. The extract range includes just the field names above the extracted table. You can select these ranges by clicking the Name box list arrow, then clicking the range name. If you click the Name Manager button in the Defined Names group on the Formulas tab, you will see these new names and the ranges associated with the names.

Looking Up Values in a Table

The Excel VLOOKUP function helps you locate specific values in a table. VLOOKUP searches vertically (V) down the far left column of a table, then reads across the row to find the value in the column you specify, much as you might look up a number in a phone book: You locate a person's name, then read across the row to find the phone number you want. Kate wants to be able to find a tour destination by entering the tour code. You will use the VLOOKUP function to accomplish this task. You begin by viewing the table name so you can refer to it in a Lookup function.

STEPS

QUICK TIP

You can change table names to better represent their content so they are easier to use in formulas. Click the table in the list of names in the Name Manager text box, click Edit, type the new table name in the Name text box, then click OK.

1. **Click the Lookup sheet tab, click the Formulas tab, then click the Name Manager button in the Defined Names group**

   The named ranges for the workbook appear in the Name Manager dialog box, as shown in Figure H-10. The Criteria and Extract ranges appear at the top of the range name list. At the bottom of the list is information about the three tables in the workbook. Table1 refers to the table on the Tours sheet, Table2 refers to the table on the Lookup sheet, and Table3 refers to the table on the Subtotals worksheet. These table names were automatically generated when the table was created by the Excel structured reference feature.

2. **Click Close**

   You want to find the tour represented by the code 675Y. The VLOOKUP function lets you find the tour name for any trip code. You will enter a trip code in cell L2 and a VLOOKUP function in cell M2.

3. **Click cell L2, enter 675Y, click cell M2, click the Lookup & Reference button in the Function Library group, then click VLOOKUP**

   The Function Arguments dialog box opens, with boxes for each of the VLOOKUP arguments. Because the value you want to find is in cell L2, L2 is the Lookup_value. The table you want to search is the table on the Lookup sheet, so its assigned name, Table2, is the Table_array.

QUICK TIP

If you want to find only the closest match for a value, enter TRUE in the Range_lookup text box. However, this can give misleading results if you are looking for an exact match. If you use FALSE and Excel can't find the value, you see an error message.

4. **With the insertion point in the Lookup_value text box, click cell L2, click the Table_array text box, then type Table2**

   The column containing the information that you want to find and display in cell M2 is the second column from the left in the table range, so the Col_index_num is 2. Because you want to find an exact match for the value in cell L1, the Range_lookup argument is FALSE.

5. **Click the Col_index_num text box, type 2, click the Range_lookup text box, then enter FALSE**

   Your completed Function Arguments dialog box should match Figure H-11.

6. **Click OK**

   Excel searches down the leftmost column of the table until it finds a value matching the one in cell L2. It finds the tour for that record, Catalonia Adventure, then displays it in cell M2. You use this function to determine the tour for one other trip code.

7. **Click cell L2, type 439U, then click the Enter button ☑ on the formula bar**

   The VLOOKUP function returns the value of Cooking in France in cell M2.

8. **Press [Ctrl][Home], then save the workbook**

Finding records using the DGET function

You can also use the DGET function to find a record in a table that matches specified criteria. For example, you could use the criteria of L1:L2 in the DGET function. When using DGET, you need to include [#All] after your table name in the formula to include the column labels that are used for the criteria range.

FIGURE H-10: Named ranges in the workbook

Created by
Advanced
Filter

Tables in the
workbook

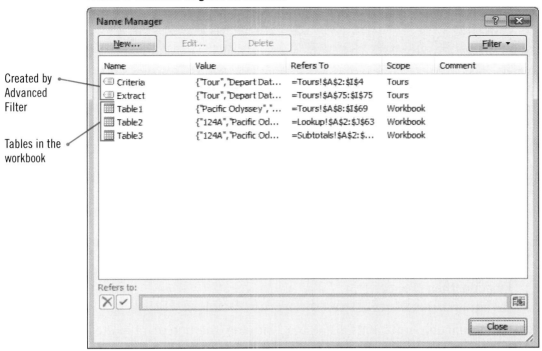

FIGURE H-11: Completed Function Arguments dialog box for VLOOKUP

Range name of
table to search

Finds exact
match

Location of
value you want
to search for

Number of
column to
search

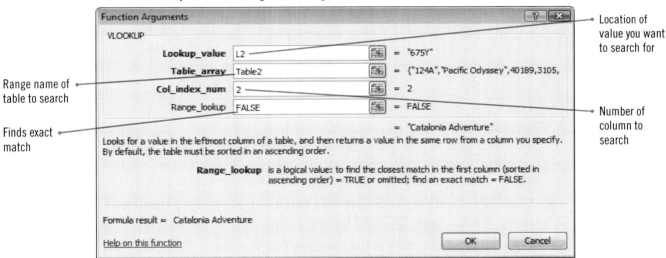

Using the HLOOKUP and MATCH functions

The VLOOKUP (Vertical Lookup) function is useful when your data is arranged vertically, in columns. The HLOOKUP (Horizontal Lookup) function is useful when your data is arranged horizontally, in rows. HLOOKUP searches horizontally across the upper row of a table until it finds the matching value, then looks down the number of rows you specify. The arguments for this function are identical to those for the VLOOKUP function, with one exception. Instead of a Col_index_ number, HLOOKUP uses a Row_index_number, which indicates the location of the row you want to search. For example, if you want to search the fourth row from the top, the Row_index_number should be 4. You can use the MATCH function when you want the position of an item in a range. The MATCH function uses the syntax: MATCH (lookup_value,lookup_array,match_ type) where lookup_value is the value you want to match in the lookup_array range. The match_type can be 0 for an exact match, 1 for matching the largest value that is less than or equal to lookup_value, or –1 for matching the smallest value that is greater than or equal to lookup_value.

Summarizing Table Data

Because a table acts much like a database, database functions allow you to summarize table data in a variety of ways. When working with a sales activity table, for example, you can use Excel to count the number of client contacts by sales representative or to total the amount sold to specific accounts by month. Table H-1 lists database functions commonly used to summarize table data. Kate is considering adding tours for the 2010 schedule. She needs your help in evaluating the number of seats available for scheduled tours.

STEPS

1. **Review the criteria range for the Pacific Odyssey tour in the range** L6:L7

   The criteria range in L6:L7 tells Excel to summarize records with the entry Pacific Odyssey in the Tour column. The functions will be in cells N6 and N7. You use this criteria range in a DSUM function to sum the seats available for only the Pacific Odyssey tours.

2. **Click cell** N6, **click the** Insert Function button **in the Function Library group, in the Search for a function text box type** database, **click** Go, **click** DSUM **under Select a function, then click** OK

   The first argument of the DSUM function is the table, or database.

> **QUICK TIP**
>
> Because the DSUM formula uses the column headings to locate and sum the table data, the header row needs to be included in the database range.

3. **In the Function Arguments dialog box, with the insertion point in the Database text box, move the pointer over the upper-left corner of the Trip Code column header until the pointer becomes** ↘, **click once, then click again**

   The first click selects the table's data range and the second click selects the entire table, including the header row. The second argument of the DSUM function is the label for the column that you want to sum. You want to total the number of available seats. The last argument for the DSUM function is the criteria that will be used to determine which values to total.

> **TROUBLE**
>
> If your Function Arguments dialog box does not match Figure H-12, click Cancel and repeat steps 2 – 4.

4. **Click the** Field text box, **then click cell** H1, **Seats Available; click the** Criteria text box **and select the range** L6:L7

   Your completed Function Arguments dialog box should match Figure H-12.

5. **Click** OK

   The result in cell N6 is 62. Excel totaled the information in the column Seats Available for those records that meet the criterion of Tour equals Pacific Odyssey. The DCOUNT and the DCOUNTA functions can help you determine the number of records meeting specified criteria in a database field. DCOUNTA counts the number of nonblank cells. You will use DCOUNTA to determine the number of tours scheduled

6. **Click cell** N7, **click** *fx* **on the formula bar, in the Search for a function text box type** database, **click** Go, **select** DCOUNTA **from the Select a function list, then click** OK

7. **With the insertion point in the Database text box, move the pointer over the upper-left corner of the Trip Code column header until the pointer becomes** ↘, **click once, click again to, click the** Field text box **and click cell** B1, **click the** Criteria text box **and select the range** L6:L7, **then click** OK

   The result in cell N7 is 4, meaning that there are four Pacific Odyssey tours scheduled for the year. You also want to display the number of seats available for the Cooking in France tours.

8. **Click cell** L7, **type** Cooking in France, **then click the** Enter button ✓ **on the formula bar**

   Figure H-13 shows that only three seats are available in the Cooking in France tours.

FIGURE H-12: Completed Function Arguments dialog box for DSUM

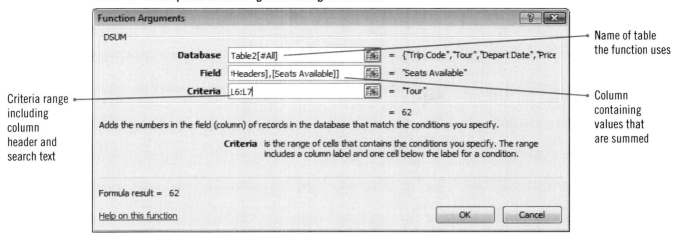

Name of table
the function uses

Criteria range
including
column
header and
search text

Column
containing
values that
are summed

FIGURE H-13: Result generated by database functions

	D	E	F	G	H	I	J	K	L	M	N
1	Price	Number of Days	Seat Capacity	Seats Reserved	Seats Available	Air Included	Meals Included		Trip Code	Tour	
2	$ 3,105	14	50	30	20	Yes	No		439U	Cooking in France	
3	$ 2,800	10	50	39	11	Yes	Yes				
4	$ 3,933	18	50	45	5	Yes	Yes				
5	$ 2,590	7	50	30	20	Yes	Yes		Criteria		
6	$ 4,200	14	50	38	12	Yes	Yes		Tour	Seats Available	3
7	$ 4,877	14	50	42	8	No	No		Cooking in France	Number of tours scheduled	2
8	$ 2,822	7	50	48	2	Yes	No				

TABLE H-1: Common database functions

function	result
DGET	Extracts a single record from a table that matches criteria you specify
DSUM	Totals numbers in a given table column that match criteria you specify
DAVERAGE	Averages numbers in a given table column that match criteria you specify
DCOUNT	Counts the cells that contain numbers in a given table column that match criteria you specify
DCOUNTA	Counts the cells that contain nonblank data in a given table column that match criteria you specify

Validating Table Data

When setting up data tables, you want to help ensure accuracy when you or others enter data. The Excel data validation feature allows you to do this by specifying what data users can enter in a range of cells. You can restrict data to whole numbers, decimal numbers, or text. You can also specify a list of acceptable entries. Once you've specified what data the program should consider valid for that cell, Excel displays an error message when invalid data is entered and can prevent users from entering any other data that it considers to be invalid. Kate wants to make sure that information in the Air Included column is entered consistently in the future. She asks you to restrict the entries in that column to two options: Yes and No. First, you select the table column you want to restrict.

STEPS

QUICK TIP
To specify a long list of valid entries, type the list in a column elsewhere in the worksheet, then type the list range in the Source text box.

1. **Click the top edge of the Air Included column header**
   The column data is selected.

2. **Click the Data tab, click the Data Validation button in the Data Tools group, click the Settings tab if necessary, click the Allow list arrow, then click List**
   Selecting the List option lets you type a list of specific options.

3. **Click the Source text box, then type Yes, No**
   You have entered the list of acceptable entries, separated by commas, as shown in Figure H-14. You want the data entry person to be able to select a valid entry from a drop-down list.

TROUBLE
If you get an invalid data error, make sure that cell I1 is not included in the selection. If I1 is included, open the Data Validation dialog box, click Clear All, click OK, then begin with step 1 again.

4. **Click the In-cell dropdown check box to select it if necessary, then click OK**
   The dialog box closes, and you return to the worksheet.

5. **Click the Home tab, click any cell in the last table row, click the Insert list arrow in the Cells group, click Insert Table Row Below, click cell I64, then click the list arrow to display the list of valid entries**
   The dropdown list is shown in Figure H-15. You could click an item in the list to have it entered in the cell, but you want to test the data restriction by entering an invalid entry.

6. **Click the list arrow to close the list, type Maybe, then press [Enter]**
   A warning dialog box appears to prevent you from entering the invalid data, as shown in Figure H-16.

7. **Click Cancel, click the list arrow, then click Yes**
   The cell accepts the valid entry. The data restriction ensures that records contain only one of the two correct entries in the Air Included column. The table is ready for future data entry.

8. **Delete the last table row, then save the workbook**

9. **Add your name to the center section of the footer, select the range L1:N7, click the Office button 🔘, click Print, under Print what, click the Selection option button, click Preview, then click Print**

Restricting cell values and data length

In addition to providing an in-cell drop-down list for data entry, you can use data validation to restrict the values that are entered into cells. For example, if you want to restrict cells to values less than a certain number, date, or time, click the Data tab, click the Data Validation button in the Data Tools group, and on the Settings tab, click the Allow list arrow, select Whole number, Decimal, Date, or Time, click the Data list arrow, select less than, then in the bottom text box, enter the maximum value. You can also limit the length of data entered into cells by choosing Text length in the Allow list, clicking the Data list arrow and selecting less than, then entering the maximum length in the Maximum text box.

FIGURE H-14: **Creating data restrictions**

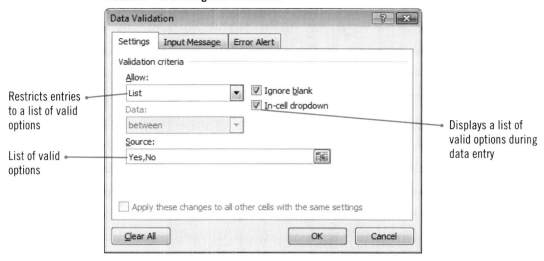

Restricts entries to a list of valid options

List of valid options

Displays a list of valid options during data entry

FIGURE H-15: **Entering data in restricted cells**

61	307R	Pacific Odyssey	12/21/2010	$ 3,105	14	50	50	0	Yes	No
62	927F	Essential India	12/30/2010	$ 3,933	18	50	31	19	Yes	Yes
63	448G	Old Japan	12/31/2010	$ 2,100	21	50	44	6	Yes	No
64								0		
65										
66										

Dropdown list

FIGURE H-16: **Invalid data warning**

Adding input messages and error alerts

You can customize the way data validation works by using the two other tabs in the Data Validation dialog box: Input Message and Error Alert. The Input Message tab lets you set a message that appears when the user selects that cell; for example, the message might contain instructions about what type of data to enter. On the Input Message tab, enter a message title and message, then click OK. The Error Alert tab lets you set one of three alert levels if a user enters invalid data. The Information level displays your message with the information icon but allows the user to proceed with data entry. The Warning level displays your information with the warning icon and gives the user the option to proceed with data entry or not. The Stop level, which you used in this lesson, displays your message and only lets the user retry or cancel data entry for that cell.

Creating Subtotals

The Excel Subtotals feature provides a quick, easy way to group and summarize a range of data. Usually, you create subtotals with the SUM function, but you can also summarize data groups with functions such as COUNT, AVERAGE, MAX, and MIN. Subtotals cannot be used in a table structure. Before you can add subtotals to a table, you must first convert the data to a range and sort it. Kate wants you to group data by tours, with subtotals for the number of seats available and the number of seats reserved. You begin by converting the table to a range.

STEPS

1. **Click the** Subtotals sheet tab, **click any cell inside the table, click the** Table Tools Design tab, **click the** Convert to Range button **in the Tools group, then click** Yes

   Before you can add the subtotals, you must first sort the data. You decide to sort it in ascending order, first by tour and then by departure date.

2. **Click the** Data tab, **click the** Sort button **in the Sort & Filter group, in the Sort dialog box click the** Sort by list arrow, **click** Tour, **then click the** Add Level button, **click the** Then by list arrow, **click** Depart Date, **verify that the order is** Oldest to Newest, **then click** OK

   You have sorted the range in ascending order, first by tour, then by departure date.

3. **Click any cell in the data range, then click the** Subtotal button **in the Outline group**

   The Subtotal dialog box opens. Here you specify the items you want subtotaled, the function you want to apply to the values, and the fields you want to summarize.

4. **Click the** At each change in list arrow, **click** Tour, **click the** Use function list arrow, **click** Sum; **in the Add subtotal to list, click the** Seats Reserved **and** Seats Available check boxes **to select them, if necessary, then click the** Meals Included check box **to deselect it**

5. **If necessary, click the** Replace current subtotals **and** Summary below data check boxes **to select them**

   Your completed Subtotal dialog box should match Figure H-17.

QUICK TIP
You can click the ▬ button to hide or the ✚ button to show a group of records in the subtotaled structure.

6. **Click** OK, **then scroll down so row 90 is visible**

   The subtotaled data appears, showing the calculated subtotals and grand total in columns G and H, as shown in Figure H-18. Notice that Excel displays an outline to the left of the worksheet, with outline buttons to control the level of detail that appears. The button number corresponds to the detail level that is displayed. You want to show the second level of detail, the subtotals and the grand total.

7. **Click the** outline symbol 2

   The subtotals and the grand totals appear.

QUICK TIP
You can remove subtotals in a worksheet by clicking the Subtotal button and clicking Remove All. The subtotals no longer appear, and the Outline feature is turned off automatically.

8. **Add your name to the center section of the footer, scale the worksheet width to print on one page, save, preview the worksheet, then print it**

9. **Close the workbook and exit Excel**

FIGURE H-17: Completed Subtotal dialog box

Field to use in grouping data

Function to apply to groups

Subtotal these fields

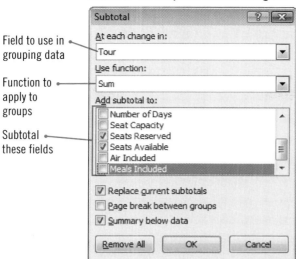

FIGURE H-18: Portion of subtotaled table

Outline symbols

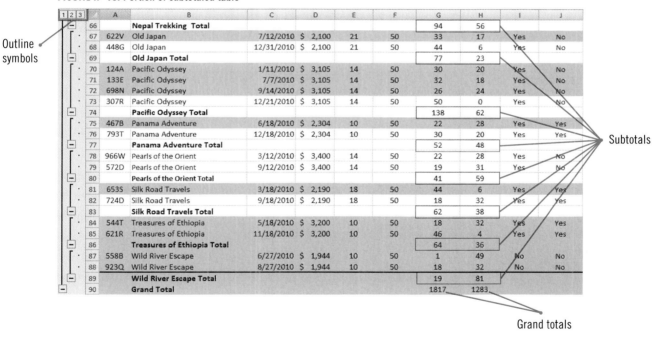

		A	B	C	D	E	F	G	H	I	J
	66		**Nepal Trekking Total**					94	56		
	67	622V	Old Japan	7/12/2010	$ 2,100	21	50	33	17	Yes	No
	68	448G	Old Japan	12/31/2010	$ 2,100	21	50	44	6	Yes	No
	69		**Old Japan Total**					77	23		
	70	124A	Pacific Odyssey	1/11/2010	$ 3,105	14	50	30	20	Yes	No
	71	133E	Pacific Odyssey	7/7/2010	$ 3,105	14	50	32	18	Yes	No
	72	698N	Pacific Odyssey	9/14/2010	$ 3,105	14	50	26	24	Yes	No
	73	307R	Pacific Odyssey	12/21/2010	$ 3,105	14	50	50	0	Yes	No
	74		**Pacific Odyssey Total**					138	62		
	75	467B	Panama Adventure	6/18/2010	$ 2,304	10	50	22	28	Yes	Yes
	76	793T	Panama Adventure	12/18/2010	$ 2,304	10	50	30	20	Yes	Yes
	77		**Panama Adventure Total**					52	48		
	78	966W	Pearls of the Orient	3/12/2010	$ 3,400	14	50	22	28	Yes	No
	79	572D	Pearls of the Orient	9/12/2010	$ 3,400	14	50	19	31	Yes	No
	80		**Pearls of the Orient Total**					41	59		
	81	653S	Silk Road Travels	3/18/2010	$ 2,190	18	50	44	6	Yes	Yes
	82	724D	Silk Road Travels	9/18/2010	$ 2,190	18	50	18	32	Yes	Yes
	83		**Silk Road Travels Total**					62	38		
	84	544T	Treasures of Ethiopia	5/18/2010	$ 3,200	10	50	18	32	Yes	Yes
	85	621R	Treasures of Ethiopia	11/18/2010	$ 3,200	10	50	46	4	Yes	Yes
	86		**Treasures of Ethiopia Total**					64	36		
	87	558B	Wild River Escape	6/27/2010	$ 1,944	10	50	1	49	No	No
	88	923Q	Wild River Escape	8/27/2010	$ 1,944	10	50	18	32	No	No
	89		**Wild River Escape Total**					19	81		
	90		**Grand Total**					1817	1283		

Subtotals

Grand totals

Practice

▼ CONCEPTS REVIEW

FIGURE H-19

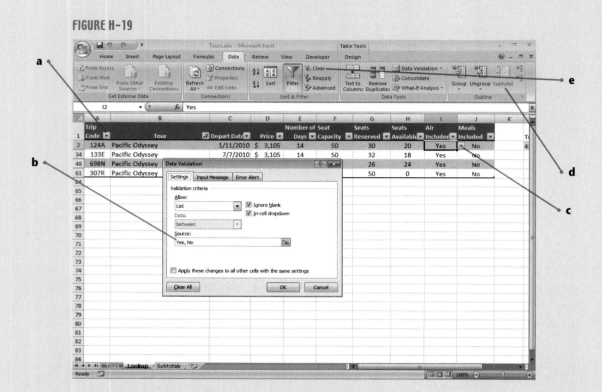

1. Which element do you click to specify acceptable data entries for a table?
2. Which element points to a field's list arrow?
3. Which element do you click to group data and summarize data in a table?
4. Which element would you click to remove a filter?
5. Which element points to an In-cell dropdown list arrow?

Match each term with the statement that best describes it.

6. DSUM
7. Data validation
8. Criteria range
9. Extracted table
10. Table_array

a. Cell range when Advanced Filter results are copied to another location
b. Range in which search conditions are set
c. Restricts table entries to specified options
d. Name of the table searched in a VLOOKUP function
e. Function used to total table values that meet specified criteria

Select the best answer from the list of choices.

11. The _____ logical condition finds records matching both listed criteria.
   a. Or
   b. And
   c. True
   d. False

12. What does it mean when you select the Or option when creating a custom filter?
   a. Both criteria must be true to find a match.
   b. Neither criterion has to be 100% true.
   c. Either criterion can be true to find a match.
   d. A custom filter requires a criteria range.

13. What must a data range have before subtotals can be inserted?

    a. Enough records to show multiple subtotals   **c.** Formatted cells

    b. Grand totals   **d.** Sorted data

14. Which function finds the position of an item in a table?

    a. MATCH   **c.** DGET

    b. VLOOKUP   **d.** HLOOKUP

▼ SKILLS REVIEW

1. Filter a table.

  a. Start Excel, open the file EX H-2.xlsx from the drive and folder where you store your Data Files, then save it as **Salary Summary**.

  b. With the Compensation sheet active, filter the table to list only records for employees in the Boston branch.

  c. Clear the filter, then add a filter that displays the records for employees in the Boston and Philadelphia branches.

  d. Redisplay all employees, then use a filter to show the three employees with the highest annual salary.

  e. Redisplay all the records, then save the workbook.

2. Create a custom filter.

  a. Create a custom filter showing employees hired before 1/1/2007 or after 12/31/2007.

  b. Create a custom filter showing employees hired between 1/1/2007 and 12/31/2007.

  c. Enter your name in the worksheet footer, save the workbook, then preview and print the filtered worksheet.

  d. Redisplay all records.

  e. Save the workbook.

3. Filter and extract a table with Advanced Filter.

  a. You want to retrieve a list of employees who were hired before 1/1/2008 and who have an annual salary of more than $80,000 a year. Define a criteria range by inserting six new rows above the table on the worksheet and copying the field names into the first row.

  b. In cell D2, enter the criterion **<1/1/2008**, then in cell G2 enter **>80000**.

  c. Click any cell in the table.

  d. Open the Advanced Filter dialog box.

  e. Indicate that you want to copy to another location, enter the criteria range **A1:J2**, verify that the List range is $A$7:$J$17, then indicate that you want to place the extracted list in the range starting at cell **A20**.

  f. Confirm that the retrieved list meets the criteria as shown in Figure H-20.

  g. Save the workbook, then preview and print the worksheet.

4. Look up values in a table.

  a. Click the Summary sheet tab. Use the Name Manager to view the table names in the workbook, then close the dialog box.

  b. You will use a lookup function to locate an employee's annual compensation; enter the Employee Number **2214** in cell A17.

  c. In cell B17, use the VLOOKUP function and enter **A17** as the Lookup_value, **Table2** as the Table_array, **10** as the Col_index_num, and **FALSE** as the Range_lookup; observe the compensation displayed for that employee number, then check it against the table to make sure it is correct.

  d. Enter another Employee Number, **4177**, in cell A17 and view the annual compensation for that employee.

  e. Format cell B17 with the Accounting format with no decimal places and the $ symbol.

  f. Save the workbook.

FIGURE H-20

	A	B	C	D	E	F	G	H	I	J
1	Employee Number	First Name	Last Name	Hire Date	Branch	Monthly Salary	Annual Salary	Annual Bonus	Benefits Dollars	Annual Compensation
2				<1/1/2008			>80000			
3										
4										
5										
6										
7	Employee Number	First Name	Last Name	Hire Date	Branch	Monthly Salary	Annual Salary	Annual Bonus	Benefits Dollars	Annual Compensation
8	1311	Mary	Lawson	2/12/2007	NY	$ 4,500	$ 54,000	$ 1,200	$ 12,420	$ 67,620
9	4522	Laurie	Wales	4/1/2008	Boston	$ 5,800	$ 69,600	$ 5,400	$ 16,008	$ 91,008
10	4177	Donna	Oahar	5/6/2006	Philadelphia	$ 7,500	$ 90,000	$ 16,000	$ 20,700	$ 126,700
11	2571	Mary	Martin	12/10/2007	Boston	$ 8,000	$ 96,000	$ 18,000	$ 22,080	$ 136,080
12	2214	Paul	Gamache	2/15/2009	Boston	$ 2,900	$ 34,800	$ 570	$ 8,004	$ 43,374
13	6587	Peter	Erickson	3/25/2007	NY	$ 2,775	$ 33,300	$ 770	$ 7,659	$ 41,729
14	2123	Erin	Mallo	6/23/2006	NY	$ 3,990	$ 47,880	$ 2,500	$ 11,012	$ 61,392
15	4439	Mark	Merry	8/3/2009	Philadelphia	$ 6,770	$ 81,240	$ 5,000	$ 18,685	$ 104,925
16	9807	Hailey	Reed	9/29/2008	Philadelphia	$ 8,600	$103,200	$ 14,000	$ 23,736	$ 140,936
17	3944	Joyce	Roy	5/12/2007	Boston	$ 3,500	$ 42,000	$ 900	$ 9,660	$ 52,560
18										
19										
20	Employee Number	First Name	Last Name	Hire Date	Branch	Monthly Salary	Annual Salary	Annual Bonus	Benefits Dollars	Annual Compensation
21	4177	Donna	Oahar	5/6/2006	Philadelphia	$ 7,500	$ 90,000	$ 16,000	$ 20,700	$ 126,700
22	2571	Mary	Martin	12/10/2007	Boston	$ 8,000	$ 96,000	$ 18,000	$ 22,080	$ 136,080
23										

5. **Summarize table data.**

   a. You want to enter a database function to average the annual salaries by branch, using the NY branch as the initial criterion. In cell E17, use the DAVERAGE function and click the top left corner of cell A1 twice to select the table and its header row as the Database, select cell G1 for the Field and select the range D16:D17 for the Criteria.

   b. Test the function further by entering the text **Philadelphia** in cell D17. When the criterion is entered, cell E17 should display 91480.

   c. Format cell E17 in Accounting format with no decimal places and the $ symbol.

   d. Save the workbook.

6. **Validation table data.**

   a. Select the data in column E of the table and set a validation criterion specifying that you want to allow a list of valid options.

   b. Enter a list of valid options that restricts the entries to **NY**, **Boston**, and **Philadelphia**. Remember to use a comma between each item in the list.

   c. Indicate that you want the options to appear in an in-cell dropdown list, then close the dialog box.

   d. Add a row to the table. Go to cell E12, then select Boston in the dropdown list.

   e. Select column F in the table and indicate that you want to restrict the data entered to only whole numbers. In the Minimum text box, enter **1000**; in the Maximum text box, enter **20000**. Close the dialog box.

   f. Click cell F12, enter **25000**, then press [Enter]. You should get an error message.

   g. Click Cancel, then enter **17000**.

   h. Complete the new record by adding an Employee Number of 1112, a First Name of Caroline, a Last Name of Dow, a Hire Date of 2/1/2010, and an Annual Bonus of $1000. Format the range F12:J12 as Accounting with no decimal places and using the $ symbol. Compare your screen to Figure H-21.

   i. Add your name to the center section of the footer, save, preview the worksheet and fit it to one page if necessary, then print it.

FIGURE H-21

7. **Create subtotals using grouping and outlines.**

   a. Click the Subtotals sheet tab.

   b. Use the Department field list arrow to sort the table in ascending order by department.

   c. Convert the table to a range.

   d. Group and create subtotals by department, using the SUM function, then click the AnnualCompensation checkbox if necessary in the Add Subtotal to list.

   e. Click the 2 outline button on the outline to display only the subtotals and the grand total. Compare your screen to Figure H-22.

   f. Enter your name in the worksheet footer, save the workbook, preview, then print the subtotals and grand total.

   g. Save the workbook, close the workbook, then exit Excel.

FIGURE H-22

▼ INDEPENDENT CHALLENGE 1

As the owner of Preserves, a gourmet food store located in Dublin, Ireland, you spend a lot of time managing your inventory. To help with this task, you have created an Excel table of your jam inventory. You want to filter the table and add subtotals and a grand total to the table. You also need to add data validation and summary information to the table.

▼ INDEPENDENT CHALLENGE 1 (CONTINUED)

a. Start Excel, open the file EX H-3.xlsx from the drive and folder where you store your Data Files, then save it as **Jams**.

b. Using the table data on the Inventory sheet, create a filter to generate a list of rhubarb jams. Enter your name in the worksheet footer, save the workbook, then preview and print the table. Clear the filter.

c. Use a Custom Filter to generate a list of jams with a quantity greater than 20. Preview, then print the table. Clear the filter.

d. Copy the labels in cells A1:F1 into A16:F16. Type **Gooseberry** in cell B17 and type **Small** in cell C17. Use the Advanced Filter with a criteria range of A16:F17 to extract a table of small gooseberry jams to the range of cells beginning in cell A20. Save the workbook, preview, then print the table with the extracted information.

e. Click the Summary sheet tab, select the table data in column B. Open the Data Validation dialog box, then indicate you want to use a validation list with the acceptable entries of **Gooseberry, Blackberry, Rhubarb**. Make sure the In-cell dropdown check box is selected.

f. Test the data validation by trying to change a cell in column B of the table to Strawberry.

g. Using Figure H-23 as a guide, enter a function in cell G18 that calculates the total quantity of blackberry jam in your store. Enter your name in the worksheet footer, save the workbook, then preview and print the worksheet.

h. Use the filter list arrow for the Type of Jam field to sort the table in ascending order by type of jam. Convert the table to a range. Insert subtotals by type of jam using the SUM function, then select Quantity in the Add Subtotal to table box. Use the appropriate button on the outline to display only the subtotals and grand total. (Note that the number of Blackberry Jams calculated in cell G22 is incorrect after subtotals are added because the subtotals are included in the database calculation.) Save the workbook, preview, then print the range containing the subtotals and grand total.

FIGURE H-23

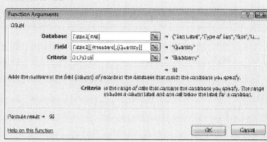

Advanced Challenge Exercise

- Clear the subtotals from the worksheet.
- Use conditional formatting to add icons to the quantity field using the following criteria: quantities greater than or equal to 20 are formatted with a green check mark, quantities greater than or equal to 10 but less than 20 are formatted with a yellow exclamation point, and quantities less than 10 are formatted with a red x. Use Figure H-24 as a guide to adding the formatting rule, then compare your Quantity values to Figure H-25. (*Hint*: You may need to click in the top Value text box for the correct value to display for the red x.)
- Save the workbook, preview then print the worksheet.

i. Close the workbook, then exit Excel.

FIGURE H-24

FIGURE H-25

	A	B	C	D	E	F
1	Jam Label	Type of Jam	Size	Unit Price	Quantity	Total
2	Tipperary Ranch	Blackberry	Medium	6.00	11	66.00
3	Galway Estate	Blackberry	Small	5.25	12	63.00
4	Wexford Hills	Blackberry	Medium	5.75	15	86.25
5	Kerry Lane	Blackberry	Small	6.55	12	78.60
6	Tipperary Ranch	Gooseberry	Small	5.75	6	34.50
7	Cork Estate	Gooseberry	Small	5.75	8	46.00
8	Wexford Hills	Gooseberry	Small	5.75	21	120.75
9	Kerry Lane	Gooseberry	Medium	7.25	18	130.50
10	Tipperary Ranch	Rhubarb	Small	6.50	5	32.50
11	Galway Estate	Rhubarb	Small	6.25	11	68.75
12	Wexford Hills	Rhubarb	Small	5.25	31	162.75
13	Kerry Lane	Rhubarb	Medium	7.55	24	181.20
14						

▼ INDEPENDENT CHALLENGE 2

You recently started a personalized pet tag business, called Paw Tags. The business sells engraved cat and dog tags. Customers order tags for their cat or dog and provide you with the name of the pet and whether they want engraving on one or both sides of the tag. You have put together an invoice table to track sales for the month of October. Now that you have this table, you would like to manipulate it in several ways. First, you want to filter the table to retrieve only tags retailing for more than a particular price and ordered during a particular part of the month. You also want to subtotal the unit price and total cost columns by tag and restrict entries in the Order Date column. Finally, you would like to add database and lookup functions to your worksheet to efficiently retrieve data from the table.

▼ INDEPENDENT CHALLENGE 2 (CONTINUED)

a. Start Excel, open the file EX H-4.xlsx from the drive and folder where you store your Data Files, then save it as **Paw Tags**.

b. Use the Advanced Filter to show tags with a price of $12.99 ordered before 10/15/2010, using cells A27:B28 to enter your criteria and filtering the table in place. (*Hint*: You don't need to specify an entire row as the criteria range.) Enter your name in the worksheet footer, save the workbook, then print the filtered table. Clear the filter, then save your work again.

c. Use the Data Validation dialog box to restrict entries to those with order dates on or after 10/1/2010 and before or on 10/31/2010. Test the data restrictions by attempting to enter an invalid date in cell D25.

d. Enter 23721 in cell F28. Enter a VLOOKUP function in cell G28 to retrieve the total based on the invoice number entered in cell F28. Make sure you have an exact match with the invoice number. Test the function with the invoice number 23718.

e. Enter the date 10/1/2010 in cell I28. Use the database function, DCOUNT, in cell J28 to count the number of invoices for the date in cell I28. Save the workbook.

f. Sort the table in ascending order by Tag, then convert the table to a range. Create subtotals showing the number of cat and dog tags in the Invoice Number column. Save your subtotaled data, then preview and print the Invoice worksheet.

Advanced Challenge Exercise

- Clear the subtotals and create a table using the data in the range A1:J25. Change the font color of the column headers to white. If the font headers are not visible, change the font color to one that contrasts with the fill color of your headers.
- Use the filtering feature to display only the Cat tags, then add a total row to display the number of cat tags in cell E26. Change the font color in cells A26 and E26 to white. If the contents of cells A26 and E26 are not visible, change the font color to one that contrasts with the fill color for those cells. Delete the total in cell J26.
- Use conditional formatting to format the cells where the Total is greater than $12.00 with light red fill and dark red text.
- Using the Total Filter arrow, sort the table by color to display the totals exceeding $12.00 on top. Filter the table by color to display only the rows with totals greater than $12.00.

g. Save the workbook, print the Invoice worksheet, close the workbook, then exit Excel.

▼ INDEPENDENT CHALLENGE 3

You are the manager of Green Mountain, a gift shop in Burlington, Vermont. You have created an Excel table that contains your order data, along with the amounts for each item ordered and the date the order was placed. You would like to manipulate this table to display product categories and ordered items meeting specific criteria. You would also like to add subtotals to the table and add database functions to total orders. Finally, you want to restrict entries in the Category column.

a. Start Excel, open the file EX H-5.xlsx from the drive and folder where you store your Data Files, then save it as **Gifts**.

b. Using the table data, create an advanced filter that retrieves, to its current location, records with dates before 9/10/2010 and whose orders were greater than $1000, using cells A37:E38 to enter your criteria for the filter. Clear the filter.

c. Create an advanced filter that extracts records with the following criteria to cell A42: orders greater than $1000 having dates either before 9/10/2010 or after 9/24/2010. (*Hint*: Recall that when you want records to meet one criterion or another, you need to place the criteria on separate lines.) Enter your name in the worksheet footer, then preview and print the worksheet.

d. Use the DSUM function in cell H2 to let worksheet users find the total order amounts for the category entered in cell G2. Format the cell containing the total order using the Accounting format with the $ symbol and no decimals. Test the DSUM function using the Food category name. (The sum for the Food category should be $5,998.) Print the worksheet.

e. Use data validation to create an in-cell drop-down that restricts category entries to Food, Clothing, Book, Personal. Use the Error Alert tab of the Data Validation dialog box to set the alert level to the Warning style with the message "Data is not valid." Test the validation in the table with valid and invalid entries.

f. Sort the table by category in ascending order. Add Subtotals to the order amounts by category. The total order amount in cell H2 will be incorrect after adding subtotals because the subtotals will be included in the database calculation.

g. Use the outline to display only category names with subtotals and the grand total.

Advanced Challenge Exercise

- Clear the subtotals from the worksheet.
- Conditionally format the 1-Month Order data using Top/Bottom Rules to emphasize the cells containing the top 10 percent with yellow fill and dark yellow text.
- Add another rule to format the bottom 10 percent in the 1-Month Order column with a light blue fill.

h. Save the workbook, preview, then print the worksheet.

i. Close the workbook, then exit Excel.

▼ REAL LIFE INDEPENDENT CHALLENGE

You decide to organize your business and personal contacts using the Excel table format. You want to use the table to look up cell, home, and work phone numbers. You also want to include addresses and a field documenting whether the contact relationship is personal or business. You enter your contact information in an Excel worksheet that you will convert to a table so you can easily filter the data. You also use lookup functions to locate phone numbers when you provide a last name in your table. Finally, you restrict the entries in one of the fields to values in drop-down lists to simplify future data entry and reduce errors.

a. Start Excel, open a new workbook, then save it as **Contacts** in the drive and folder where you store your Data Files.

b. Use the structure of Table H-2 to enter at least six of your personal and business contacts into a worksheet. (*Hint*: You will need to format the Zip column using the Zip Code type of the Special category.) In the Relationship field, enter either Business or Personal. If you don't have phone numbers for all the phone fields, leave them blank.

TABLE H-2

Last name	First name	Cell phone	Home phone	Work phone	Street address	City	State	Zip	Relationship

c. Use the worksheet information to create a table. Use the Name Manager dialog box to edit the table name to Contacts.

d. Create a filter that retrieves records of personal contacts. Clear the filter.

e. Create a filter that retrieves records of business contacts. Clear the filter.

f. Restrict the Relationship field entries to Business or Personal. Provide an in-cell drop-down list allowing the selection of these two options. Add an input message of **Select from the dropdown list**. Add an Information level error message of **Choose Business or Personal**. Test the validation by adding a new record to your table.

g. Below your table, create a phone lookup area with the following labels in adjacent cells: **Last name**, **Cell phone**, **Home phone**, **Work phone**.

h. Enter one of the last names from your table under the label Last Name in your phone lookup area.

i. In the phone lookup area, enter lookup functions to locate the cell phone, home phone, and work phone numbers for the contact last name that you entered in the previous step. Make sure you match the last name exactly.

j. Enter your name in the center section of the worksheet footer, save the workbook, preview, then print the worksheet on one page.

k. Close the workbook, then exit Excel.

▼ VISUAL WORKSHOP

Open the file EX H-6.xlsx from the drive and folder where you save your Data Files, then save it as **Schedule**. Complete the worksheet as shown in Figure H-26. Cells B18:E18 contain lookup functions that find the instructor, day, time, and room for the course entered in cell A18. Use HIS101 in cell A18 to test your lookup functions. The range A22:G27 is extracted from the table using the criteria in cells A20:A21. Add your name to the worksheet footer, save the workbook, then preview and print the worksheet.

FIGURE H-26

	A	B	C	D	E	F	G
1	Spring 2011 Schedule of History Classes						
2							
3	Course number	ID #	Time	Day	Room	Credits	Instructor
4	HIS100	1245	8:00 - 9:00	M,W,F	126	3	Walsh
5	HIS101	1356	8:00 - 9:30	T,TH	136	3	Guan
6	HIS102	1567	9:00 - 10:00	M,W,F	150	3	Marshall
7	HIS103	1897	10:00 - 11:30	T,TH	226	3	Benson
8	HIS104	3456	2:00 - 3:30	M,W,F	129	4	Paulson
9	HIS200	4678	12:00 - 1:30	T,TH	156	3	Dash
10	HIS300	7562	3:00 - 4:30	M,W,F	228	4	Christopher
11	HIS400	9823	11:00 - 12:00	M,W,F	103	3	Robbinson
12	HIS500	7123	3:00 - 4:30	T,TH	214	3	Matthews
13							
14							
15							
16							
17	Course Number	Instructor	Day	Time	Room		
18	HIS101	Guan	T,TH	8:00 - 9:30	136		
19							
20	Day						
21	M,W,F						
22	Course number	ID #	Time	Day	Room	Credits	Instructor
23	HIS100	1245	8:00 - 9:00	M,W,F	126	3	Walsh
24	HIS102	1567	9:00 - 10:00	M,W,F	150	3	Marshall
25	HIS104	3456	2:00 - 3:30	M,W,F	129	4	Paulson
26	HIS300	7562	3:00 - 4:30	M,W,F	228	4	Christopher
27	HIS400	9823	11:00 - 12:00	M,W,F	103	3	Robbinson
28							

Automating Worksheet Tasks

Files You Will Need:

EX I-1.xlsx

A **macro** is a set of instructions that performs tasks in the order you specify. You create macros to automate Excel tasks that you perform frequently. Because they perform tasks rapidly, macros can save you a great deal of time. For example, if you usually enter your name and date in a worksheet footer, you can record the keystrokes in an Excel macro that enters the text and inserts the current date automatically when you run the macro. In this unit, you will plan and design a simple macro, then record and run it. You will then edit the macro and explore ways to make it more easily available as you work.  Kate Morgan, the vice president of sales at Quest, wants you to create a macro for the sales division. The macro needs to automatically insert text that identifies the worksheet as a sales division document.

OBJECTIVES

Plan a macro

Enable a macro

Record a macro

Run a macro

Edit a macro

Use shortcut keys with macros

Use the Personal Macro Workbook

Assign a macro to a button

Planning a Macro

You create macros for Excel tasks that you perform frequently. For example, you can create a macro to enter and format text or to save and print a worksheet. To create a macro, you record the series of actions or write the instructions in a special programming language. Because the sequence of actions is important, you need to plan the macro carefully before you record it. Kate wants you to create a macro for the sales division that inserts the text "Sales Division" in the upper-left corner of any worksheet. You work with her to plan the macro.

DETAILS

To plan a macro, use the following guidelines:

- **Assign the macro a descriptive name**
  The first character of a macro name must be a letter; the remaining characters can be letters, numbers, or underscores. Letters can be uppercase or lowercase. Spaces are not allowed in macro names; use underscores in place of spaces. (Press [Shift][-] to enter an underscore character.) Kate wants you to name the macro "DivStamp". See Table I-1 for a list of macros that could be created to automate other tasks at Quest.

- **Write out the steps the macro will perform**
  This planning helps eliminate careless errors. Kate writes a description of the macro she wants, as shown in Figure I-1.

- **Decide how you will perform the actions you want to record**
  You can use the mouse, the keyboard, or a combination of the two. Kate wants you to use both the mouse and the keyboard.

- **Practice the steps you want Excel to record, and write them down**
  Kate has written down the sequence of actions she wants you to include in the macro.

- **Decide where to store the description of the macro and the macro itself**
  Macros can be stored in an active workbook, in a new workbook, or in the **Personal Macro Workbook**, a special workbook used only for macro storage. Kate asks you to store the macro in a new workbook.

FIGURE I-1: Paper description of planned macro

Macro to create stamp with the division name

Name:	DivStamp
Description:	Adds a stamp to the top left of the worksheet, identifying it as a sales division worksheet
Steps:	1. Position the cell pointer in cell A1.
	2. Type Sales Division, then click the Enter button.
	3. Click the Format button, then click Format Cells.
	4. Click the Font tab, under Font style, click Bold; under Underline; click Single; under Color; click Red; then click OK.

TABLE I-1: Possible macros and their descriptive names

description of macro	descriptive name
Enter a frequently used proper name, such as Kate Morgan	KateMorgan
Enter a frequently used company name, such as Quest	Company_Name
Print the active worksheet on a single page, in landscape orientation	FitToLand
Add a footer to a worksheet	FooterStamp
Show a generic view of a worksheet using the default print and display settings	GenericView

Enabling a Macro

Because a macro may contain a virus—destructive software that can damage your computer files—the default security setting in Excel disables macros from running. Although a workbook containing a macro will open, if macros are disabled, they will not function. You can manually change the Excel security setting to allow macros to run if you know a macro came from a trusted source. When saving a workbook with a macro, you need to save it as a macro-enabled workbook with the extension xlsm. ⬛⬛⬛ Kate asks you to change the security level to enable all macros. You will change the security level back to the default setting after you create and run your macros.

STEPS

1. **Start Excel, click the** Save button 🔲 **on the Quick Access Toolbar, in the Save As dialog box click the** Save as type list arrow, **click** Excel Macro-Enabled Workbook (*.xlsm), **then in the File name text box type** Macro Workbook

QUICK TIP

If the Developer tab is displayed on your Ribbon, skip steps three and four.

2. **Navigate to the drive and folder where you store your Data Files, then click** Save
   The security settings that enable macros are available on the Developer tab.

3. **Click the** Microsoft Office button 🔵, **then click the** Excel Options button **at the bottom of the menu**
   The Excel Options dialog box opens, as shown in Figure I-2.

4. **If necessary, click** Popular **in the category list, click the** Show Developer tab in the Ribbon check box **to select it if necessary, then click** OK
   The Developer tab appears on the Ribbon. You are ready to change the security settings.

5. **Click the** Developer tab, **then click the** Macro Security button **in the Code group**
   The Trust Center dialog box opens, as shown in Figure I-3.

6. **Click** Macro Settings **if necessary, click the** Enable all macros (not recommended; potentially dangerous code can run) option button **to select it, then click** OK
   The dialog box closes. Macros remain enabled until you disable them by deselecting the Enable all macros option. As you work with Excel, you should disable macros when you are not working with them.

FIGURE I-2: Excel Options dialog box

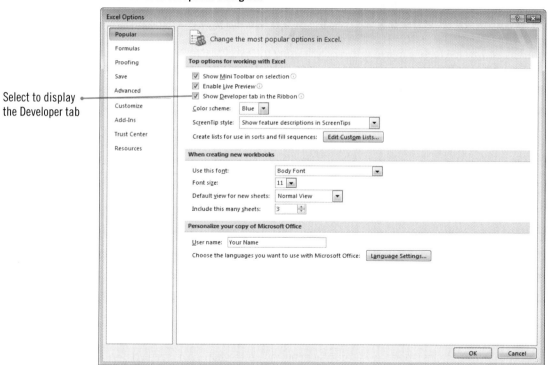

Select to display the Developer tab

FIGURE I-3: Trust Center dialog box

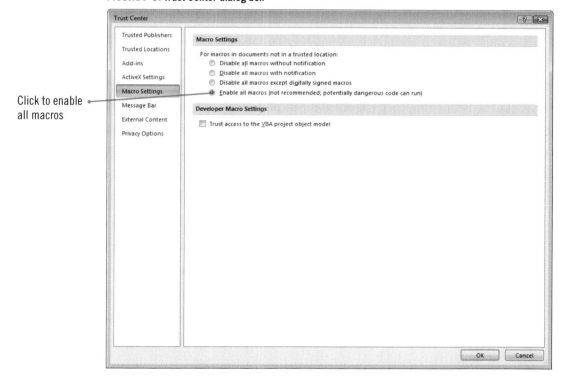

Click to enable all macros

Excel 2007

Disabling macros

To prevent viruses from running on your computer, you should disable all macros when you are not working with them. To disable macros, click the Developer tab, then click the Macro Security button in the Code group. Clicking any of the first three options will disable

macros. The first option will disable all macros without notifying you. The second option will notify you when macros are disabled, and the third option will allow only digitally signed macros to run.

Recording a Macro

The easiest way to create a macro is to record it using the Excel Macro Recorder. You turn the Macro Recorder on, name the macro, enter the keystrokes and select the commands you want the macro to perform, then stop the recorder. As you record the macro, Excel automatically translates each action into program code that you can later view and modify. You can take as long as you want to record the macro; a recorded macro contains only your actions, not the amount of time you took to record it. ▓▓▓▓▓ Kate wants you to create a macro that enters a division "stamp" in cell A1 of the active worksheet. You create this macro by recording your actions.

STEPS

QUICK TIP
You can also click the Record Macro button in the Code group on the Developer tab to record a new macro.

1. **Click the Record Macro button 🖳 on the left side of the status bar**

   The Record Macro dialog box opens, as shown in Figure I-4. The default name Macro1 is selected. You can either assign this name or enter a new name. This dialog box also lets you assign a shortcut key for running the macro and assign a storage location for the macro.

2. **Type DivStamp in the Macro name text box**

3. **If the Store macro in list box does not display This Workbook, click the list arrow and select This Workbook**

4. **Type your name in the Description text box, then click OK**

   The dialog box closes and the Record Macro button on the status bar is replaced with a Stop Recording button. Take your time performing the steps below. Excel records every keystroke, menu selection, and mouse action that you make.

5. **Press [Ctrl][Home]**

   When you begin an Excel session, macros record absolute cell references. By beginning the recording in cell A1, you ensure that the macro includes the instruction to select cell A1 as the first step, in cases where A1 is not already selected.

QUICK TIP
You can press [Ctrl][Enter] instead of clicking the Enter button.

6. **Type Sales Division in cell A1, then click the Enter button ✓ on the Formula Bar**

7. **Click the Home tab, click the Format button in the Cells group, then click Format Cells**

8. **Click the Font tab, in the Font style list box click Bold, click the Underline list arrow and click Single, click the Color list arrow and click the Red, Accent 2 Theme color (first row, sixth color from the left), then compare your dialog box to Figure I-5**

QUICK TIP
You can also click the Stop Recording button in the Code group on the Developer tab to stop recording a macro.

9. **Click OK, click the Stop Recording button 🔲 on the left side of the status bar, click cell D1 to deselect cell A1, then save the workbook**

   Figure I-6 shows the result of recording the macro.

FIGURE I-4: Record Macro dialog box

Type macro name here →

Type your name and description of macro here →

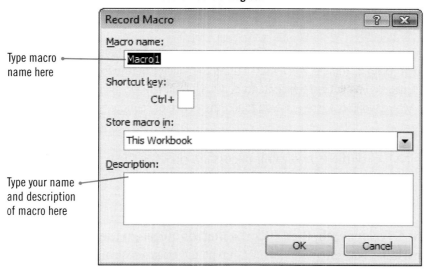

FIGURE I-5: Font tab of the Format Cells dialog box

Macro will apply these formatting attributes to the text

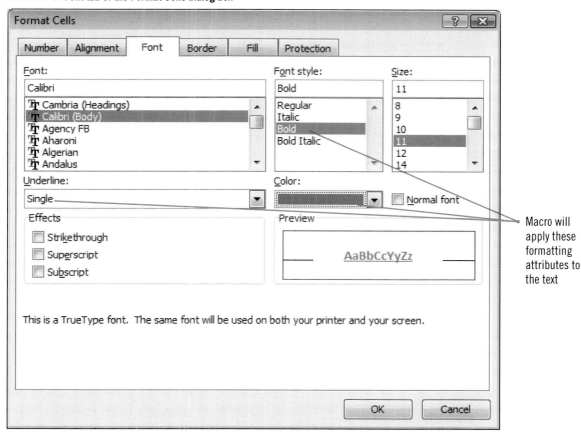

FIGURE I-6: Sales Division stamp

	A	B	C
1	Sales Division		
2			
3			
4			

Running a Macro

Once you record a macro, you should test it to make sure that the actions it performs are correct. To test a macro, you **run** (play) it. You can run a macro using the Macros button in the Code group of the Developer tab. ▨▨▨▨ Kate asks you to clear the contents of cell A1 and then test the DivStamp macro. After you run the macro in the Macro workbook, she asks you to test the macro once more from a newly opened workbook.

STEPS

1. **Click cell A1, click the Home tab if necessary, click the Clear button ▨▨ in the Editing group, click Clear All, then click any other cell to deselect cell A1**
    When you delete only the contents of a cell, any formatting still remains in the cell. By using the Clear All option you can be sure that the cell is free of contents and formatting.

2. **Click the Developer tab, then click the Macros button in the Code group**
    The Macro dialog box, shown in Figure I-7, lists all the macros contained in the open workbooks. If other people have used your computer, other macros may be listed.

3. **Make sure DivStamp is selected, as you watch cell A1, click Run, then deselect cell A1**
    The macro quickly plays back the steps you recorded in the previous lesson. When the macro is finished, your screen should look like Figure I-8. As long as the workbook containing the macro remains open, you can run the macro in any open workbook.

4. **Click the Microsoft Office button ▨, click New, then in the New Workbook dialog box click Create**
    Because the Macro Workbook.xlsm is still open, you can use its macros.

5. **Deselect cell A1, click the Macros button in the Code group, make sure 'Macro Workbook.xlsm'!DivStamp is selected, click Run, then deselect cell A1**
    When multiple workbooks are open, the macro name in the Macro dialog box includes the workbook name between single quotation marks, followed by an exclamation point, indicating that the macro is outside the active workbook. Because you only used this workbook to test the macro, you don't need to save it.

6. **Close Book2.xlsx without saving changes**
    The Macro Workbook.xlsm workbook remains open.

FIGURE I-7: **Macro dialog box**

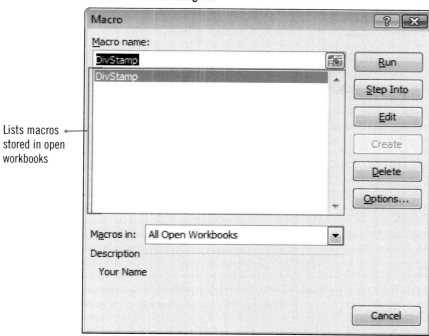

Lists macros stored in open workbooks

FIGURE I-8: **Result of running DivStamp macro**

Formatted text inserted into cell A1

Running a macro automatically

You can create a macro that automatically performs certain tasks when the workbook it is saved in is opened. This is useful for actions you want to do every time you open a workbook. For example, you may import data from an external data source into the workbook or format the worksheet data in a certain way. To create a macro that will automatically run when the workbook is opened, you need to name the macro Auto_Open and save it in the workbook.

Editing a Macro

When you use the Macro Recorder to create a macro, the program instructions, called **program code**, are recorded automatically in the **Visual Basic for Applications (VBA)** programming language. Each macro is stored as a **module**, or program code container, attached to the workbook. After you record a macro, you might need to change it. If you have a lot of changes to make, it might be best to record the macro again. But if you need to make only minor adjustments, you can edit the macro code directly using the **Visual Basic Editor**, a program that lets you display and edit your macro code. Kate wants you to modify the DivStamp macro to change the point size of the department stamp to 14.

STEPS

1. **Make sure the Macro Workbook.xlsm workbook is open, click the Macros button in the Code group, make sure DivStamp is selected, then click Edit**

   The Visual Basic Editor starts, showing three windows: the Project Explorer window, the Properties window, and the Code window, as shown in Figure I-9.

   > **TROUBLE**
   > If the Properties window does not appear in the lower-left portion of your screen, click the Properties Window button 📇 in the Visual Basic Standard Toolbar, then resize it as shown in the figure if necessary.

2. **Click Module 1 in the Project Explorer window if it's not already selected, then examine the steps in the macro, comparing your screen to Figure I-9**

   The name of the macro and your name appear at the top of the module window. Below this area, Excel has translated your keystrokes and commands into macro code. When you open and make selections in a dialog box during macro recording, Excel automatically stores all the dialog box settings in the macro code. For example, the line `.FontStyle = "Bold"` was generated when you clicked Bold in the Format Cells dialog box. You also see lines of code that you didn't generate directly while recording the DivStamp macro, for example, `.Name = "Calibri"`.

3. **In the line `.Size = 11`, double-click 11 to select it, then type 14**

   Because Module1 is attached to the workbook and not stored as a separate file, any changes to the module are saved automatically when you save the workbook.

4. **Click File on the Visual Basic Editor menu bar, click Print, click OK to print the module, then review the printout**

   > **QUICK TIP**
   > You can return to Excel without closing the module by clicking the View Microsoft Excel button 🗷 on the Visual Basic Editor toolbar.

5. **Click File on the menu bar, then click Close and Return to Microsoft Excel**

   You want to rerun the DivStamp macro to make sure the macro reflects the change you made using the Visual Basic Editor. You begin by clearing the division name from cell A1.

6. **Click cell A1, click the Home tab, click the Clear button 🖉 in the Editing group, then click Clear All**

   > **QUICK TIP**
   > Another way to start the Visual Basic Editor is to click the Developer tab, then click the Visual Basic button in the Code group.

7. **Click any other cell to deselect cell A1, click the Developer tab, click the Macros button in the Code group, make sure DivStamp is selected, click Run, then deselect cell A1**

   The department stamp is now in 14-point type, as shown in Figure I-10.

8. **Save the workbook**

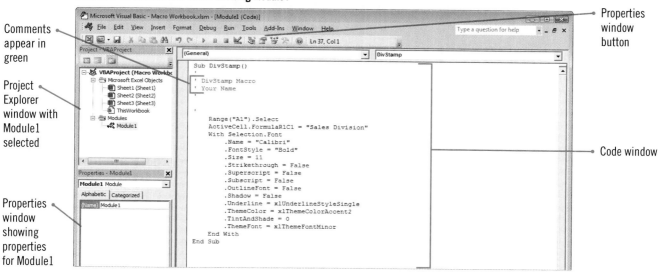

FIGURE I-9: Visual Basic Editor showing Module1

Comments appear in green

Project Explorer window with Module1 selected

Properties window showing properties for Module1

Properties window button

Code window

```
Sub DivStamp()
'
' DivStamp Macro
' Your Name
'

'
    Range("A1").Select
    ActiveCell.FormulaR1C1 = "Sales Division"
    With Selection.Font
        .Name = "Calibri"
        .FontStyle = "Bold"
        .Size = 11
        .Strikethrough = False
        .Superscript = False
        .Subscript = False
        .OutlineFont = False
        .Shadow = False
        .Underline = xlUnderlineStyleSingle
        .ThemeColor = xlThemeColorAccent2
        .TintAndShade = 0
        .ThemeFont = xlThemeFontMinor
    End With
End Sub
```

FIGURE I-10: Result of running edited DivStamp macro

Font size is enlarged to 14-point

	A	B	C
1	**Sales Division**		
2			
3			
4			

Adding comments to Visual Basic code

With practice, you will be able to interpret the lines of macro code. Others who use your macro, however, might want to know the function of a particular line. You can explain the code by adding comments to the macro. **Comments** are explanatory text added to the lines of code. When you enter a comment, you must type an apostrophe (') before the comment text. Otherwise, the program tries to interpret it as a command. On the screen, comments appear in green after you press [Enter], as shown in Figure I-9. You can also insert blank lines as comments in the macro code to make the code more readable. To do this, type an apostrophe, then press [Enter].

Using Shortcut Keys with Macros

In addition to running a macro from the Macro dialog box, you can run a macro by using a shortcut key combination that you assign to the macro. Using shortcut keys saves you time by reducing the number of actions you need to take to run a macro. You assign shortcut key combinations in the Record Macro dialog box.  Kate also wants you to create a macro called CompanyName to enter the company name into a worksheet. You assign a shortcut key combination to run the macro.

STEPS

1. **Click cell B2**

   You want to record the macro in cell B2, but you want the macro to enter the company name anywhere in a worksheet. Therefore, you do not begin the macro with an instruction to position the cell pointer, as you did in the DivStamp macro.

2. **Click the Record Macro button 📷 on the status bar**

   The Record Macro dialog box opens. Notice the option Shortcut key: Ctrl+ followed by a blank box. You can type a letter (A-Z) in the Shortcut key text box to assign the key combination of [Ctrl] plus that letter to run the macro. Because some common Excel shortcuts use the [Ctrl][letter] combination, such as [Ctrl][C] for Copy, you decide to use the key combination [Ctrl][Shift] plus a letter to avoid overriding any of these shortcut key combinations.

   > **QUICK TIP**
   > Be careful when choosing letters for a keyboard shortcut. The letters entered in the shortcut key text box are case sensitive.

3. **With the default macro name selected, type CompanyName, click the Shortcut key text box, press and hold [Shift], type C, then in the Description box type your name**

   You have assigned the shortcut key combination [Ctrl][Shift][C] to the CompanyName macro. After you create the macro, you will use this shortcut key combination to run it. Compare your screen with Figure I-11. You are ready to record the CompanyName macro.

4. **Click OK to close the dialog box**

5. **Type Quest in cell B2, click the Enter button ✓ on the formula bar, press [Ctrl][I] to italicize the text, click the Stop Recording button ◼ on the status bar, then deselect cell B2**

   Quest appears in italics in cell B2. You are ready to run the macro in cell A5 using the shortcut key combination.

6. **Click cell A5, press and hold [Ctrl][Shift], type C, then deselect the cell**

   The company name appears in cell A5, as shown in Figure I-12. The macro played back in the selected cell (A5) instead of the cell where it was recorded (B2) because you did not begin recording the macro by clicking cell B2.

FIGURE I-11: **Record Macro dialog box with shortcut key assigned**

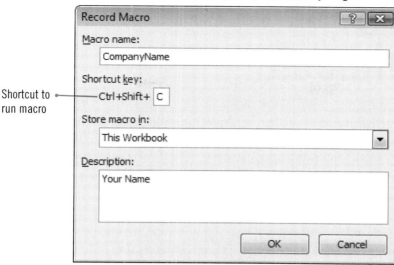

Shortcut to run macro

FIGURE I-12: **Result of running the CompanyName macro**

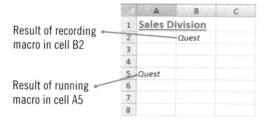

Result of recording macro in cell B2

Result of running macro in cell A5

Using Relative Referencing when creating a macro

By default, Excel records absolute cell references in macros. You can record a macro's actions based on the relative position of the active cell by clicking the Use Relative References button in the Code group prior to recording the action. For example, when you create a macro using the default setting of absolute referencing, bolding the range A1:D1 will always bold that range when the macro is run. However, if you click the Use Relative References button when recording the macro before bolding the range, then running the macro will not necessarily result in bolding the range A1:D1. The range that will be bolded will depend on the location of the active cell when the macro is run. If the active cell is A4, then the range A4:D4 will be bolded. Selecting the Use Relative References button highlights the button

name, indicating it is active, as shown in Figure I-13. The button remains active until you click it again to deselect it. This is called a **toggle**, meaning that it acts like an off/on switch: it retains the relative reference setting until you click it again to turn it off or you exit Excel.

FIGURE I-13: **Use Relative References button selected**

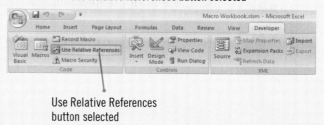

Use Relative References button selected

Using the Personal Macro Workbook

When you create a macro, it is automatically stored in the workbook in which you created it. But if you wanted to use that macro in another workbook, you would have to copy the macro to that workbook. Instead, it's easier to store commonly used macros in a Personal Macro Workbook. The **Personal Macro Workbook** is an Excel file that is always available, unless you specify otherwise, and gives you access to all the macros it contains, regardless of which workbooks are open. The Personal Macro Workbook file is automatically created the first time you choose to store a macro in it, and is named PERSONAL.XLSB. You can add additional macros to the Personal Macro Workbook by saving them in the workbook. By default, the PERSONAL.XLSB workbook opens each time you start Excel, but you don't see it because Excel designates it as a hidden file.  Kate often likes to print her worksheets in landscape orientation with one-inch left, right, top, and bottom margins. She wants you to create a macro that automatically formats a worksheet for printing this way. Because she wants to use this macro in future workbooks, she asks you to store the macro in the Personal Macro Workbook.

STEPS

1. **Click the Record New Macro button 📖 on the status bar**
   The Record Macro dialog box opens.

2. **Type FormatPrint in the Macro name text box, click the Shortcut key text box, press and hold [Shift], type F, then click the Store macro in list arrow**
   You have named the macro FormatPrint and assigned it the shortcut combination [Ctrl][Shift][F]. Notice that This Workbook is selected by default, indicating that Excel automatically stores macros in the active workbook, as shown in Figure I-14. You also can choose to store the macro in a new workbook or in the Personal Macro Workbook.

TROUBLE

If a dialog box appears saying that a macro is already assigned to this shortcut combination choose another letter for a keyboard shortcut. If a dialog box appears with the message that a macro named FormatPrint already exists, click Yes to replace it.

3. **Click Personal Macro Workbook, in the Description text box enter your name, then click OK**
   The recorder is on, and you are ready to record the macro keystrokes.

4. **Click the Page Layout tab, click the Orientation button in the Page Setup group, click Landscape, click the Margins button in the Page Setup group, click Custom Margins, then enter 1 in the Top, Left, Bottom, and Right text boxes**
   Compare your margin settings to Figure I-15.

5. **Click OK, then click the Stop Recording button 🔳 on the status bar**
   You want to test the macro.

TROUBLE

You may have to wait a few moments for the macro to finish. If you are using a different letter for the shortcut key combination, type that letter instead of the letter F.

6. **Activate Sheet2, in cell A1 type Macro Test, press [Enter], press and hold [Ctrl][Shift], then type F**
   The FormatPrint macro plays back the sequence of commands.

7. **Preview Sheet2 and verify that the orientation is landscape and the margins are one inch on the left, right, top, and bottom**

8. **Close Print Preview and save the workbook**

FIGURE I-14: **Record Macro dialog box showing macro storage options**

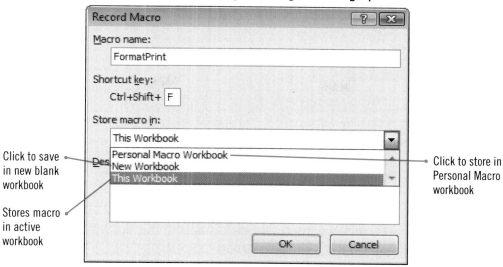

Click to save in new blank workbook

Stores macro in active workbook

Click to store in Personal Macro workbook

FIGURE I-15: **Margin settings for the FormatPrint macro**

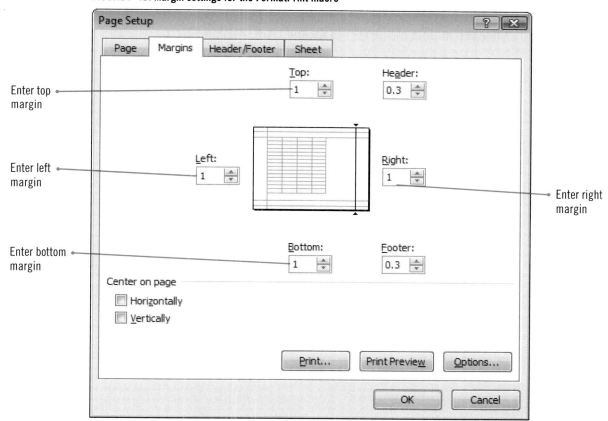

Enter top margin

Enter left margin

Enter bottom margin

Enter right margin

Working with the Personal Macro Workbook

Once you use the Personal Macro Workbook, it opens automatically each time you start Excel so you can add macros to it. By default, the Personal Macro Workbook is hidden in Excel as a precautionary measure so you don't accidentally delete anything from it. If you need to delete a macro from the Personal Macro Workbook, click the View tab, click Unhide in the Window group, click PERSONAL.XLSB, then click OK. To hide the Personal Macro Workbook, make it the active workbook, click the View tab, then click Hide in the Window group.

Assigning a Macro to a Button

When you create macros for others who will use your workbook, you might want to make the macros more visible so they're easier to use. In addition to using shortcut keys, you can run a macro by assigning it to a button on your worksheet. Then when you click the button the macro will run.  To make it easier for people in the sales division to run the DivStamp macro, Kate asks you to assign it to a button on the workbook. You begin by creating the button.

STEPS

1. **Click Sheet3, click the Insert tab, click Shapes in the Illustrations group, then click the first rectangle in the Rectangles group**
   The mouse pointer changes to a + symbol.

2. **Click at the top-left corner of cell A8 and drag the pointer to the lower-right corner of cell B9**
   Compare your screen to Figure I-16.

QUICK TIP

When you print a worksheet with a macro button, the button will print, just like any worksheet object.

3. **Click the middle of the rectangle and type Division Macro**
   Now that you have created the button, you are ready to assign the macro to it.

4. **Right-click the new button, then on the shortcut menu click Assign Macro**
   The Assign Macro dialog box opens.

5. **Click DivStamp under Macro name, then click OK**
   You have assigned the DivStamp macro to the button.

6. **Click any cell to deselect the button, then click the button**
   The DivStamp macro plays and the text Sales Division appears in cell A1, as shown in Figure I-17.

7. **Save the workbook, print Sheet3, close the workbook, then exit Excel clicking No when asked to save changes to the Personal Macro Workbook**

FIGURE I-16: **Button shape**

Rectangle shape will become button

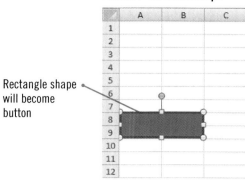

FIGURE I-17: **Sheet3 with the Sales Division text**

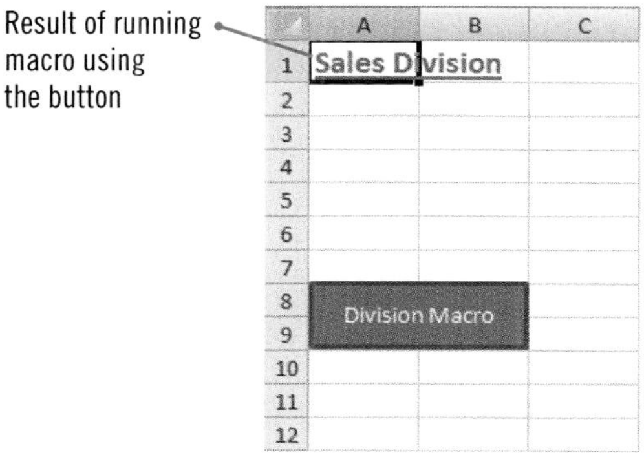

Result of running macro using the button

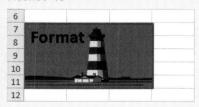

Formatting a macro button

You can format macro buttons using 3-D effects, clip art, photographs, fills, and shadows. To format a button, right-click it and select Format Shape from the shortcut menu. In the Format Shape dialog box you can select the Fill, Line Color, Line Style, Shadow, 3-D Format, 3-D Rotation, Picture, or Text Box. To add an image to the button, click Fill, then click the Picture or texture fill option button. To insert a picture from a file, click the File button, select a picture, then click Insert. To insert a clip art picture, click Clip Art, select a picture, then click OK. You may need to resize your button to fully display a picture. You may also want to move the text on

the button if it overlaps the image. Figure I-18 shows a button formatted with clip art.

FIGURE I-18

Practice

▼ CONCEPTS REVIEW

FIGURE I-19

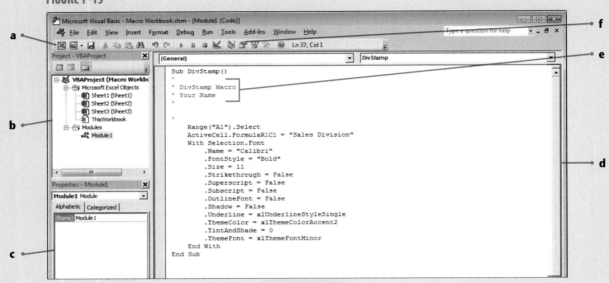

1. **Which element points to the Properties window?**
2. **Which element points to the Code window?**
3. **Which element points to the Properties Window button?**
4. **Which element do you click to return to Excel without closing the module?**
5. **Which element points to a comment?**
6. **Which element points to the Project Explorer window?**

Match each term or button with the statement that best describes it.

7. **Visual Basic Editor**
8. **Comments**
9. **Personal Macro Workbook**
10. **Virus**
11. **Macro**

    a. Set of instructions that perform a task in a specified order
    b. Statements that appear in green explaining the macro
    c. Destructive software that can damage computer files
    d. Used to make changes to macro code
    e. Used to store commonly used macros

Select the best answer from the list of choices.

12. Which of the following is the best candidate for a macro?

a. Often-used sequences of commands or actions

b. Nonsequential tasks

c. Seldom-used commands or tasks

d. One-button or one-keystroke commands

13. You can open the Visual Basic Editor by clicking the _____ button in the Macro dialog box.

a. Programs

b. Visual Basic Editor

c. Modules

d. Edit

14. A Macro named _____ will automatically run when the workbook it is saved in opens.

a. Macro1

b. Default

c. Auto_Open

d. Open_Macro

15. Which of the following is NOT true about editing a macro?

a. You edit macros using the Visual Basic Editor.

b. A macro cannot be edited and must be recorded again.

c. You can type changes directly in the existing program code.

d. You can make more than one editing change in a macro.

16. Why is it important to plan a macro?

a. Planning helps prevent careless errors from being introduced into the macro.

b. Macros can't be deleted.

c. It is impossible to edit a macro.

d. Macros won't be stored if they contain errors.

17. Macros are recorded with relative references:

a. Only if the Use Relative References button is selected.

b. In all cases.

c. By default.

d. Only if the Use Absolute References button is not selected.

18. You can run macros:

a. From the Macro dialog box.

b. From shortcut key combinations.

c. From a button on the worksheet.

d. Using all of the above.

19. Macro security settings can be changed using the _____ tab.

a. Security

b. Home

c. Developer

d. Review

▼ SKILLS REVIEW

1. Plan and enable a macro.

a. You need to plan a macro that enters and formats your name and e-mail address in a worksheet.

b. Write out the steps the macro will perform.

c. Write out how the macro could be used in a workbook.

d. Start Excel, open a new workbook, then save it as a Macro-Enabled workbook named **Macros** in the drive and folder where you store your Data Files. (*Hint*: The file will have the file extension xlsm.)

e. Use the Excel Options feature to display the Developer tab if it is not showing in the Ribbon.

f. Using the Trust Center dialog box, enable all macros.

2. Record a macro.

a. You want to record a macro that enters and formats your name and e-mail address in a worksheet using the steps below.

b. Name the macro **MyEmail**, store it in the current workbook, and make sure your name appears as the person who recorded the macro.

c. Record the macro, entering your name in cell A1 and your email address in cell A2.

d. Resize column A to fit the information entirely in that column.

e. Add an outside border around the range A1:A2 and format the font using purple from the Standard Colors.

f. Add bold formatting to the text in the range A1:A2.

g. Stop the recorder and save the workbook.

3. Run a macro.

  a. Clear cell entries and formats in the range affected by the macro, then resize the width of column A to 8.43.

  b. Run the MyEmail macro to place your name and e-mail information in the range A1:A2.

  c. On the worksheet, clear all the cell entries and formats generated by running the MyEmail macro. Resize the width of column A to 8.43.

  d. Save the workbook.

4. Edit a macro.

  a. Open the MyEmail macro in the Visual Basic Editor.

  b. Change the line of code above the last line from Selection.Font.Bold = True to Selection.Font.Bold = False.

FIGURE I-20

	A	B
1	Your Name	
2	yourname@yourschool.edu	
3		
4		
5		

  c. Use the Close and Return to Microsoft Excel option on the File menu to return to Excel.

  d. Test the macro on Sheet1 and compare your worksheet to Figure I-20 verifying that the text is not bold.

  e. Save the workbook.

5. Use shortcut keys with macros.

  a. You want to record a macro that enters your e-mail address in italics with a font color of red in the selected cell of a worksheet, using the steps below.

  b. Record the macro called **EmailStamp** in the current workbook, assigning your macro the shortcut key combination [Ctrl][Shift][E], storing it in the current workbook, with your name in the description.

  c. After you record the macro, clear the contents and formats from the cell containing your e-mail address that you used to record the macro.

  d. Use the shortcut key combination to run the EmailStamp macro in a cell other than the one it was recorded in. Compare your macro result to Figure I-21. Your email address may appear in a different cell.

FIGURE I-21

B	C	D	E	F
	yourname@yourschool.edu			

  e. Save the workbook.

6. Use the Personal Macro Workbook.

  a. Using Sheet1, record a new macro called **FitToLand** and store it in the Personal Macro workbook with your name in the Description text box. If you already have a macro named FitToLand replace that macro. The macro should set the print orientation to landscape.

  b. After you record the macro, activate Sheet2, and enter **Test data for FitToLand macro** in cell A1.

  c. Verify that the orientation for Sheet2 is set to portrait.

  d. Run the macro. (You may have to wait a few moments.)

  e. Preview Sheet2 and verify that it is now in Landscape orientation.

  f. Save the workbook.

FIGURE I-22

7. Assign a macro to a button.

  a. Enter **Button Test** in cell A1 of Sheet3.

  b. Using the rectangle shape, draw a rectangle in the range A7:B8.

  c. Label the button with the text **Landscape**.

  d. Assign the macro PERSONAL.XLSB!FitToLand to the button.

  e. Verify that the orientation of Sheet3 is set to portrait.

  f. Run the FitToLand macro using the button.

  g. Preview the worksheet and verify that it is in landscape view.

  h. Add your name to the Sheet3 footer, save the workbook, then print Sheet3.

  i. Compare your printed worksheet to Figure I-22, close the workbook then exit Excel without saving the FitToLand macro in the Personal Macro Workbook.

▼ INDEPENDENT CHALLENGE 1

As a computer-support employee of Portland Marketing Group, you need to develop ways to help your fellow employees work more efficiently. Employees have asked for Excel macros that can do the following:

- Adjust the column widths to display all column data in a worksheet.
- Place the department name of Marketing in red font in cell A1 (the width of A1 should be increased if necessary).

a. Plan and write the steps necessary for each macro.

b. Start Excel, open the Data file EX I-1.xlsx from the drive and folder where you store your Data Files, then save it as a macro-enabled workbook called **Marketing Macros**.

c. Check your macro security on the Developer tab to be sure that macros are enabled.

d. Create a macro named **ColumnFit**, save it in the Marketing Macros.xlsm workbook, assign the ColumnFit macro a shortcut key combination of [Ctrl][Shift][C], and add your name in the description area for the macro. Record the macro using the following steps.

e. Record the ColumnFit macro to adjust a worksheet's column widths to display all data. (*Hint*: Select the entire sheet, click the Home tab, click the Format button in the Cells group, then select AutoFit Column Width.) End the macro recording.

f. Format the widths of columns A through G to 8.43, then test the ColumnFit macro with the shortcut key combination [Ctrl][Shift][C].

g. Using Sheet2, create a macro named **DepartmentName** and save it in the Marketing Macros.xlsm workbook. Assign the macro a shortcut key combination of [Ctrl][Shift][D], and add your name in the description area for the macro.

h. Record the DepartmentName macro. The macro should do the following:
- Place Marketing in a red font in cell A1 of a worksheet
- Change the font size of Marketing in cell A1 to 14-point
- Increase the width of column A to fit the Marketing label

i. Clear the text and formats from cell A1 and reformat the width of column A to 8.43. Test the DepartmentName macro using the shortcut key combination [Ctrl][Shift][D].

j. Edit the DepartmentName macro in the Visual Basic Editor to change the font to 13-point. Close the Visual Basic Editor and return to Excel.

k. Add a rectangle button to the Sheet2 in the range A6:B7. Label the button with the text **Department Name**.

l. Assign the DepartmentName macro to the button.

m. Clear the text and formats from cell A1 and reformat the width of column A to 8.43. Use the button to run the DepartmentName macro. Check the font to be sure it is 13-point. Compare your screen to Figure I-23.

FIGURE I-23

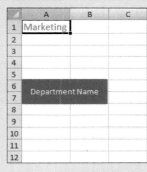

Advanced Challenge Exercise

- Format the button using the fill color of your choice. (*Hint*: Right-click the button and select Format Shape from the shortcut menu.)
- Format the button to add the 3-D effect of your choice.
- Add a shadow in the color of your choice to the button.

n. Save the workbook, print the module containing the program code for both macros, then close the workbook and exit Excel.

▼ INDEPENDENT CHALLENGE 2

You are an administrative assistant at the Toronto branch of Rare Books, a provider of out-of-print books. As part of your work, you create spreadsheets with sales projections for different titles. You frequently have to change the print settings so that workbooks print in landscape orientation with custom margins of one inch on the top and bottom. You have decided that it's time to create a macro to streamline this process.

a. Plan and write the steps necessary to create the macro.

b. Check your macro security settings to confirm that macros are enabled.

c. Start Excel, create a new workbook, then save it as a macro-enabled file named **Books Macro** in the drive and folder where you store your Data Files.

d. Create a macro that changes the page orientation to landscape and adds custom margins of one inch on the top and bottom of the page. Name the macro **Format**, add your name in the description, assign it the shortcut key combination [Ctrl][Shift][Z], and store it in the current workbook.

e. Go to Sheet2 and enter the text **Macro Test** in cell A1. Test the macro using the shortcut key combination of [Ctrl][Shift][Z].

f. Enter the text **Macro Test** in cell A1 of Sheet 3, add a rectangular button with the text Format to run the Format macro, then test the macro using the button.

g. Print the module for the macro.

h. Save and close the workbook, then exit Excel.

▼ INDEPENDENT CHALLENGE 3

You are the eastern region sales manager of Confetti, a national party supplies store. You manage the Boston, New York, and Philadelphia stores and frequently create workbooks with data from the three locations. It's tedious to change the tab names and colors every time you open a new workbook, so you decide to create a macro that will add the store locations and colors to your three default worksheet tabs, as shown in Figure I-24.

a. Plan and write the steps to create the macro described above.

b. Start Excel and open a new workbook.

c. Create the macro using the plan from step a, name it **SheetFormat**, assign it the shortcut key combination [Ctrl][Shift][Z], store it in the Personal Macro Workbook, and add your name in the description area.

d. After recording the macro, close the workbook without saving it.

e. Open a new workbook, then save it as a macro-enabled workbook named **Store Test** in the drive and folder where you store your Data Files. Use the shortcut key combination of [Ctrl][Shift][Z] to test the macro in the new workbook.

f. Unhide the PERSONAL.XLSB workbook. (*Hint*: Click the View tab, click the Unhide button in the Window group, then click PERSONAL.XLSB.)

g. Edit the SheetFormat macro using Figure I-25 as a guide, changing the Sheet3 name from Philadelphia to Phil. (*Hint*: There are three instances of Philadelphia that need to be changed.)

h. Open a new workbook, then save it as a macro-enabled workbook named **Store Test New** in the drive and folder where you store your data files. Test the edited macro using the shortcut key combination of [Ctrl][Shift][Z].

i. Save the workbook, print the module for the macro, then close the module and return to Excel.

FIGURE I-24

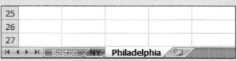

FIGURE I-25

```
Sub SheetFormat()
'
' SheetFormat Macro
' Your Name
'
' Keyboard Shortcut: Ctrl+Shift+Z
'
    Sheets("Sheet1").Select
    Sheets("Sheet1").Name = "Boston"
    Sheets("Sheet2").Select
    Sheets("Sheet2").Name = "NY"
    Sheets("Sheet3").Select
    Sheets("Sheet3").Name = "Phil"
    Sheets("Boston").Select
    With ActiveWorkbook.Sheets("Boston").Tab
        .Color = 255
        .TintAndShade = 0
    End With
    Sheets("NY").Select
    With ActiveWorkbook.Sheets("NY").Tab
        .Color = 5287936
        .TintAndShade = 0
    End With
    Sheets("Phil").Select
    With ActiveWorkbook.Sheets("Phil").Tab
        .Color = 65535
        .TintAndShade = 0
    End With
End Sub
```

▼ INDEPENDENT CHALLENGE 3 (CONTINUED)

j. Hide the PERSONAL.XLSB workbook. (*Hint*: With the PERSONAL.XLSB workbook active, click the View tab, then click the Hide button in the Window group.)

k. Close the workbook, click No to save the PERSONAL.XLSB changes, then exit Excel.

▼ REAL LIFE INDEPENDENT CHALLENGE

Excel can be a helpful tool in keeping track of hours worked at a job or on a project. A macro can speed up the repetitive process of entering a formula to total your hours each week.

a. Start Excel, create a new workbook, then save it as **Hours** in the drive and folder where you store your data files. Be sure to save it as a macro-enabled file.

b. If necessary, change your security settings to enable macros.

c. Use Table I-2 as a guide in entering labels and hours into a worksheet tracking your work or project effort.

d. Create a macro named **TotalHours** in the cell adjacent to the Total label that can be activated by the [Ctrl][Shift][T] key combination. Save the macro in the Hours workbook and add your name in the description area.

e. The TotalHours macro should do the following:
- Total the hours for the week.
- Boldface the Total amount and the Total label to its left.

f. Test the macro using the key combination [Ctrl][Shift][T].

g. Add a button to the range A11:B12 with the label Total.

h. Assign the TotalHours macro to the Total button.

i. Test the macro using the button.

j. Enter your name in the footer, save your workbook, then print the results of the macro.

k. Open the macro in the Visual Basic Editor, then print the macro code.

TABLE I-2

Monday	5
Tuesday	6
Wednesday	3
Thursday	8
Friday	9
Saturday	5
Sunday	0
Total	

Advanced Challenge Exercise

- Edit the macro code to add a comment with a description of your work or project.
- Add another comment with your email address.
- Above the keyboard comment enter the comment "Macro can be run using the Total button."
- Print the macro code.

l. Return to Excel, save and close the workbook, then exit Excel.

▼ VISUAL WORKSHOP

Start Excel, create a new workbook, then save it as a macro-enabled workbook with the name **Yearly Data** in the drive and folder where you save your Data Files. Create a macro with the name **Quarters** in the Yearly Data workbook that enters labels for the first, second, third, and fourth quarters. Use the macro recorder to create the macro, using the code shown in Figure I-26 as a guide for the placement and font style of the labels, and the shortcut key combination to run the macro. The code also specifies the column width format for the labels. Test the macro, edit the macro code as necessary, then print the module.

FIGURE I-26

```
Sub Quarters()
'
' Quarters Macro
' Your Name
'
' Keyboard Shortcut: Ctrl+Shift+Q
'
    Range("A1").Select
    ActiveCell.FormulaR1C1 = "First Quarter"
    Range("B1").Select
    ActiveCell.FormulaR1C1 = "Second Quarter"
    Range("C1").Select
    ActiveCell.FormulaR1C1 = "Third Quarter"
    Range("D1").Select
    ActiveCell.FormulaR1C1 = "Fourth Quarter"
    Columns("A:D").Select
    Selection.Columns.AutoFit
    Range("A1:D1").Select
    Selection.Font.Bold = True
End Sub
```

Enhancing Charts

Although Excel offers a variety of eye-catching chart types, you can customize your charts by adjusting data and chart features and by adding special formatting and graphics so that your data presentation has greater impact. In this unit, you learn to enhance your charts by manipulating chart data, formatting axes, and rotating the chart. You clarify your data display by adding a data table, special text effects, a picture, and trendlines. As you enhance your charts, keep in mind that too much customization can be distracting; your goal in enhancing charts should be to communicate your data more clearly and accurately. Quest's vice president of sales, Kate Morgan, has requested charts comparing sales in the Quest regions over the first two quarters. You will produce these charts and enhance them to improve their appearance and make the worksheet data more accessible.

OBJECTIVES

Customize a data series

Change a data source and add data labels

Format the axes of a chart

Add a data table to a chart

Rotate a chart

Enhance a chart with WordArt

Add a picture to a chart

Identify data trends

Customizing a Data Series

A **data series** is the sequence of values that Excel uses to **plot**, or create, a chart. You can format the data series in a chart to make the chart more attractive and easier to read. As with other Excel elements, you can change the borders, patterns, or colors of a data series. ▰▰▰▰ Kate wants you to create a chart showing the sales for each region in January and February. You begin by creating a column chart, which you will customize to make it easier to compare the sales for each region.

STEPS

1. **Start Excel, open the file EX J-1.xlsx from the drive and folder where you store your Data Files, then save it as Region Sales**

   Kate wants to see how each region performed over January and February before adding the March data. The first step is to select the data you want to appear in the chart. In this case, you want the row labels in cells A3:A6 and the data for January and February in cells B2:C6, including the column labels.

2. **Select the range A2:C6**

   TROUBLE

   If your chart overlaps the worksheet data, you can drag it to move it below row 6.

3. **Click the Insert tab, click the Column button in the Charts group, then click the 3-D Clustered Column chart (the first chart in the 3-D Column group)**

   The column graph compares the January and February sales for each branch, as shown in Figure J-1. You decide to display the data so that it is easier to compare the monthly sales for each branch.

4. **Click the Switch Row/Column button in the Data group**

   The legend now contains the region data, and the horizontal axis groups the bars by month. Kate can now easily compare the branch sales for each month. The graph will be easier to read if the U.S. and Canada data series are plotted in colors that are easier to distinguish.

   QUICK TIP

   You can also format a data series by clicking the data series on the chart, clicking the Chart Tools Layout tab, then clicking the Format Selection button.

5. **Right-click the Jan U.S. data series bar (the leftmost bar on the graph), click Format Data Series from the shortcut menu, click Fill in the left pane of the Format Data Series dialog box, click the Solid fill option button, click the Color list arrow, select Lime, Accent 6 in the Theme Colors group, then click Close**

   Now the U.S. data series is easy to distinguish from the Canada data series.

6. **Select the Chart Area, then drag the chart to place its upper-left corner in cell A8**

   You can resize a chart by dragging its corner sizing handles. When a chart is resized this way, all of the elements are resized to maintain its appearance.

7. **Drag the chart's lower-right sizing handle to fit the chart in the range A8:H23, then compare your chart to Figure J-2**

8. **Save the workbook**

Adding width and depth to data series

You can change the gap depth and the gap width in 3-D bar or column charts by right-clicking one of the data series of the chart then clicking Format Data Series from the shortcut menu. With Series Option selected in the left pane of the Format Data Series dialog box you can move the Gap Depth and Gap Width sliders from No Gap or 0% to Large Gap or 500%. Increasing the gap width adds space between each set of data on the chart by increasing the width of chart's data series. Increasing the gap depth adds depth to all categories of data.

FIGURE J-1: Chart comparing January and February sales for each region

Chart data

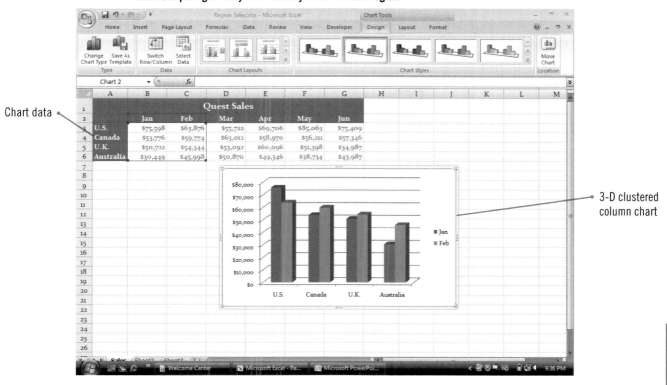

3-D clustered
column chart

FIGURE J-2: Chart comparing region sales in January and February

Customized
U.S. data
series

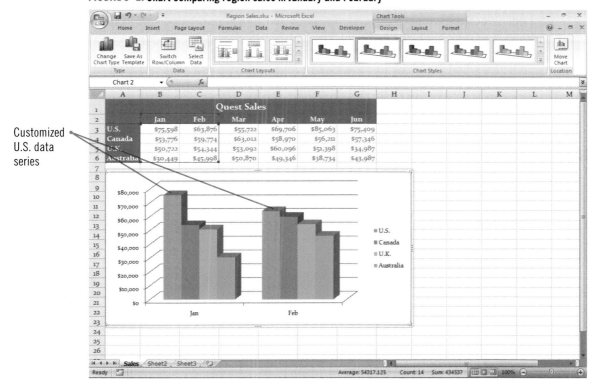

Changing a Data Source and Adding Data Labels

As you update your workbooks with new data, you may also need to add data series to (or delete them from) a chart. Excel makes it easy to revise a chart's data source and to rearrange chart data. To communicate chart data more clearly, you can add descriptive text, called a **data label**, which appears above a data marker in a chart.  Kate wants you to create a chart showing the branch sales for the first quarter. You need to add the March data to your chart so that it reflects the first-quarter sales. Kate asks you to add data labels to clarify the charted data and to make the chart more attractive. It will be easier to compare the branch sales in a 3-D column chart that is not clustered.

STEPS

1. **Click the Chart Tools Design tab, click the Change Chart Type button in the Type group, in the Change Chart Type dialog box click 3-D Column (the last chart in the first row), then click OK**

   The chart bars are no longer clustered. You want to change the data view to compare branch sales for each month in the new chart type.

2. **Click the Switch Row/Column button in the Data group**

   The labels that were in the legend are now on the horizontal axis. You want to add the March data to the chart.

3. **Click the Select Data button in the Data group**

   The Select Data Source dialog box opens.

   > **QUICK TIP**
   > You can also add data to a chart by selecting the chart and dragging the corner of the data border to the right to include the new worksheet data.

4. **Verify that the range in the Chart data range text box is selected, on the Sales worksheet select the range A2:D6, verify that =Sales!$A$2:$D$6 appears in the Chart data range text box, then click OK**

   The March data series appears on the chart, as shown in Figure J-3. You want to change all of the column colors to make them more attractive and decide to use one of the preformatted chart styles.

5. **Click the More button ▼ in the Chart Styles group, then click Style 26**

   The bars are now three shades of blue with gradients. You can quickly add data labels to your chart using one of the predefined chart layouts in the Chart Layouts gallery.

   > **QUICK TIP**
   > You can also add or delete data labels using the Data Labels button in the Labels group on the Chart Tools Layout tab.

6. **Click the More button ▼ in the Chart Layouts group, then click Layout 4**

   Data labels showing the exact value of each data point now appear above each bar. The data labels are crowded together. You decide to resize the chart so that the data labels are easier to read.

7. **Drag the chart's lower-right sizing handle to fit the chart in the range A8:J27, then compare your chart to Figure J-4**

Representing proportional relationships

Pie charts are often used to show the relative sizes of items in a data series by displaying the proportional relationships of entities in a data series to the sum. Pie charts represent the contribution of each value to a total in either a 2-D or 3-D format. For example if you want to show the part of a budget a department uses in an organization, you can create a pie chart and display the data labels as percentages. The percentages represent the parts of the whole pie for each of the departments.

To annotate a pie chart so it displays the percentage share of each item in a data series, select the chart, click the Chart Tools Layout tab, click the Data Labels button in the Labels group, select the position for the data labels, click the Data Labels button again, click More Data Label Options, click the Percentage check box to select it, deselect the Value check box, then click Close. Some of the layouts in the Chart Layouts group of the Chart Tools Design tab also feature percentage labels.

FIGURE J-3: Chart with March data series added

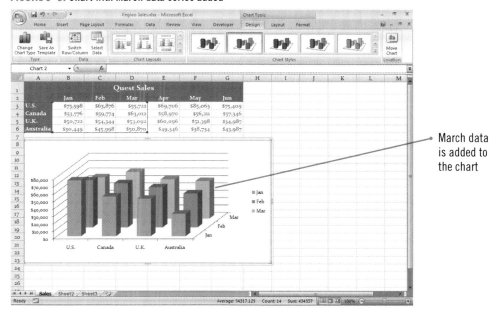

March data
is added to
the chart

FIGURE J-4: Chart with data labels

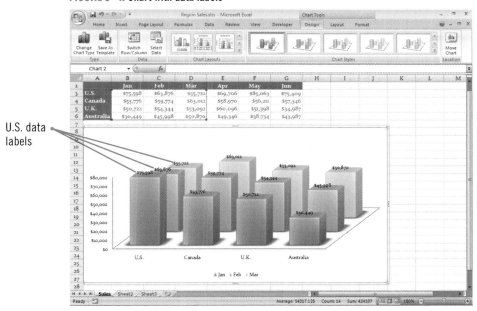

U.S. data
labels

Moving, removing, and formatting legends

To change the position of a legend or to remove it, click the Chart Tools Layout tab, click the Legend button in the Labels group, then select the desired legend position or select None to remove the legend. To format a legend's position, fill, border color and style, or shadows, click More Legend Options at the bottom of the Legend menu. You can add textured fills or pictures and customize the border and shadow characteristics. If you position the Format Legend dialog box next to the legend, you can use the Excel Live Preview feature to try out different effects, such as those shown in Figure J-5. To change a legend's font size, right-click the legend text, click Font on the shortcut menu, then adjust the font size in the Font dialog box. You can also drag a legend to the location of your choice.

FIGURE J-5: Formatted legend

Jan   Feb   Mar

Formatting the Axes of a Chart

Excel plots and formats chart data and places the chart axes within the chart's **plot area**. Data values in two-dimensional charts are plotted on the vertical y-axis (often called the **value axis** because it usually shows value levels). Categories are plotted on the horizontal x-axis (often called the **category axis** because it usually shows data categories). Excel creates a scale for the value (*y*) axis based on the highest and lowest values in the series and places intervals along the scale. A three-dimensional (3-D) chart, like the one in Figure J-6, has three axes; the x-axis remains the category axis, but the z-axis becomes the value axis and the y-axis becomes the measure for the chart's depth and is not visible. In 3-D charts, the value (*z*) axis usually contains the scale. For a summary of the axes Excel uses to plot data, see Table J-1. You can override the Excel default formats for chart axes at any time by using the Format Axis dialog box. ▄▄▟▟ Kate asks you to increase the maximum number on the value axis and change the axis number format. She would also like you to add axes titles to explain the plotted data.

STEPS

1. **Click the chart to select it if necessary, click the** Chart Tools Layout tab, **click the** Axes button **in the Axes group, point to** Primary Vertical Axis, **then click** More Primary Vertical Axis Options

    The Format Axis dialog box opens. The minimum, maximum, and unit Axis Options are set to Auto, and the default scale settings appear in the text boxes on the right. You can override any of these settings by clicking the Fixed option buttons and entering new values.

QUICK TIP
You can change the scale of the axis: Click the Chart Tools Layout tab, click the Axes button in the Axes group, point to Primary Vertical Axis, click More Primary Vertical Axes Options, click the Fixed option button in the Major unit group, then type the new scale interval value in the Fixed text box.

2. **With Axis Options selected in the list on the left, click the** Fixed option button **in the Maximum line, press [Tab], in the Fixed text box type** 90000, **then click** Close

    Now 90,000 appears as the maximum value on the value axis, and the chart bar heights adjust to reflect the new value. Next, you want the vertical axis values to appear without zeroes to make the chart data easier to read.

3. **Click the** Axes button **in the Axes group, point to** Primary Vertical Axis, **then click** Show Axis in Thousands

    The values are reduced to two digits and the word "Thousands" appears in a text box to the left of the values. You decide that vertical and horizontal axis titles would improve the clarity of the chart information.

4. **Click the** Axis Titles button **in the Labels group, point to** Primary Vertical Axis Title, **then click** Rotated Title

    A text box containing the text Axis Title appears on the vertical axis, next to Thousands.

5. **Type** Sales, **then click outside the text box to deselect it**

    The word Sales appears in the Vertical axis label. You decide to label the horizontal axis.

6. **Click the** Axis Titles button **in the Labels group, point to** Primary Horizontal Axis Title, **click** Title Below Axis, **type** Regions, **then click outside the text box to deselect it**

7. **Drag the** Thousands text box **on the vertical axis lower in the Chart Area to match Figure J-7, then deselect it**

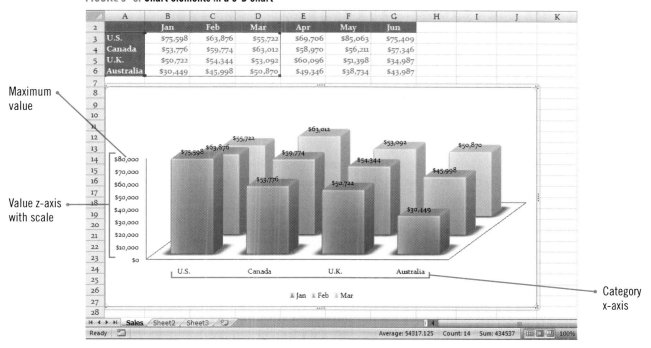

FIGURE J-6: Chart elements in a 3-D chart

Maximum value

Value z-axis with scale

Category x-axis

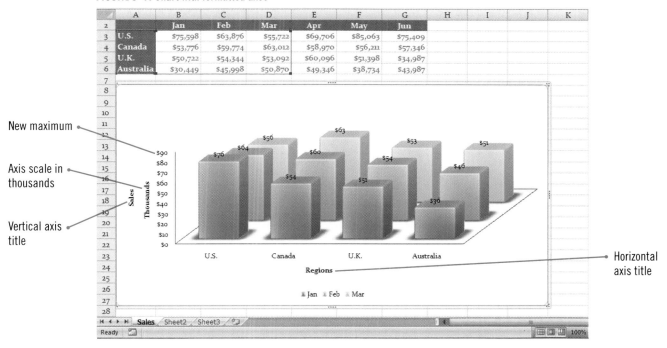

FIGURE J-7: Chart with formatted axes

New maximum

Axis scale in thousands

Vertical axis title

Horizontal axis title

TABLE J-1: Axes used by Excel for chart formatting

axes in a two-dimensional chart	axes in a three-dimensional chart
Category (x) axis (horizontal)	Category (x) axis (horizontal)
Value (y) axis (vertical)	Series (y) axis (depth)
	Value (z) axis (vertical)

Adding a Data Table to a Chart

A **data table** is a grid containing the chart data, attached to the bottom of a chart. Data tables are useful because they display—directly on the chart itself—the data you used to generate a chart. You can display data tables in line, area, column, and bar charts, and print them automatically along with a chart. It's good practice to add data tables to charts that are stored separately from worksheet data.  Kate wants you to move the chart to its own worksheet and add a data table to emphasize the chart's first-quarter data.

STEPS

1. **Click the chart object to select it if necessary, click the** Chart Tools Design tab, **then click the** Move Chart button **in the Location group**
   The Move Chart dialog box opens. You want to place the chart on a new sheet named First-Quarter Chart.

2. **Click the** New sheet option button, **type** First Quarter Chart **in the New sheet text box, then click** OK

3. **Click the** Chart Tools Layout tab, **click the** Data Table button **in the Labels group, then click** Show Data Table with Legend Keys
   A data table with the first-quarter data and a key to the legend appears at the bottom of the chart, as shown in Figure J-8. The data table would stand out more if it were formatted.

> **QUICK TIP**
> You can also add a data table by selecting a chart with a data table from the Chart Layouts gallery.

4. **Click the** Data Table button, **then click** More Data Table Options
   The Format Data Table dialog box opens.

5. **Click** Border Color **in the left pane, click the** Solid line option button **to select it, click the** Color list arrow, **click the** Lime, Accent 6 color (first row, last color) **in the Theme Colors section, click** Close, **then click the chart area to deselect the data table.**
   The data table appears with green lines, as shown in Figure J-9.

> **QUICK TIP**
> To hide a data table, click the Data Table button in the Labels group, then click None.

6. **Save the workbook**

Using the Modeless Format dialog box

Many of the buttons on the Chart Tools Layout tab have a "More ...Options " command at the bottom of the menu that appears when you click them. For example, clicking the Data Table button allows you to click More Data Table Options. The Format dialog box that opens when you click it allows you to format the selected data table. But while the dialog box is open, you can also click and format other elements. The Format dialog boxes are **modeless**, which means when they are open, you can click on other chart elements and then change their formatting in the same dialog box, whose options adjust to reflect the selected element. You are not restricted to changing only one object—i.e., you are not in a single **mode**, or limited set of possible choices. For example if the Format Data Table dialog box is open and you click a data label, the dialog box changes to Format Data Labels. If you click the legend, the dialog box becomes the Format Legend dialog box, allowing you to modify the legend characteristics.

FIGURE J-8: **Chart with data table**

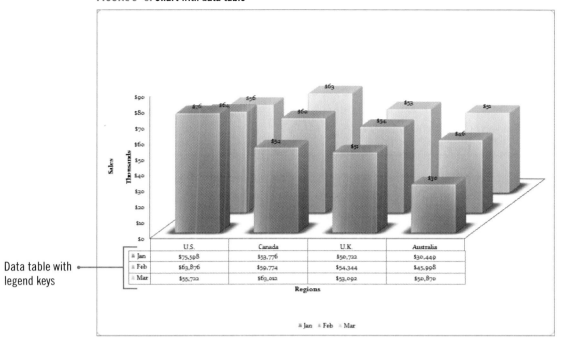

Data table with legend keys

FIGURE J-9: **Chart with formatted data table**

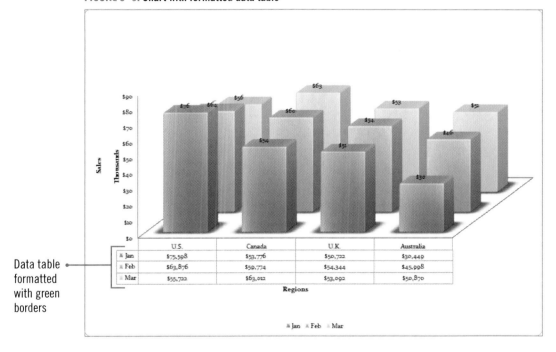

Data table formatted with green borders

Rotating a Chart

Three-dimensional (3-D) charts do not always display data in the most effective way. In many cases, one or more of a chart's data points can obscure the view of other data points, making the chart difficult to read. By rotating and/or changing the chart's depth, you can make the data easier to see. ▰▰▰▰ Kate wants you to rotate the chart and increase the depth. You will begin by hiding the data table so it doesn't overlap the view of the data.

STEPS

1. **Click the chart to select it if necessary, click the Chart Tools Layout tab, click the Data Table button in the Labels group, then click None**

2. **Click the 3-D Rotation button in the Background group, then if necessary click 3-D Rotation in the list on the left pane of the Format Chart Area dialog box**
   The 3-D rotation options are shown in Figure J-10.

3. **In the Chart Scale section, click the Right Angle Axes check box to deselect it, double-click the X: text box in the Rotation section, then enter 25**
   The X: Rotation setting rotates the chart to the left and right. You can also click the Left and Right buttons to rotate the chart.

QUICK TIP
You can also click the Up and Down buttons in the Rotation area of the dialog box to rotate the chart up and down.

4. **Double-click the Y: text box, then enter 20**
   The Y: Rotation setting rotates the chart up and down. You decide to change the depth of the columns.

5. **Double-click the Depth (% of base) text box in the Chart Scale section, then enter 200**

6. **Click Close, then compare your chart to Figure J-11**
   The chart columns now appear deeper and less crowded, making the chart easier to read.

7. **Save the workbook**

Making 3-D charts easier to read

In addition to rotating a chart there are other ways to view smaller data points that may be obscured by larger data markers in the front of a 3-D chart. To reverse the order that the data series are charted you can click the Axes button in the Axes group of the Chart Tools Layout tab, point to Depth Axis, click More Depth Axis Options, click the Series in reverse order check box in the Format Axis dialog box to select it, then click Close. Another way to see smaller data series in the back of a 3-D chart is to add transparency to the large data markers in the front of the chart. To do this you can right-click the data series that you want to make transparent, click Format Data Series in the shortcut menu, click Fill in the Format Data Series dialog box, click either the Solid fill or Gradient fill option buttons, move the slider on the Transparency bar to a percentage that allows you to see the other data series on the chart, then click Close. If you have a picture on the chart's back wall, adding transparency to the series in front of it makes more of the picture visible.

FIGURE J-10: 3-D rotation options

X rotation

Y rotation

Depth

Left and right buttons

Up and down buttons

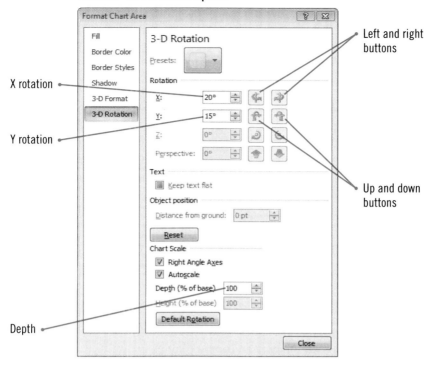

FIGURE J-11: Chart with increased depth and rotation

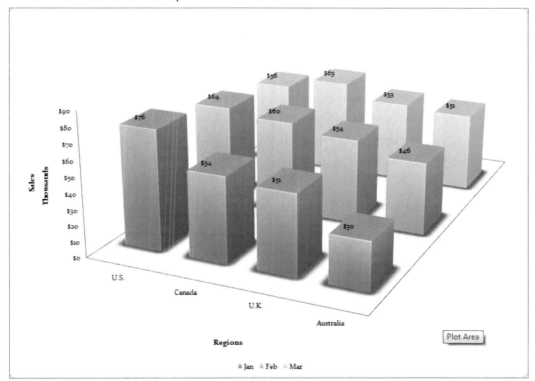

Charting data accurately

The purpose of a chart is to help viewers to interpret the worksheet data. When creating charts, you need to make sure that your chart accurately portrays your data. Charts can sometimes misrepresent data and thus mislead people. For example, you can change the y-axis units or its starting value to make charted sales values appear larger than they are. Even though you may have correctly labeled the sales values on the chart, the height of the data points will lead people viewing the chart to think the sales are higher than the labeled values. So use caution when you modify charts to make sure you accurately represent your data.

Enhancing a Chart with WordArt

You can enhance your chart or worksheet titles using **WordArt**, which is preformatted text. Once you've added WordArt text to your worksheet or chart, you can edit or format it by adding 3-D effects and shadows. WordArt text is a shape rather than text. This means that you cannot treat WordArt objects as if they were labels entered in a cell; that is, you cannot sort, use the spelling checker, or use their cell references in formulas.  Kate wants you to add a WordArt title to the first-quarter chart. You will begin by adding a title to the chart.

STEPS

QUICK TIP
To delete a chart title, right-click it, then select Delete from the shortcut menu. You can also select the chart title and press [Delete].

1. **Click the chart to select it if necessary, click the** Chart Tools Layout tab, **click the** Chart Title button **in the Labels group, then click** Above Chart
   A chart title text box appears above the chart.

2. **Select the** Chart Title text **in the text box, then type** First Quarter Sales

3. **Drag to select the** chart title **text if necessary, click the** Chart Tools Format tab, **then click the** More button ⬇ **in the WordArt Styles group**
   The WordArt Gallery opens, as shown in Figure J-12. This is where you select the style for your text.

4. **Click** Gradient Fill - Accent 4, Reflection **(the last style in the fourth row), then click outside the chart title to deselect it**
   The title text becomes formatted with capital letters with a gradient turquoise fill, a white background, and a light shadow. You decide the chart title would look better if it were closer to the chart.

5. **Place the pointer over the edge of First Quarter Sales (the WordArt title), drag** First Quarter Sales **down closer to the chart**
   Adding the title caused the vertical axis label and the vertical axis title to overlap.

6. **Drag the vertical axis label to the right, as shown in Figure J-13**

7. **Click on the chart to deselect any items**

Adding WordArt to a worksheet

You can use WordArt to add interest to the text on a worksheet. To insert WordArt, click the Insert tab, click the WordArt button in the Text group, choose a WordArt Style from the gallery, then replace the WordArt text "Your Text Here" with your text. After selecting the text, you can use the Text Fill list arrow in the WordArt Styles group to add a solid, picture, gradient, or texture fill to your text. The Text

Outline list arrow in the WordArt Styles group allows you to add color, weight, and dashes to the text outline. You can use the Text Effects button in the WordArt Styles group to add shadows, reflections, glows, bevels, 3-D rotations, and transformations to the WordArt text.

FIGURE J-12: **WordArt Styles gallery**

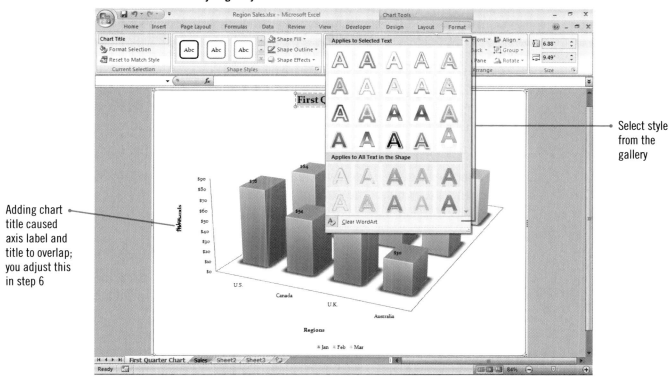

Adding chart title caused axis label and title to overlap; you adjust this in step 6

Select style from the gallery

FIGURE J-13: **Chart with WordArt title**

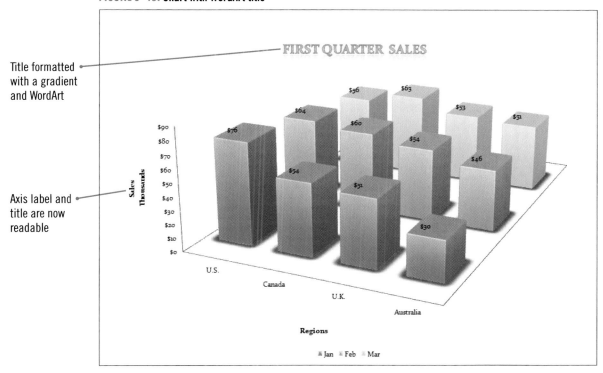

Title formatted with a gradient and WordArt

Axis label and title are now readable

FIRST QUARTER SALES

Rotating chart labels

You can rotate the category labels on a chart so that longer labels won't appear crowded. Select the Category Axis on the chart, click the Chart Tools Format tab, click the Format Selection button in the Current Selection group, click Alignment in the left pane of the dialog box, click the Text direction list arrow, then select the rotation option for the labels. In a two-dimensional chart, you can also select a custom angle for the axis labels.

Adding a Picture to a Chart

You can further enhance your chart by adding a picture to the data markers, chart area, plot area, legend, or chart walls and floors. However, you want to keep your chart as clean and simple as possible, so use pictures sparingly. When you add a picture to a chart element, its purpose should be to enhance the message the chart data communicates, rather than to call attention to the image itself. Kate wants you to add the Quest logo to the back wall of the chart to identify the company data.

STEPS

1. **Click the chart to select it if necessary, click the Chart Tools Format tab, then click the Chart Elements list arrow in the Current Selection group**

   The chart elements that can be formatted are displayed as shown in Figure J-14.

2. **Click Back Wall**

   The back wall of the chart is selected, as shown by the four small circles on its corners.

3. **Click the Format Selection button in the Current Selection group, click the Picture or texture fill option button to select it in the Format Wall dialog box, then click the File button under Insert from**

   The Insert Picture dialog box opens, allowing you to navigate to the logo image.

4. **Navigate to the location where you store your Data Files, click the chartlogo.gif file, click Insert, then click Close**

   The Quest logo appears on the back wall of the chart.

5. **Move the chart title if necessary to view the top of the logo, then compare your chart to Figure J-15**

6. **Click the Insert tab, click the Header & Footer button in the Text group, click the Custom Footer button on the Header/Footer tab, enter your name in the center section text box, click OK, then click OK again**

7. **Preview then print the First-Quarter Chart sheet**

Creating a chart template

After you create a custom chart with specific formatting, you can save it as a chart template. Chart templates can be opened and reused later, and the applied formatting will be available. Chart templates have the file extension crtx. If you use a custom chart frequently, you can save the template as the default chart type. To save a chart as a chart template, click the Chart Tools Design tab, click Save As Template in the Type group, enter a filename in the Save Chart Template dialog box, then click Save. Your chart template will be saved in the Templates\Charts folder. When you want to format a chart like a chart template, you need to apply the template. Select your chart, click the Insert tab, click a chart type in the Charts group, click All Chart Types, click the Templates folder in the Change Chart Type dialog box, select a template in the My Templates area, then click OK.

FIGURE J-14: Chart elements list

Chart Elements
list arrow

Click to select a
chart element

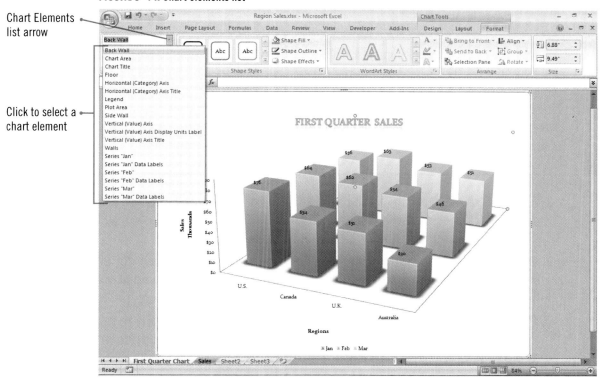

FIGURE J-15: First Quarter chart with picture inserted

Logo
inserted on
back wall
of chart

Identifying Data Trends

You often use charts to visually represent data over a period of time. To emphasize patterns in data, you can add trendlines to your charts. A **trendline** is a series of data points on a line that shows data values representing the general direction in a data series. In some business situations, you can use trendlines to predict future data based on past trends. ▨▨▨ Kate wants you to compare the U.S. and U.K. sales performance over the first two quarters and to project sales for each region in the following three months, assuming past trends. You begin by charting the six months sales data in a 2-D Column chart.

STEPS

1. **Click the** Sales sheet tab, **scroll to the top of the worksheet if necessary, select the** range A2:G6, **click the** Insert tab, **click the** Column button **in the Charts group, then click the** Clustered Column button **(First chart in the 2-D Column group)**

2. **Drag the chart left until its upper-left corner is at the upper left corner of cell** A8, **drag the** middle-right sizing handle **right to the border between column G and column H**
   You are ready to add a trendline for the U.S. data series.

3. **Click the** U.S. January data point **(the leftmost column in the chart) to select the U.S. data series, click the** Chart Tools Layout tab, **click the** Trendline button **in the Analysis group, then click** Linear Trendline
   A linear trendline identifying U.S. sales trends in the first six months is added to the chart, along with an entry in the legend identifying the line. You need to compare the U.S. sales trend with the U.K. sales trend.

4. **Click the** U.K. January data point **(the third column in the chart) to select the U.K. data series, click the** Trendline button, **then click** Linear Trendline
   The chart now has two trendlines, making it easy to compare the sales trends of the U.S. and the U.K. branches. Now you want to project the next three months sales for the U.S. and U.K. sales branches based on the past six months trends.

TROUBLE
If you have trouble selecting the trend-line you can click the Layout tab, click the Chart Elements list arrow in the Current Selection group, then select Series "U.S." Trendline1.

5. **Click the** U.S. data series trendline, **click the** Trendline button, **then click** More Trendline Options
   The Format Trendline dialog box opens, as shown in Figure J-16.

6. **In the Forecast section, enter** 3 **in the Forward text box, click** Close, **click the** U.K. data series trendline, **click the** Trendline button, **click** More Trendline Options, **enter** 3 **in the Forward text box, then click** Close
   The trendlines project three additional months, predicting the future sales trends for the U.S. and U.K. regions. The two trendlines look identical, so you decide to format them.

7. **Click the** U.S. data series trendline, **click the** Trendline button, **click** More Trendline Options, **click the** Custom option button **in the Trendline name section, then type** U.S. Trends **in the Custom text box**

8. **Click** Line Color **in the left pane of the dialog box, click the** Solid line option button, **click the** Color list arrow, **select** Red **in the Standard colors section, click** Line Style **in the left pane, click the** Dash type list arrow, **select the** Dash option, **then click** Close
   The U.S. data series trendline is now a red dashed line and is clearly identified in the legend.

9. **Select the** U.K. data series trendline, **repeat steps 7 and 8 but using the name** U.K. Trends **and a** Green **dashed line, then click outside the chart and go to cell** A1

10. **Compare your chart to Figure J-17, enter your name in the center section of the Sales sheet footer, save the workbook, preview and print the Sales sheet, then exit Excel**

FIGURE J-16: Format Trendline dialog box

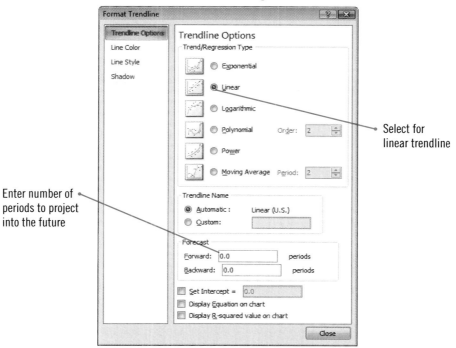

Enter number of periods to project into the future

Select for linear trendline

FIGURE J-17: Sales chart with trendlines for U.S. and U.K. data

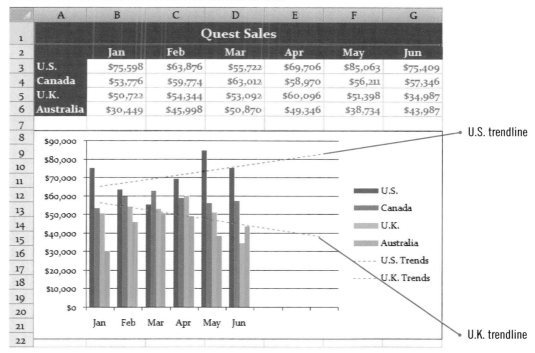

	A	B	C	D	E	F	G
1				Quest Sales			
2		Jan	Feb	Mar	Apr	May	Jun
3	U.S.	$75,598	$63,876	$55,722	$69,706	$85,063	$75,409
4	Canada	$53,776	$59,774	$63,012	$58,970	$56,211	$57,346
5	U.K.	$50,722	$54,344	$53,092	$60,096	$51,398	$34,987
6	Australia	$30,449	$45,998	$50,870	$49,346	$38,734	$43,987

U.S. trendline

U.K. trendline

Choosing the right trendline for your chart

Trendlines can help you forecast where your data is headed and understand its past values. This type of data analysis is called **regression analysis** in mathematics. You can choose from four types of trendlines: Linear, Exponential, Linear Forecast, and Two Period Moving Average. A **linear trendline** is used for data series with data points that have the pattern of a line. An exponential trendline is a curved line that is used when data values increase or decrease quickly. You cannot use an exponential trendline if your data contains negative values. A linear forecast trendline is a linear trendline with a two-period forecast. A two-period moving average smoothes out fluctuations in data by averaging the data points.

Practice

If you have a SAM user profile, you may have access to hands-on instruction, practice, and assessment of the skills covered in this unit. Log in to your SAM account (http://sam2007.course.com/) to launch any assigned training activities or exams that relate to the skills covered in this unit.

▼ CONCEPTS REVIEW

FIGURE J-18

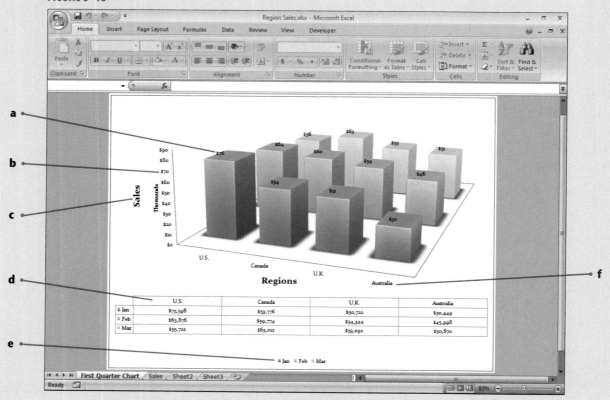

1. Which element points to the chart legend?
2. Which element points to a data table?
3. Which element points to a data label?
4. Which element points to a vertical axis title?
5. Which element points to the value axis?
6. Which element points to the category axis?

Match each term with the statement that best describes it.

7. Data series
8. Plot area
9. x-axis
10. y-axis
11. z-axis

a. Category axis
b. Depth in a 3-D chart
c. Vertical axis in a 3-D chart
d. Sequence of values plotted on a chart
e. Location holding data charted on the axes

Select the best answer from the list of choices.

12. Which of the following is true regarding WordArt?

    a. Spelling errors in WordArt can be detected by the spell checker.

    b. Cell references to WordArt can be used in formulas.

    c. Cells containing WordArt can be sorted.

    d. WordArt is a shape.

13. In 2-dimensional charts, the y-axis is the:

    a. Category axis.   **c.** 2-D axis.

    b. Depth axis.   **d.** Value axis.

14. A chart's scale:

    a. Always appears on the z-axis.   **c.** Always appears on the x-axis.

    b. Can be adjusted.   **d.** Always appears on the y-axis.

15. Which Chart Tools tab is used to format the axes of a chart?

    a. Layout   **c.** Format

    b. Design   **d.** Insert

16. What is a data table?

    a. The data used to create a chart, displayed in a grid

    b. A customized data series

    c. A grid with chart data displayed above a chart

    d. A three-dimensional arrangement of data on the y-axis

17. A chart template is saved with the extension:

    a. crtx   **c.** xlsx

    b. tem   **d.** xlsm

18. Which of the following is false regarding trendlines?

    a. Trendlines visually represent patterns in past data.

    b. Trendlines are used to predict future data.

    c. Six types of trendlines can be added to a chart.

    d. Trendlines can be formatted to stand out on a chart.

▼ SKILLS REVIEW

1. Customize a data series.

    a. Start Excel, open the file EX J-2.xlsx from the drive and folder where you save your Data Files, then save it as **Pastry Sales**.

    b. With the Sales sheet active, select the range A2:D6.

    c. Create a 3-D column chart using the selected data. (*Hint*: Do not choose the 3-D clustered column chart.)

    d. Move and resize the chart to fit in the range A8:G20.

    e. Change the color of the January data series to a light blue color in the Standard Colors group.

    f. Save the workbook.

2. Change a data source and add data labels.

    a. Add the April, May, and June data to the chart.

    b. Change the chart view by exchanging the row and column data.

    c. Resize the chart to fill the range A8:J28 to display the new data.

    d. Change the chart view back to show the months in the legend by exchanging the row and column data. Apply Chart Layout 4 to add data labels to your chart. Delete the data labels for all but the June series. (*Hint*: Click one of the data labels in the series, then press [Delete].) Move any June data labels that are difficult to view.

    e. Save the workbook.

3. Format the axes of a chart.

    a. Change the display of the vertical axis values to thousands.

    b. Move the thousands label lower along the axis so it appears between $3 and $5.

    c. Set the value axis maximum to 7000.

    d. Add a horizontal axis title below the chart. Label the axis **Products**.

    e. Move the horizontal axis title so it appears between Cookies and Brownies.

    f. Save the workbook.

4. Add a data table to a chart.

    a. Move the chart to its own sheet named **Sales Chart**.

    b. Add a data table with legend keys.

    c. Move the horizontal axis title up to a location above the data table between Cookies and Brownies. Move the vertical thousands label to the right so that it is closer to the chart.

    d. Format the data table to change the border color to the standard color purple.

    e. Enter your name in the center section of the Sales Chart footer. Preview, then print the chart.

    f. Save the workbook, then compare your screen to Figure J-19.

5. Rotate a chart.

    a. Apply Chart Layout 1. (*Hint*: This will remove the data table, the data labels, and the horizontal title.)

    b. Set the X: rotation to 70 degrees.

    c. Set the Y: rotation to 20 degrees.

    d. Change the depth to 180% of the base.

    e. Move the thousands label to the left of the vertical axis, then save the workbook.

6. Enhance a chart with WordArt.

    a. Add a chart title of **Pastry Sales** to the top of the chart. Format the chart title with WordArt Gradient Fill – Accent 1.

    b. Add a linear gradient fill to the title, with a transparency of 90%. (*Hint*: On the Chart Tools Layout tab, use the Chart Title button in the Labels group.)

    c. Position the new title approximately half way across the top of the chart and closer to the chart.

    d. Save the workbook.

7. Add a picture to a chart.

    a. Select the back chart wall.

    b. Format the back wall fill with the picture cookie.gif from the drive and folder where you store your Data Files.

    c. Save the workbook.

    d. Preview the worksheet.

    e. Print the worksheet, then compare your printout to Figure J-20.

FIGURE J-19

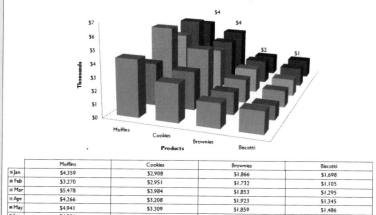

	Muffins	Cookies	Brownies	Biscotti
▪ Jan	$4,359	$2,908	$1,866	$1,698
▪ Feb	$3,270	$2,951	$1,732	$1,105
▪ Mar	$5,478	$3,984	$1,853	$1,295
▪ Apr	$4,266	$3,208	$1,923	$1,345
▪ May	$4,941	$3,309	$1,859	$1,486
▪ Jun	$4,234	$3,586	$1,530	$1,455

▪ Jan ▪ Feb ▪ Mar ▪ Apr ▪ May ▪ Jun

FIGURE J-20

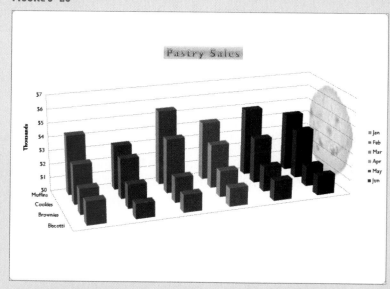

▼ SKILLS REVIEW (CONTINUED)

8. Identify data trends.

a. Activate the Sales sheet and scroll to the top of the worksheet.

b. Create a 2-D line chart using the data in the range A2:G6, then move and resize the chart to fit in the range A8:G20.

c. Add a linear trendline to the Muffins data series.

d. Change the trendline color to red and the line style to dash.

e. Set the forward option to six periods to view the future trend, then compare your screen to Figure J-21.

f. Add your name to the center footer section, save the workbook, then preview and print the worksheet.

g. Exit Excel.

FIGURE J-21

	A	B	C	D	E	F	G
1				Nancy's Pastry			
2		Jan	Feb	Mar	Apr	May	Jun
3	Muffins	$4,359	$3,270	$5,478	$4,266	$4,941	$4,234
4	Cookies	$2,908	$2,951	$3,984	$3,208	$3,309	$3,586
5	Brownies	$1,866	$1,732	$1,853	$1,923	$1,859	$1,530
6	Biscotti	$1,698	$1,105	$1,295	$1,345	$1,486	$1,455

(Chart showing $6,000 to $0 scale, Jan–Jun, with series: Muffins, Cookies, Brownies, Biscotti, Linear (Muffins))

▼ INDEPENDENT CHALLENGE 1

You are the assistant to the vice president of marketing at the Metro-West Philharmonic located outside of Boston. The vice president has asked you to chart some information from a recent survey of the Philharmonic's customers. Your administrative assistant has entered the survey data in an Excel worksheet, which you will use to create two charts.

a. Start Excel, open the file titled EX J-3.xlsx from the drive and folder where you store your Data Files, then save it as **Customer Survey**.

b. Using the data in A2:B7 of the Education data worksheet, create a 3-D pie chart (the first chart in the 3-D Pie group) on the worksheet.

c. Add a title of **Education Data** above the chart. Format the title using Word Art Gradient Fill - Accent 6, Inner Shadow.

d. Move the chart to a separate sheet named **Education Chart**. Format the chart using chart Style 13. Add data labels to the outside end of the data points. Format the legend text in 14-point bold. (*Hint*: Use the font options on the Home tab or the Mini toolbar.)

e. Select the Bachelor's degree pie slice by clicking the chart, then clicking the Bachelor's degree slice. Change the slice color to the standard color of purple. (*Hint*: On the Chart Tools Format tab, click the Format Selection button in the Current Selection group and use the Format Data Point dialog box.) Compare your chart to Figure J-22

f. On the Family data worksheet, use the data in A2:B6 to create a standard clustered column (The first chart in the 2-D Column group) chart.

g. Delete the legend. (*Hint*: Select the legend and press [Delete].)

h. Place the chart on a new sheet named **Family Chart**. Format the chart using chart Style 5.

i. Add a chart title of **Family Data** above the chart and format the title using WordArt Style Gradient Fill - Black, Outline - White, Outer Shadow.

j. Title the category axis **Number of Children**. Format the category axis title in 14-point bold. (*Hint*: Use the font options on the Home tab or use the Mini toolbar.)

k. Enter your name in the center sections of the footers of the Family Chart and Education Chart sheets.

l. Save the workbook, then preview and print the Family Chart and the Education Chart sheets.

m. Close the workbook and exit Excel.

FIGURE J-22

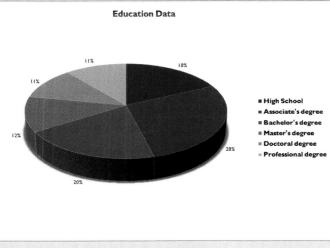

Education Data

- High School
- Associate's degree
- Bachelor's degree
- Master's degree
- Doctoral degree
- Professional degree

▼ INDEPENDENT CHALLENGE 2

You were voted employee of the month for January at Careers, an employment agency. Your manager has asked you to assemble a brief presentation on your placements during January to show to the newly hired staff. You decide to include a chart showing your placements in each of three job categories: technical, business, and medical.

a. Start Excel and save a new workbook as Careers in the drive and folder where you store your Data Files.

b. Enter worksheet labels and your own data on a worksheet named January Placements. Use Table J-2 as a guide for the worksheet layout.

c. Create a clustered bar chart (the first chart in the 2-D Bar group) on the worksheet, showing your placements. Format the chart using Chart Style 11. Make sure the Office theme is selected.

d. Display data values using Chart Layout 4.

e. Add a chart title of January Placements above the chart and format it using WordArt Style Fill - None, Outline - Accent 2.

f. Delete the chart legend.

g. Add new data to the worksheet for the Academic job category.

h. Add the new data to the chart.

i. Move the chart to a sheet named January Chart.

j. Add a horizontal axis title of Number of Placements and format the title in 14-point bold font.

k. Change the value scale if necessary to fit your sales data and improve its readability.

l. Add a data table to the chart. Format the data table lines to display in red.

TABLE J-2

Job Category	Number of Placements
Technical	
Business	
Medical	

Advanced Challenge Exercise

- Change the name of the chart's data series name in the legend to Placements. (*Hint*: On the Chart Tools Design tab, use the Select Data button and use the editing features in the Select Data Source dialog box. Change the existing Series name to Placements.)
- Use the Format Data Series dialog box to add a shadow with a format of your choice to the bars in the chart.
- Add a bevel with a format of your choice to the bars in the chart.
- Change the fill color for the bars to one of the theme colors.

m. Enter your name in the center section of the January Chart sheet footer, save the workbook, then preview and print the sheet.

n. Close the workbook and exit Excel.

▼ INDEPENDENT CHALLENGE 3

You manage the Pine Hills Pro Shop. You meet twice a year with the store owner to discuss store sales trends. You decide to use a chart to represent the sales trends for the department's product categories. You begin by charting the sales for the first five months of the year. Then you add data to the chart and analyze the sales trend using a trendline. Lastly, you enhance the chart by adding a data table, titles, and a picture.

a. Start Excel, open the file EX J-4.xlsx from the drive and folder where you store your Data Files, then save the workbook as Golf Sales.

b. Create a 2-D line chart on the worksheet showing the January through May sales information. Move the chart and resize it if necessary.

c. Format the Clubs data series and the Cart rentals data series using colors of your choice.

d. Add the June data from Table J-3 to the worksheet. Add the June data series to the chart.

e. Move the chart to its own sheet named Jan - June and add a data table without legend keys. Format the data table line color using the color of your choice.

f. Add a chart title of January - June Sales using the Centered Overlay position. Format the chart title using the WordArt Style of your choice.

TABLE J-3

Jun
$3,409
$5,187
$3,450
$3,709

▼ INDEPENDENT CHALLENGE 3 (CONTINUED)

g. Add a rotated title of **Sales** in 20-point bold to the vertical axis.

h. Add a linear trendline to the Clubs data series.

i. Change the color of the trendline to red and format the width in 2-pt dash style.

j. Insert the golfball.gif picture from the drive and folder where your Data Files are stored into the legend area of the chart.

Advanced Challenge Exercise

- Move the legend to the left side of the chart. Move the vertical axis title to the right if necessary.
- Remove the horizontal chart gridlines.
- Change the value axis scale to increment by 500.
- Add a gradient fill of your choice to the plot area.
- Drag the legend to the plot area and add a clip art background. Adjust the transparency of the legend background and the font color, if necessary, so that the legend text is readable.

k. Enter your name in the center footer section of the chart sheet, save the workbook, then preview and print the chart.

l. Close the workbook and exit Excel.

▼ REAL LIFE INDEPENDENT CHALLENGE

This Independent Challenge requires a Web connection.

Stock charts are used to graph a stock's high, low, and closing prices. You will create a stock chart using four weeks of high, low, and close prices for a stock that you are interested in tracking.

a. Start Excel, save a new workbook as **Stock Chart** in the drive and folder where you store your Data Files.

b. Use the search engine of your choice to research the high, low, and close prices for a stock over the past four weeks.

c. Create a worksheet with the data from your chart. Use Table J-4 as a guide for the worksheet structure. Apply a document theme of your choice.

d. Create a High-Low-Close stock chart using your worksheet data. (*Hint*: To find the stock charts, click the Other Charts button.)

e. Format the horizontal axis to change the major unit to seven days.

f. Change the color of the high-low lines to the standard color of dark red.

TABLE J-4

Stock Name			
Date	High	Low	Close

g. Add a rotated vertical axis title of **Stock Price**. Format the title in 14-point bold.

h. Delete the chart legend.

i. Add a chart title with your stock name. Format the title with a WordArt style of your choice from the WordArt Styles gallery.

j. Add data labels above the data series. (*Hint*: Use the Data Labels button on the Layout tab.) Delete the High and Low labels but keep the Close data labels. Add a line to the chart title with the text **Closing Prices**.

k. Format the chart area using a gradient and transparency of your choice. Format the plot area with a clip art fill related to the company or its product. Adjust the clip art transparency as necessary to view the chart.

l. Enter your name in the center footer section of the worksheet, save the workbook, then preview and print the sheet in landscape orientation on one page.

m. Close the workbook and exit Excel.

▼ VISUAL WORKSHOP

Open the file EX J-5.xlsx from the drive and folder where you store your Data Files, and create the custom chart shown in Figure J-23. Save the workbook as **Tea Sales**. Study the chart and worksheet carefully to make sure you select the displayed chart type with all the enhancements shown. Enter your name in the center section of the worksheet footer, then preview and print the worksheet in landscape orientation on one page.

FIGURE J-23

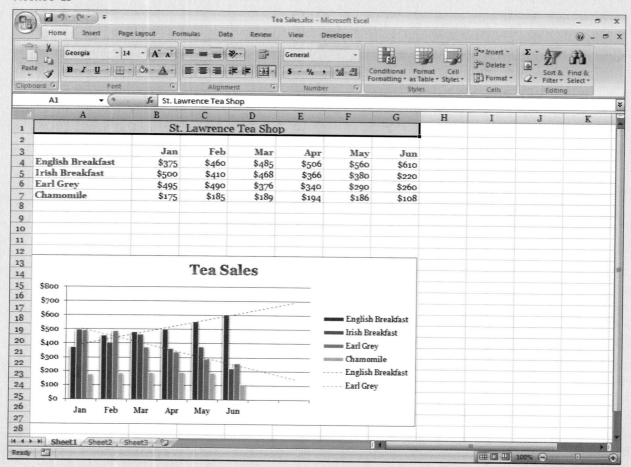

Sharing Excel Files and Incorporating Web Information

The Web as well as private networks are often used to share Excel files, allowing others to review, revise, and provide feedback on worksheet data. Information from the Web can easily be incorporated into workbooks, providing up-to-date information in the worksheets. Kate Morgan, the vice president of sales for Quest, wants to share information with corporate office employees and branch managers using the company's intranet and the Web.

OBJECTIVES

Share Excel files

Set up a shared workbook for multiple users

Track revisions in a shared workbook

Apply and modify passwords

Work with XML schemas

Import and export XML data

Run Web queries to retrieve external data

Import and export HTML data

Sharing Excel Files

Microsoft Excel provides many different ways to share spreadsheets with people in your office, in your organization, or anywhere on the Web. When you share workbooks, you have to consider how you will protect information that you don't want everyone to see and how you can control revisions others will make to your files. Some information you want to use might not be in Excel format. Because there is a great deal of information published on the Web in HTML format, Excel allows you to import HTML to your worksheets. XML is better suited than HTML for storing and exchanging data, so businesses store data in XML files and exchange XML data both internally and externally. Excel allows you to easily import XML data as well. You can export worksheet data to an HTML or XML file. You can also retrieve data from the Web using queries. Kate considers the best way to share her Excel workbooks with corporate employees and branch managers.

DETAILS

To share worksheet information, consider the following issues:

* **Allowing others to use a workbook**

  When you share Excel files with others, you need to set up your workbooks so that several users can **share** them, which means they can simultaneously open them from a network server, modify them electronically, and return their revisions to you for incorporation with others' changes. You can view each user's name and the date each change was made. Kate wants to obtain feedback on Quest sales data from the branch managers.

* **Controlling access to workbooks on a server**

  When you place a workbook on a network server, you will likely want to control who can open and change it. You can do this using Excel passwords. Kate assigns a password to her workbook and gives the workbook to the corporate staff and branch managers, along with the password, so only they can open the workbook and revise it.

* **HTML data**

  You can paste data from a Web page into a worksheet and then manipulate and format it using Excel. You can also save Excel workbook information in HTML format so it can be published on an intranet or on the Web. Kate decides to publish the worksheet with the North American sales information in HTML format on the company intranet, as shown in Figure N-1.

* **Working with XML data**

  You can import XML data into an Excel workbook. Once the data is in a workbook, you can manage and analyze it using Excel tools. You can also export Excel data in XML format to create an XML file. Storing data in XML format allows you to use it in different situations. For example, a company may store all of its sales data in an XML file and make different parts of the file available to various departments such as marketing and accounting. These departments can extract information that is relevant to their purposes from the file. A subset of the same XML file might be sent to vendors or other business associates who only require certain types of sales data stored in the XML file. Kate decides to import XML files that contain sales information from the Miami and New York branches to get a sales summary for Quest's eastern region.

* **Using an Excel query to retrieve data from the Web**

  You can use built-in Excel queries to import stock quotes and currency rates from the MSN Money Website. These queries import data from the Web into an Excel workbook, where you can organize and manipulate the information using Excel spreadsheet and graphics tools. Kate decides to use a query to get currency rate information for her analysis of the sales data from the Quest Canada branches, as shown in Figure N-2.

FIGURE N-1: North America sales information displayed in a Web browser

Excel data
published
in browser

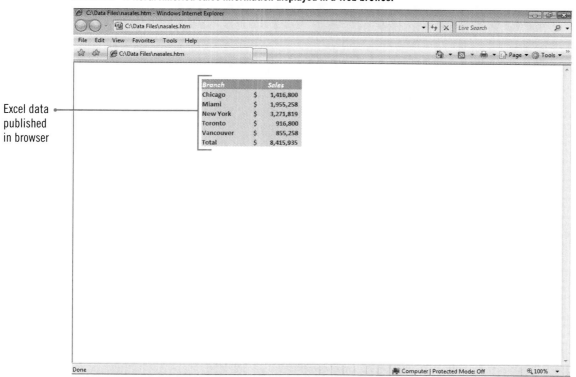

FIGURE N-2: Data retrieved from the Web using a Web query

Excel worksheet
with imported
currency
information

	A	B	C	D
1	**Currency Rates Provided by MSN Money**			
2	Click here to visit MSN Money			
3				
4	**Name**	**In US$**	**Per US$**	
5	United States Dollar (b) vs Argentine Peso Spot	0.32165	3.109	
6	Australian Dollar Futures Spot Price	0.74571	1.341	
7	Bahraini Dinar to US Dollar	2.6491	0.377	
8	Bolivian Boliviano to US Dollar	0.125	8	
9	Brazilian Real to US Dollar	0.45981	2.175	
10	British Pound Futures Spot Price	1.8713	0.534	
11	Canadian Dollar Futures Spot Price	0.89414	1.118	
12	United States Dollar (b) vs Chilean Peso Spot	0.00186	537	
13	Chinese Yuan to US Dollar	0.12639	7.912	
14	United States Dollar (b) vs Colombia Peso Spot	0.00042	2400	
15	United States Dollar (b) vs Cypriot Pound Spot	2.1716	0.461	
16	Czech Koruna to US Dollar	0.04473	22.357	
17	Danish Krone to US Dollar	0.16998	5.883	
18	United States Dollar (b) vs Ecuadorian Sucre Spot	0.00004	25030	
19	United States Dollar (b) vs Euro Spot	1.2674	0.789	
20	Hong Kong Dollar to US Dollar	0.12834	7.792	
21	United States Dollar (b) vs Hungary Forint Spot	0.00464	215.5	
22	Indian Rupee to US Dollar	0.02184	45.798	
23	United States Dollar (b) vs Indonesian Rupiah Spot	0.00011	9206	
24	Japanese Yen Futures Spot Price	0.00846	118.2	

Sheet1 / Sheet2 / Sheet3

Ready

Excel 2007

Setting Up a Shared Workbook for Multiple Users

You can make an Excel file a **shared workbook** so that several users can open and modify it at the same time. This is useful for workbooks that you want others to review on a network server, where the workbook is equally accessible to all network users. When you share a workbook, you can have Excel keep a list of all changes to the workbook, which you can view and print at any time. ██████ Kate asks you to help her put a shared workbook containing customer and sales data on the company's network. She wants to get feedback from selected corporate staff and branch managers before presenting the information at the next corporate staff meeting. You begin by making her Excel file a shared workbook.

STEPS

1. **Start Excel, open the file EX N-1.xlsx from the drive and folder where you store your Data Files, then save it as Sales Information**

   The workbook with the sales information opens, displaying two worksheets. The first contains tour sales data for the Quest U.S. branches; the second is a breakdown of the branch sales by sales associate.

> **QUICK TIP**
> The Advanced tab of the Share Workbook dialog box allows you to specify the length of time the change history is saved and when the file will be updated with the changes.

2. **Click the Review tab, then click the Share Workbook button in the Changes group**

   The Share Workbook dialog box opens, as shown in Figure N-3.

3. **Click the Editing tab, if necessary**

   The dialog box lists the names of people who are currently using the workbook. You are the only user, so your name, or the name of the person entered as the computer user, appears, along with the current date and time.

> **QUICK TIP**
> You can remove users from the list by clicking their names and clicking Remove User.

4. **Click to select the check box next to Allow changes by more than one user at the same time. This also allows workbook merging., then click OK**

   A dialog box appears, asking if you want to save the workbook. This will resave it as a shared workbook.

5. **Click OK**

   Excel saves the file as a shared workbook. The title bar now reads Sales Information.xlsx [Shared], as shown in Figure N-4. This version replaces the unshared version.

Managing shared workbooks

A workbook remains shared as long as the Allow Changes by more than one user at the same time option is checked. Once you've obtained input from other users and no longer need to collaborate with them or keep a record of their changes, you can return a shared workbook to unshared status. To do this, click the Review tab, click the Share Workbook button in the Changes group, then deselect the Allow changes by more than one user at the same time option on the Editing tab of the Share Workbook dialog box.

FIGURE N-3: Share Workbook dialog box

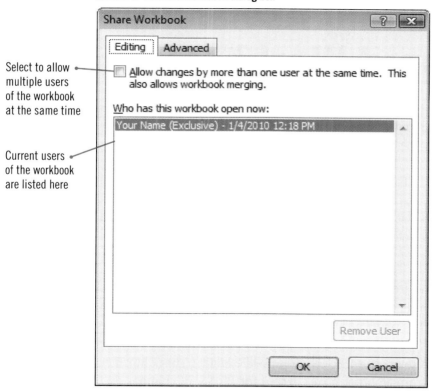

Select to allow multiple users of the workbook at the same time

Current users of the workbook are listed here

Excel 2007

FIGURE N-4: Shared workbook

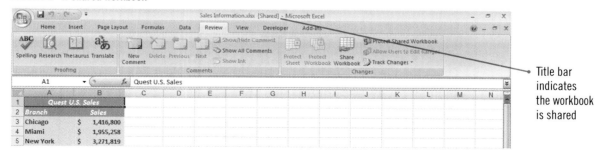

Title bar indicates the workbook is shared

Merging workbooks

Instead of putting the shared workbook on a server, you might want to distribute copies to your reviewers via e-mail. Once everyone has entered their changes and returned their copies to you, you can merge the changed copies into one master workbook that will contain all the changes. Each copy you distribute must be designated as shared, and the Change History feature on the Advanced tab of the Share Workbook dialog box must be activated. Occasionally a conflict occurs when two users are trying to edit the same cells in a shared workbook. In this case, the second person to save the file will see a Resolve Conflicts dialog box and need to choose Accept Mine or Accept Other. To merge workbooks, you need to add the Compare and Merge Workbooks command to the Quick Access Toolbar by clicking the Office button, clicking Excel Options, and clicking Customize. Click All Commands in the Choose commands from list, click Compare and Merge Workbooks, click Add, then click OK. Once you get the changed copies back, open the master copy of the workbook, then click Compare and Merge Workbooks. The Select Files to Merge Into Current Workbook dialog box opens. Select the workbooks you want to merge (you can use the [Ctrl] key to select more than one workbook), then click OK.

Tracking Revisions in a Shared Workbook

When you share workbooks, it is often helpful to **track** modifications, or identify who made which changes. You can accept the changes you agree with, and if you disagree with any changes, you can reject them. When you activate the Excel change tracking feature, changes appear in a different color for each user. Each change is identified with the username and date. In addition to highlighting changes, Excel keeps track of changes in a **change history**, a list of all changes that you can place on a separate work-sheet so you can review them all at once. ▰▰▰▰ Kate asks you to set up the shared Sales Information workbook so that all future changes will be tracked. You will then open a workbook that is on the server and review the changes and the change history.

STEPS

1. **Click the Track Changes button in the Changes group, then click Highlight Changes**

    The Highlight Changes dialog box opens, as shown in Figure N-5, allowing you to turn on change tracking. You can also specify which changes to highlight and whether you want to display changes on the screen or save the change history in a separate worksheet.

2. **Click to select the Track changes while editing check box if necessary, remove check marks from all other boxes except for Highlight changes on screen, click OK, then click OK in the dialog box that informs you that you have yet to make changes**

    Leaving the When, Who, and Where check boxes blank allows you to track all changes.

3. **Click the Sales by Rep sheet tab, change the sales figure for Sanchez in cell C3 to 190,000, press [Enter], then move the mouse pointer over the cell you just changed**

    A border with a small triangle in the upper-left corner appears around the cell you changed, and a ScreenTip appears with your name, the date, the time, and details about the change, as shown in Figure N-6.

4. **Save and close the workbook**

5. **Open the file EX N-2.xlsx from the drive and folder where you store your Data Files, then save it as Sales Information Edits**

    Jose Silva has made changes to a version of this workbook. You want to view the details of these changes and accept the ones that appear to be correct.

6. **Click the Review tab if necessary, click the Track Changes button in the Changes group, click Accept/Reject Changes, click the When check box in the Select Changes to Accept or Reject dialog box to deselect it, then click OK**

    You will accept the first four changes that Jose made to the workbook and reject his last change.

7. **Click Accept four times to approve the first four changes, then click Reject to undo Jose's fifth change**

8. **Click the Track Changes button in the Changes group, click Highlight Changes, click the When check box in the Highlight Changes dialog box to deselect it, click to select the List changes on a new sheet check box, then click OK**

    The History sheet appears, as shown in Figure N-7, with Jose's changes in a filtered list.

9. **Click the Insert tab, click the Header & Footer button in the Text group, click OK to unfreeze the sheet panes, enter your name in the center section of the History sheet header, print the History sheet, save the workbook, observe that the History sheet closes automatically, then close the workbook**

    The change history printout shows all of Jose's changes to the workbook.

FIGURE N-5: Highlight Changes dialog box

Select to show
changes to the
worksheet

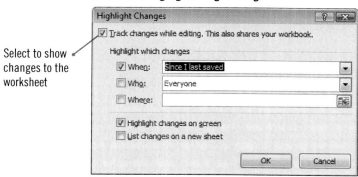

FIGURE N-6: Tracked change

Triangle in corner
indicates cell has
been changed

ScreenTip provides
details of changes
to the cell

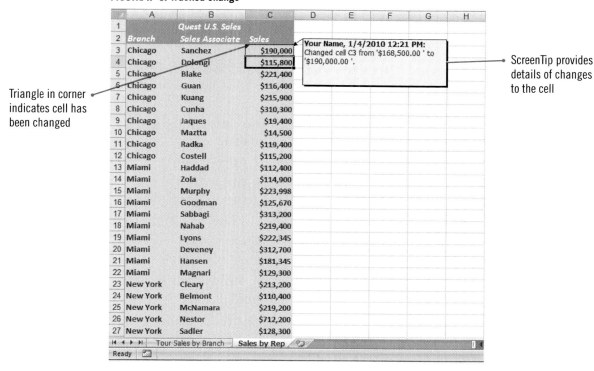

FIGURE N-7: History sheet tab with change history

Details of changes
to the worksheet

History tab

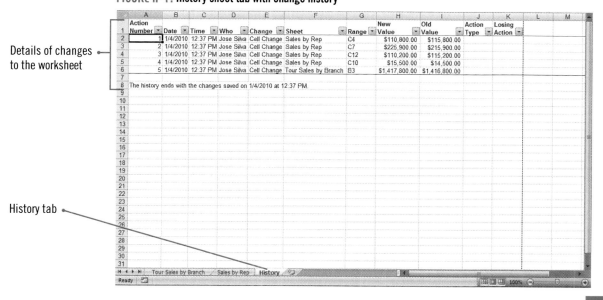

Excel 2007

Applying and Modifying Passwords

When you place a shared workbook on a server, you may want to use a password so that only authorized people will be able to open it or make changes to it. However, it's important to remember that *if you lose your password, you will not be able to open or change the workbook.* Passwords are case sensitive, so you must type them exactly as you want users to type them, with the same spacing and using the same case. It is a good idea to include uppercase and lowercase letters and numbers in a password. 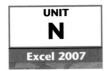 Kate wants you to put the workbook with sales information on one of the company's servers. You decide to save a copy of the workbook with two passwords: one that users will need to open it, and another that they will use to make changes to it.

STEPS

1. **Open the file** EX N-1.xlsx **from the drive and folder where you store your Data Files, click the** Office button, **click** Save As, **click the** Tools list arrow **in the bottom of the Save As dialog box, then click** General Options

   The General Options dialog box opens, with two password boxes: one to open the workbook, and one to allow changes to the workbook, as shown in Figure N-8.

2. **In the Password to open text box, type** QSTmanager01

   Be sure to type the letters in the correct cases. This is the password that users must type to open the workbook. When you enter passwords, the characters you type are masked with bullets (• • •) for security purposes.

3. **Press [Tab], in the Password to modify text box, type** QSTsales02, **then click** OK

   This is the password that users must type to make changes to the workbook. A dialog box asks you to verify the first password by reentering it.

4. **Enter** QSTmanager01 **in the first Confirm Password dialog box, click** OK, **enter** QSTsales02 **in the second Confirm Password dialog box, then click** OK

5. **Change the filename to** Sales Information PW, **navigate to the location where you store your Data Files, click** Save, **then close the workbook**

6. **Reopen the workbook** Sales Information PW, **enter the password** QSTmanager01 **when prompted for a password, click** OK, **then enter** QSTsales02 **to obtain write access**

   The Password dialog box is shown in Figure N-9. Obtaining write access for a workbook allows you to modify it.

7. **Click** OK, **change the sales figure for the Chicago branch in cell B3 to** 1,500,000, **then press [Enter]**

   You were able to make this change because you obtained write access privileges using the password "QSTsales02."

8. **Save and close the workbook**

FIGURE N-8: General Options dialog box

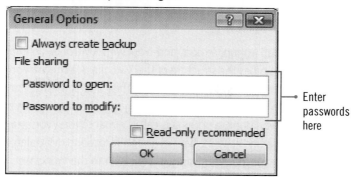

Enter passwords here

FIGURE N-9: Password entry prompt

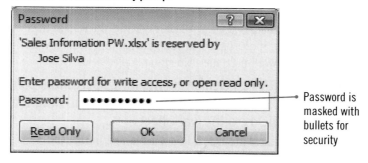

Password is masked with bullets for security

Removing passwords

You can change or delete a workbook's password if you know what it is. Open the workbook, click the Office button, then click Save As. In the Save As dialog box, click the Tools list arrow, then click General Options. Double-click to highlight the symbols for the existing passwords in the Password to open or Password to modify text boxes, press [Delete], click OK, change the filename if desired, then click Save.

Working with XML Schemas

Using Excel you can import, export, and work with XML data. To import XML data, Excel requires a file called a schema that describes the structure of the XML file. A **schema** contains the rules for the XML file by listing all of the fields in the XML document and their characteristics, such as the type of data they contain. A schema is used to **validate** XML data, making sure the data follows the rules given in the file. Once a schema is attached to a workbook, a schema is called a map. When you **map** an element to a worksheet, you place the element name on the worksheet in a specific location. Mapping XML elements allows you to choose the XML data from a file that you want to work with in the worksheet. ▓▓▓▓▓ Kate has been given XML files containing sales information from the U.S. branches. She asks you to prepare a workbook to import the sales representatives' XML data. You begin by adding a schema to a worksheet that describes the XML data.

STEPS

TROUBLE
If the Developer tab does not appear on your ribbon, click the Office button, click Excel Options, select the Show Developer tab in the Ribbon check box, then click OK.

1. **Create a new workbook, save it as Sales Reps in the drive and folder where you store your Data Files, click the Developer tab, then click the Source button in the XML group**

   The XML Source pane opens. This is where you specify a schema, or map, to import. A schema has the extension .xsd. Kate has provided you with a schema she received from the IT department describing the XML file structure.

2. **Click the XML Maps button at the bottom of the task pane**

   The XML Maps dialog box opens, listing the XML maps or schemas in the workbook. There are no schemas in the Sales Reps workbook at this time, as shown in Figure N-10.

QUICK TIP
You can delete a map from a workbook by clicking the XML Maps button at the bottom of the XML Source task pane to open the XML Maps dialog box. In the dialog box select the map that you want to delete, click Delete, then click OK.

3. **Click Add in the XML Maps dialog box, navigate to the folder containing your Data Files in the Select XML Source dialog box, click EX N-3.xsd, click Open, then click OK**

   The schema elements appear in the XML Source task pane. Elements in a schema describe data similarly to the way field names in an Excel table describe the data in their columns. You choose the schema elements from the XML Source pane that you want to work with on your worksheet and map them to the worksheet. Once on the worksheet, the elements are called fields.

4. **Click the BRANCH element in the XML Source task pane and drag it to cell A1 on the worksheet, then use Figure N-11 as a guide to drag the FNAME, LNAME, SALES, and ENUMBER fields to the worksheet**

   The mapped elements appear in bolded format in the XML Source pane. The fields on the worksheet have filter arrows because Excel automatically creates a table on the worksheet as you map the schema elements. You decide to remove the ENUMBER field from the table.

QUICK TIP
Make sure that you right-click the ENUMBER element in the XML Source task pane and not the field on the worksheet.

5. **Right-click the ENUMBER element in the XML Source task pane, then click Remove element**

   ENUMBER is no longer formatted in bold because it is no longer mapped to the worksheet. This means that when XML data is imported, the ENUMBER field will not be populated with data. However, the field name remains in the table on the worksheet.

6. **Drag the table resizing arrow up and to the left to remove cell E1 from the table**

   Because you plan to import XML data from different files, you want to be sure that data from one file will not overwrite data from another file when it is imported into the worksheet. You also want to be sure that Excel validates the imported data against the rules specified in the schema.

7. **Click any cell in the table, click the Developer tab, then click the Map Properties button in the XML group**

   The XML Map Properties dialog box opens, as shown in Figure N-12.

8. **Click the Validate data against schema for import and export check box to select it, click the Append new data to existing XML tables option button to select it, then click OK**

   You are ready to import XML data into your worksheet.

FIGURE N-10: **XML Maps dialog box**

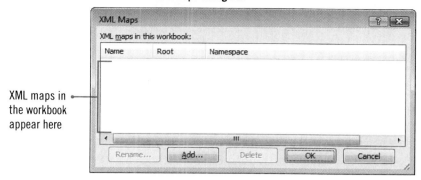

XML maps in the workbook appear here

FIGURE N-11: **XML elements mapped to the worksheet**

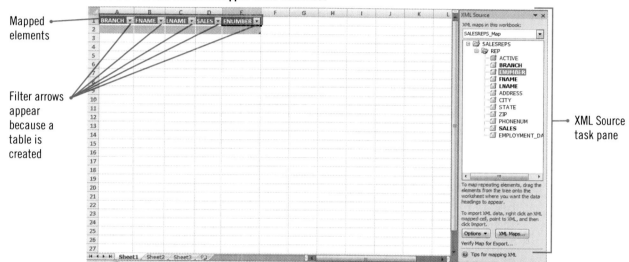

Mapped elements

Filter arrows appear because a table is created

XML Source task pane

FIGURE N-12: **XML Map Properties dialog box**

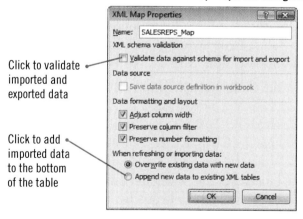

Click to validate imported and exported data

Click to add imported data to the bottom of the table

Learning more about XML

XML is a universal data format for business and industry information sharing. Using XML you can store structured information related to services, products, or business transactions and easily share and exchange the information with others. XML provides a way to express structure in data. Structured data is tagged, or marked up, to indicate its content. For example, an XML data marker (tag) that contains an item's cost might be named COST. Excel's ability to work with XML data allows you to access the large amount of information stored in the XML format. For example, organizations have developed many XML applications with a specific focus, such as MathML (Mathematical Markup Language) and RETML (Real Estate Transaction Markup Language).

Importing and Exporting XML Data

After the mapping is complete, you can import any XML file with a structure that conforms to the workbook schema. The mapped elements on the worksheet will fill with (or be **populated** with) data from the XML file. If an element is not mapped on the worksheet, then its data will not be imported. Once you import the XML data, you can analyze it using Excel tools. You can also export data from an Excel workbook to an XML file. 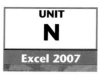 Kate asks you to combine the sales data for the Miami and New York branches that are contained in XML files. She would like you to add a total for the combined branches and export the data from Excel to an XML file.

STEPS

1. **Click cell A1, click the Developer tab if necessary, then click the Import button in the XML group**

   The Import XML dialog box opens.

2. **Navigate to the folder containing your Data Files, click EX N-4.xml, then click Import**

   The worksheet is populated with data from the XML file that contains the Miami sales rep information. The data for only the mapped elements are imported. You decide to add the sales rep data for the New York branch to the worksheet.

3. **Click the Import button in the XML group, navigate to the folder containing your Data Files in the Import XML dialog box, click EX N-5.xml, then click Import**

   The New York branch sales rep data is added to the Miami branch data. You decide to total the sales figures for all sales reps.

4. **Click the Table Tools Design tab, then click the Total Row check box to select it**

   The total sales amount of 4999777 appears in cell D25. You decide to format the table.

5. **Select the range of cells D2:D25, click the Home tab, click the Accounting Number Format button $ in the Number group, click the Decrease Decimal button in the Number group twice, click the Table Tools Design tab, click the More button in the Table Styles group, select Table Style Light 19, then click cell A1**

   Compare your completed table to Figure N-13.

6. **Enter your name in the center section of the worksheet footer, then preview and print the table**

   You will export the combined sales rep data as an XML file. Because not all of the elements in the schema were mapped to fields in your Excel table, you do not want the data exported from the table to be validated against the schema.

7. **Click any cell in the table, click the Developer tab, click the Map Properties button in the XML group, then click the Validate data against schema for import and export check box to deselect it**

   The Map Properties dialog box with the validation turned off is shown in Figure N-14. You are ready to export the XML data.

8. **Click OK, click the Export button in the XML group, navigate to the folder containing your Data Files in the Export XML dialog box, enter the name eastreps in the File name text box, click Export, then save and close the workbook**

   The sales data is saved in your Data File location in XML format, in the file called eastreps.xml.

FIGURE N-13: **Completed table with combined sales rep data**

	A	B	C	D	E
1	BRANCH	FNAME	LNAME	SALES	
2	Miami	Ed	Murphy	$ 223,998	
3	Miami	Kathy	Goodman	$ 125,670	
4	Miami	Laurie	Sabbagi	$ 313,200	
5	Miami	Bert	Nahab	$ 219,400	
6	Miami	Kate	Deveney	$ 312,700	
7	Miami	Mary	Lyons	$ 222,345	
8	Miami	Ed	Hansen	$ 181,345	
9	Miami	Dawn	Magnari	$ 129,300	
10	New York	Katherine	Cleary	$ 213,200	
11	New York	Edward	Belmont	$ 110,400	
12	New York	Mel	McNamara	$ 219,200	
13	New York	Virginia	Nestor	$ 712,200	
14	New York	Julio	Sadler	$ 128,300	
15	New York	Ann	Lee	$ 314,200	
16	New York	John	Bloomberg	$ 210,400	
17	New York	Pat	Harrington	$ 217,300	
18	New York	William	Galvin	$ 113,452	
19	New York	Ed	McCarthy	$ 239,300	
20	New York	George	Ryan	$ 112,300	
21	New York	Rod	Stedman	$ 123,567	
22	New York	Al	Tessier	$ 218,200	
23	New York	Kathy	Vodel	$ 210,400	
24	New York	Ken	Perkins	$ 129,400	
25	Total			$ 4,999,777	
26					
27					

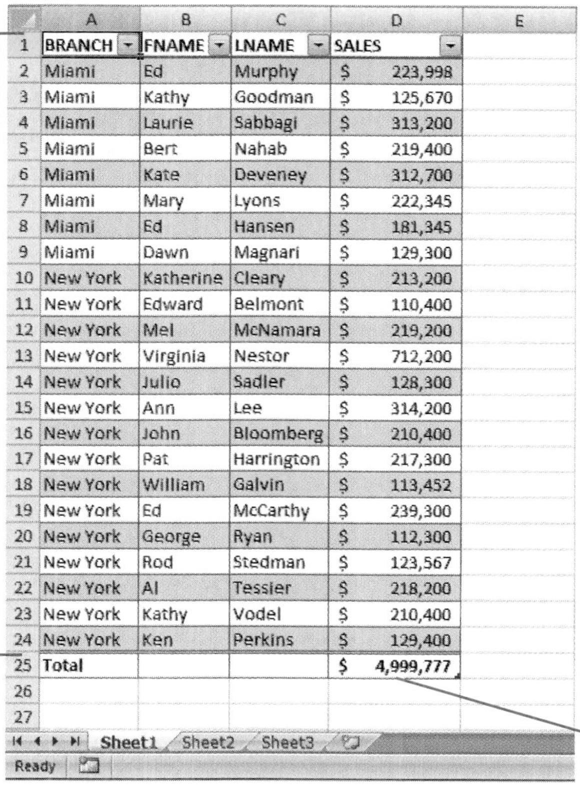

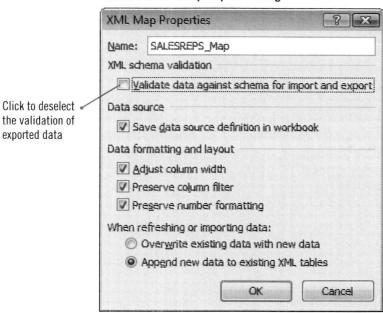

Imported data is formatted

Total sales

FIGURE N-14: **XML Map Properties dialog box**

Click to deselect the validation of exported data

Importing XML data without a schema

You can import XML data without a schema and Excel will create one for you. In this situation all of the XML elements are mapped to the Excel worksheet, and the data in all of the fields is populated using the XML file. When a schema is not used, you are unable to validate the data that is imported. You also need to delete all of the fields in the table that you will not use in the worksheet, which can be time consuming.

Running Web Queries to Retrieve External Data

Often you'll want to incorporate information from the Web into an Excel worksheet for analysis. Using Excel, you can obtain data from a Web site by running a **Web query**, then save the information in an existing or new Excel workbook. You must be connected to the Internet to run a Web query. You can save Web queries to use them again later; a saved query has an .iqy file extension. Several Web query files come with Excel. ██████ As part of an effort to summarize the North American sales for Quest, Kate needs to obtain currency rate information for the Canadian dollar to adjust the data from the Toronto and Vancouver branches. She asks you to run a Web query to obtain the most current currency rate information from the Web.

STEPS

1. **Create a new workbook, then save it as Currency Rates in the drive and folder where you store your Data Files**

TROUBLE

Depending on the size of your monitor and the Add-Ins you have installed, you might not see a Get External Data group; you may instead see a Get External Data button. If so, click the Get External Data button, then click the Existing Connections button.

2. **Click the Data tab, then click Existing Connections in the Get External Data group**

   The Existing Connections dialog box opens, with all of the connections displayed, including the queries that come with Excel.

3. **Click MSN MoneyCentral Investor Currency Rates in the Connection files on this computer area if necessary, then click Open**

   The Import Data dialog box opens, as shown in Figure N-15. Here you specify the worksheet location where you want the imported data to appear.

4. **Make sure the Existing worksheet option button is selected, click cell A1 if necessary to place =$A$1 in the Existing worksheet text box, then click OK**

   Currency rate information from the Web is placed in the workbook, as shown in Figure N-16. Kate wants you to obtain the previous closing exchange rate of the Canadian dollar.

TROUBLE

If you do not see Canadian Dollar to US Dollar in column A, choose the link that will convert Canadian currency into US currency.

5. **Click the Canadian Dollar to US Dollar link**

   A Web page opens in your browser displaying currency rate details for the Canadian dollar, as shown in Figure N-17.

6. **Close your browser window, add your name to the center header section of the worksheet, save the workbook, print the first page of the worksheet, then close the workbook and exit Excel**

Creating your own Web queries

The easiest way to retrieve data from a particular Web page on a regular basis is to create a customized Web query. Click the Data tab, click the From Web button in the Get External Data group (or click the Get External Data button and click the From Web button). In the Address text box in the New Web Query dialog box, type the address of the Web page from which you want to retrieve data, then click Go. Click the yellow arrows next to the information you want to bring into a worksheet or click the upper-left arrow to import the entire page, verify that the information that you want to import has a green checkmark next to it, then click Import. The Import Data dialog box opens and allows you to specify where you want the imported data placed in the worksheet. You can save a query for future use by clicking the Save Query button 🖳 in the New Web Query dialog box before you click Import. The query is saved as a file with an .iqy file extension.

FIGURE N-15: Import Data dialog box

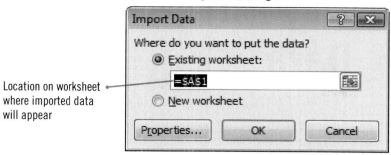

Location on worksheet where imported data will appear

FIGURE N-16: Currency rates quote

Currency rates from the Web

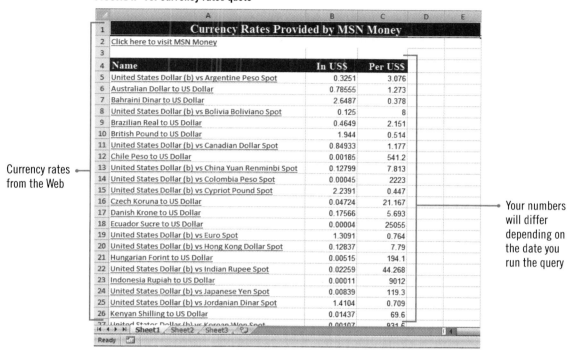

Your numbers will differ depending on the date you run the query

FIGURE N-17: Rate details for the Canadian dollar

Your values will differ depending on the date you run the query

Importing and Exporting HTML Data

Although you can open HTML files directly in Excel, most often the information that you want to include in a worksheet is published on the Web and you don't have the HTML file. In this situation you can import the HTML data by copying the data on the Web page and pasting it into an Excel worksheet. This allows you to bring in only the information that you need from the Web page to your worksheet. Once the HTML data is in your worksheet you can analyze the imported information using Excel features. You can also export worksheet data as an HTML file that can be shared on the Web. 🗃️ The Toronto and Vancouver branch managers have published the Canada branch sales information on the company intranet. Kate asks you to import the published sales data into an Excel worksheet so she can summarize it using Excel tools. She also wants you to export the summarized data to an HTML file so that it can be shared with all of the North American branch managers. You begin by copying the Canada sales information on the Web page.

STEPS

QUICK TIP
You can also open the htm file by navigating directly to your Data Files folder and double-clicking the filename.

1. **In Windows Explorer, navigate to the drive and folder containing your Data Files, double-click the EX N-6.htm file to open it in your browser, then copy the two table rows on the Web page containing the Toronto and Vancouver sales information**
    You are ready to paste the information from the Web page into an Excel worksheet

2. **Start Excel, open the file EX N-1.xlsx from the drive and folder where you store your Data Files, then save it as North America Sales**

3. **Click cell A6 on the Tour Sales by Branch sheet, click the Home tab, click the Paste list arrow in the Clipboard group, click Paste Special, click HTML in the As: list if necessary, then click OK**
    The Canada sales information is added to the U.S. sales data. You decide to total the sales and format the new data.

4. **Click the Paste Options list arrow 📋▾, select Match Destination Formatting, click cell A8, type Total, press [Tab], click the Sum button Σ in the Editing group, then press [Enter]**

5. **Select the range A5:B5, click the Format Painter button 🖌 in the Clipboard group, select the range A6:B8, then click cell A1**
    Compare your worksheet to Figure N-18. Kate is finished with the analysis and formatting of the North America branches. She wants the combined information published in a Web page.

6. **Click the Office button, then click Save As**
    The Save As dialog box opens. This dialog box allows you to specify what workbook components you want to publish.

7. **Navigate to the folder containing your Data Files, click the Save as type list arrow, click Web Page (*.htm; *.html), edit the filename to read nasales.htm, click the Selection: Sheet option button, click Publish, then click Publish again**
    The HTML file is saved in your Data Files folder.

8. **In Windows Explorer, navigate to the drive and folder containing your Data Files, then double-click the file nasales.htm**
    The HTML version of your worksheet opens in your default browser, similar to Figure N-19.

9. **Close your browser window, click the Excel window to activate it if necessary, enter your name in the center footer section of the Tour Sales by Branch worksheet, save the workbook, preview then print the worksheet, close the workbook, then exit Excel**

FIGURE N-18: Worksheet with North America sales data

Formatted table with
two rows added from
HTML file

	A	B
1	Quest U.S. Sales	
2	Branch	Sales
3	Chicago	$ 1,416,800
4	Miami	$ 1,955,258
5	New York	$ 3,271,819
6	Toronto	$ 916,800
7	Vancouver	$ 855,258
8	Total	$ 8,415,935
9		

FIGURE N-19: North America Sales as Web page

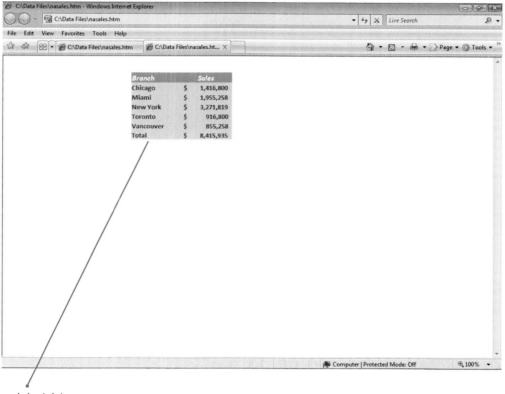

Excel worksheet data
displayed in a browser

Adding Web hyperlinks to a worksheet

In Excel worksheets, you can create hyperlinks to information on the Web. Every Web page is identified by a unique Web address called a Uniform Resource Locator (URL). To create a hyperlink to a Web page, click the cell for which you want to create a hyperlink, click the Insert tab, click the Hyperlink button in the Links group, under Link to: make sure Existing File or Web Page is selected, specify the target for the hyperlink (the URL) in the Address text box, then click OK. If there is text in the cell, the text format changes to become a blue underlined hyperlink or the color the current workbook theme uses for hyperlinks. If there is no text in the cell, the Web site's URL appears in the cell.

Practice

▼ CONCEPTS REVIEW

FIGURE N-20

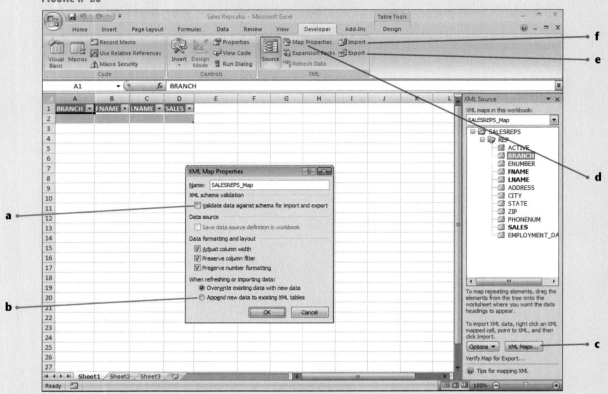

1. **Which element do you click to add a schema to an Excel workbook?**
2. **Which element do you click to bring in XML data to a workbook table?**
3. **Which element do you click to check imported XML data using the schema rules?**
4. **Which element do you click to add imported XML data below existing data in a table?**
5. **Which element do you click to save workbook data to an XML file?**
6. **Which element do you click to change the way XML data is imported and exported?**

Match each item with the statement that best describes it.

7. **iqy**
8. **Shared workbook**
9. **xsd**
10. **Change history**
11. **Password**

a. The file extension for an XML schema
b. A record of edits others have made to a worksheet
c. Used to protect a workbook from unauthorized use
d. The file extension for a Web query
e. A file used by many people on a network

Sharing Excel Files and Incorporating Web Information

Select the best answer from the list of choices.

12. Which of the following is the best example of a password for a workbook?

a. myfile

b. myFile

c. MYFILE

d. myFile08

13. Which of the following allows you to import data from the Web?

a. Web Wizard

b. Table query

c. Web query

d. Data query

14. The process of selecting XML elements to include on a worksheet is called:

a. Mapping.

b. Selecting.

c. Loading.

d. Sharing.

15. A file that describes the structure of XML data is called a:

a. Layout.

b. Query.

c. Schema.

d. Detail File.

▼ SKILLS REVIEW

1. Set up a shared workbook for multiple users.

a. Start Excel, open the file EX N-7.xlsx from the drive and folder where you store your Data Files, then save it as **Sales**.

b. Use the Share Workbook option on the Review tab to set up the workbook so that more than one person can use it at one time.

2. Track revisions in a shared workbook.

a. Change the Seattle sales to **$30,000** for the first quarter and **$40,000** for the second quarter.

b. Save the file.

c. Display the History sheet by opening the Highlight Changes dialog box, deselecting the When check box, then selecting the option for List changes on a new sheet.

d. Compare your History sheet to Figure N-21, enter your name in the History sheet footer, then print the History sheet.

e. Save and close the workbook.

FIGURE N-21

	A	B	C	D	E	F	G	H	I	J	K	L	M	N	O
1	Action Number	Date	Time	Who	Change	Sheet	Range	New Value	Old Value	Action Type	Losing Action				
2	1	10/1/2010	1:20 PM	Your Name	Cell Change	Sales	C2	$30,000.00	$21,000.00						
3	2	10/1/2010	1:20 PM	Your Name	Cell Change	Sales	D2	$40,000.00	$28,000.00						
4															
5	The history ends with the changes saved on 10/1/2010 at 1:20 PM.														
6															

3. Apply and modify passwords.

a. Open the file EX N-7.xlsx from the drive and folder where you store your Data Files, open the Save As dialog box, then open the General Options dialog box.

b. Set the password to open the workbook as **Sales10** and the password to modify it as **FirstHalf02**.

c. Save the password-protected file as **Sales PW** in the location where you store your Data Files.

d. Close the workbook.

e. Use the assigned passwords to reopen the workbook and verify that you can change it by adding your name in the center section of the Sales sheet footer, save the workbook, print the Sales worksheet, then close the workbook.

4. Work with XML schemas.

a. Create a new workbook, then save it as **Contact Information** in the drive and folder where you store your Data Files.

b. Open the XML Source pane and add the XML schema EX N-8.xsd to the workbook.

c. Map the FNAME element to cell A1 on the worksheet, LNAME to cell B1, PHONENUM to cell C1, and EMPLOYMENT_DATE to cell D1.

d. Remove the EMPLOYMENT_DATE element from the map and delete the field from the table.

e. Use the XML Map Properties dialog box to make sure imported XML data is validated using the schema.

5. **Import and export XML data.**
   a. Import the XML file EX N-9.xml into the workbook.
   b. Sort the worksheet list in ascending order by LNAME.
   c. Add the Table Style Medium 24 to the table, and compare your screen to Figure N-22.
   d. Enter your name in the center section of the worksheet footer, save the workbook, then print the table.
   e. Use the XML Map Properties dialog box to turn off the validation for imported and exported worksheet data, export the worksheet data to an XML file named **contact**, save and close the workbook, then close the XML Source pane.

FIGURE N-22

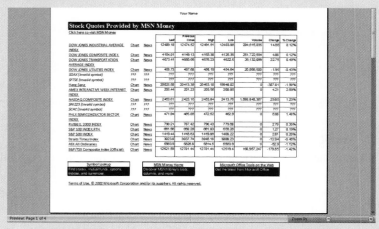

	A	B	C
1	FNAME ▼	LNAME ↓↑	PHONENUM ▼
2	Kate	Donovan	503-302-1163
3	Jane	Goodly	503-367-4156
4	Ed	Jones	503-392-8163
5	Kerry	Manney	503-722-9163
6	Laurie	Mason	503-932-9966
7	Ken	Mellon	503-272-9456
8	Bill	Neely	503-322-3163
9	Mary	Shelly	503-322-3163
10			

6. **Run Web queries to retrieve external data.**
   a. Create a new workbook, then save it as **Quotes** in the location where you store your Data Files.
   b. Use the Existing Connections dialog box to select the Web query MSN MoneyCentral Investor Major Indices.
   c. Specify that you want to place the data to cell A1 of the current worksheet.
   d. Enter your name in the center section of the worksheet header, change the page orientation to landscape, save the workbook, preview the worksheet, compare your screen to Figure N-23, then print the first page of the worksheet.
   e. Close the workbook.

FIGURE N-23

7. **Import and export HTML data.**
   a. Open the file EX N-7.xlsx from the drive and folder where you store your Data Files, then save it as **Sales_2**.
   b. Open the file EX N-10.htm in your browser from the drive and folder where you store your Data Files. Copy the data in the four rows of the Web page and paste it below the data in the Sales sheet of the Sales_2 workbook.
   c. On the Sales sheet, enter **Total** in cell A27 and use AutoSum in cell D27 to total the values in column D.
   d. Adjust the formatting for the new rows to match the other rows on the Sales sheet, add your name to the center section of the worksheet footer, save the workbook, then preview and print the Sales sheet.
   e. Save the data on the Sales sheet as an HTML file with the name **sales_2.htm**.
   f. Exit Excel, open the sales_2.htm file in your browser, print the Web page from your browser, compare your screen to Figure N-24, close your browser, close the workbook.

FIGURE N-24

▼ INDEPENDENT CHALLENGE 1

Shore College has three campuses, North, West, and South. The deans of the campuses work together on the scheduling of classes using shared Excel workbooks. As the registrar for the college, you are preparing the fall schedule as a shared workbook for the three campus deans. They will each make changes to the location data, and you will review all three workbooks and accept their changes.

a. Start Excel, open the file EX N-11.xlsx from the drive and folder where you store your Data Files, then save it as **Shore College**. The workbook has been shared so the other deans can modify it. Close the workbook.

b. Open the file EX N-12.xlsx from the drive and folder where you store your Data Files, then save it as **West Campus**. This workbook is a copy of the original that Joe Peabody has reviewed and changed.

c. Use the Accept or Reject dialog box to accept the change Joe made to the workbook. Save and close the workbook.

d. Open the file EX N-13.xlsx from the drive and folder where you store your Data Files, then save it as **North Campus**. Nancy Brown has reviewed this workbook and made a change.

e. Use the Accept or Reject dialog box to accept the change Nancy made. Save and close the workbook.

f. Open the file EX N-14.xlsx from the drive and folder where you store your Data Files, then save it as **South Campus**.

g. Use the Accept or Reject dialog box to accept the change made to the workbook by Maureen Alberto.

h. Use the Highlight Changes dialog box to highlight Maureen's change on the screen. Review the ScreenTip details.

i. Use the Highlight Changes dialog box to create a History worksheet detailing Maureen's change to the workbook. Add your name to the left section of the History sheet footer, then print the History worksheet. Save and close the workbook.

Advanced Challenge Exercise

- Open the file EX N-11.xlsx from the drive and folder where you store your Data Files, then save it as **Merged Schedule_ACE**. Notice that the locations for the first three courses are W121, N234, and S312, respectively.
- Add the Compare and Merge Workbooks command to the Quick Access Toolbar for the Merged Schedule_ACE workbook. Do not add it to the Quick Access Toolbar for all workbooks.
- Merge the files North Campus.xlsx, South Campus.xlsx, and West Campus.xlsx into the Merged Schedule workbook. Notice the new locations for the first three courses in the worksheet. Compare your merged data with Figure N-25.
- Enter your name in the Fall 2010 worksheet footer, then save the workbook.
- Print the merged 2010 worksheet, then close the workbook.

j. Exit Excel.

FIGURE N-25

	A	B	C	D	E	F
1	Code	Term	Start Time	End Time	Days	Location
2	1124	Fall 2010	8:00 a.m.	8:50 a.m.	M, W, F	W100
3	1128	Fall 2010	8:00 a.m.	8:50 a.m.	M, W, F	N200
4	1135	Fall 2010	8:00 a.m.	8:50 a.m.	M, W, F	S300
5	1140	Fall 2010	9:00 a.m.	10:15 a.m.	T, TH	W214
6	1145	Fall 2010	9:00 a.m.	10:15 a.m.	T, TH	N134
7	1151	Fall 2010	9:00 a.m.	10:15 a.m.	T, TH	S230
8	1156	Fall 2010	1:00 p.m.	1:50 p.m.	M, W, F	W101
9	1162	Fall 2010	1:00 p.m.	1:50 p.m.	M, W, F	N214
10	1167	Fall 2010	1:00 p.m.	1:50 p.m.	M, W, F	S213
11	1173	Fall 2010	3:00 p.m.	4:15 p.m.	T, TH	W132
12	1178	Fall 2010	3:00 p.m.	4:15 p.m.	T, TH	N154
13	1183	Fall 2010	3:00 p.m.	4:15 p.m.	T, TH	S215
14						

▼ INDEPENDENT CHALLENGE 2

The Montreal Athletic Club is a fitness center with five facilities in the greater Montreal area. As the general manager you are responsible for setting and publishing the membership rate information. You decide to run a special promotion offering a 10 percent discount off of the current membership prices. You will also add two new membership categories to help attract younger members. The membership rate information is published on the company Web site. You will copy the rate information from the Web page and work with it in Excel to calculate the special discounted rates. You will save the new rate information as an HTML file so it can be published on the Web.

a. Open the file EX N-15.htm from the drive and folder where you store your Data Files to display it in your browser.

b. Start Excel, create a new workbook, then save it as **Membership Rates** in the drive and folder where you store your Data Files.

▼ INDEPENDENT CHALLENGE 2 (CONTINUED)

c. Copy the five rows of data from the table in the EX N-15 file and paste them in the Membership Rates workbook. Adjust the column widths and formatting as necessary. Close the EX N-15.htm file.

d. Add the new membership data from Table N-1 in rows 6 and 7 of the worksheet.

TABLE N-1

Teen	320
Youth	150

e. Enter **Special** in cell C1 and calculate each special rate in column C by discounting the prices in column B by 10%. (*Hint*: Multiply each price by .90).

f. Format the price information in columns B and C with the Accounting format using the $ English (Canada) symbol with two decimal places.

g. Add the passwords **Members11** to open the Membership Rates workbook and **Fitness01** to modify it. Save and close the workbook, then reopen it by entering the passwords.

h. Verify that you can modify the workbook by formatting the worksheet using colors of your choice. Compare your worksheet data to Figure N-26.

i. Add your name to the center footer section of the worksheet, save the workbook, then preview and print the worksheet.

j. Save the worksheet data in HTML format using the name **prices.htm**. Close the workbook and exit Excel.

k. Open the prices.htm page in your browser and print the page.

l. Close your browser.

FIGURE N-26

	A	B	C
1	Membership	Price	Special
2	Family	$ 975.00	$ 877.50
3	Adult	$ 670.00	$ 603.00
4	Senior	$ 500.00	$ 450.00
5	College	$ 450.00	$ 405.00
6	Teen	$ 320.00	$ 288.00
7	Youth	$ 150.00	$ 135.00
8			

▼ INDEPENDENT CHALLENGE 3

You are the director of development at a local educational nonprofit institution. You are preparing the phone lists for your annual fundraising phone-a-thon. The donor information for the organization is in an XML file, which you will bring into Excel to organize. You will use an XML schema to map only the donors' names and phone numbers to the worksheet. This will allow you to import the donor data and limit the information that is distributed to the phone-a-thon volunteers. You will export your worksheet data as XML for future use.

a. Start Excel, create a new workbook, then save it as **Donors** in the drive and folder where you store your Data Files.

b. Add the map EX N-16.xsd from the drive and folder where you store your Data Files to the workbook.

c. Map the FNAME element to cell A1, LNAME to cell B1, and PHONENUM to cell C1.

d. Import the XML data in file EX N-17.xml from the drive and folder where you store your Data Files. Make sure the data is validated using the schema as it is imported.

e. Add the Table Style Medium 10 to the table. Change the field name in cell A1 to **FIRST NAME**, change the field name in cell B1 to **LAST NAME**, and change the field name in cell C1 to **PHONE NUMBER**. Widen the columns as necessary to accommodate the full field names.

f. Sort the list in ascending order by LAST NAME. Compare your sorted list to Figure N-27.

g. Export the worksheet data to an XML file named **phonelist**.

FIGURE N-27

	A	B	C
1	FIRST NAME	LAST NAME	PHONE NUMBER
2	Virginia	Alexander	312-765-8756
3	Ellen	Atkins	773-167-4156
4	Shelley	Connolly	312-322-3163
5	Bill	Duran	312-322-3163
6	Katherine	Gonzales	773-379-0092
7	Keith	Jackson	773-220-9456
8	Edward	Land	312-299-4298
9	Julio	Mendez	312-765-8756
10	Laurie	Ng	312-932-9966
11	Mel	Zoll	312-765-8756
12			

▼ INDEPENDENT CHALLENGE 3 (CONTINUED)

Advanced Challenge Exercise

- Add the map EX N-18.xsd from the drive and folder where you store your Data Files to the worksheet.
- Using the INFO_Map, map the DNUMBER element to cell A14 and LEVEL to cell B14.
- Import the XML data in file EX N-19.xml from the drive and folder where you store your Data Files.

h. Enter your name in the center section of the worksheet header, save the workbook, then print the worksheet.

i. Close the workbook and exit Excel.

▼ REAL LIFE INDEPENDENT CHALLENGE

You can track the history of a stock using published Web quotes that can be entered into Excel worksheets for analysis. To eliminate the data entry step, you will use the MSN MoneyCentral Investor Stock Quotes Web query in Excel. You will run the query from an Excel workbook using the symbol of a stock that you are interested in following. The stock information will be automatically inserted into your worksheet.

a. Start Excel, create a new workbook, then save it as **Stock Analysis** in the drive and folder where you store your Data Files.

b. Run the Web Query MSN MoneyCentral Investor Stock Quotes to obtain a quote for the stock that you are interested in. Enter the symbol for your stock in the Enter Parameter Value dialog box, as shown in Figure N-28. (*Hint*: Microsoft's symbol is MSFT. Once you run the query, you can use the Symbol Lookup hyperlink to find symbols of companies that you are interested in researching.)

c. Display the chart of your stock data by clicking the Chart link on the worksheet.

FIGURE N-28

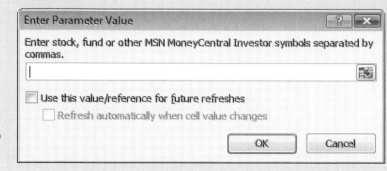

d. Print the Chart page showing the stock price history from your browser.

e. Close your browser and return to the workbook.

f. Place the name of the company that you are researching in cell A20. Use the name in cell A20 to add a hyperlink to the company's Web site. (*Hint*: Click the Insert tab, then click the Hyperlink button in the Links group.)

g. Test the link, then close the browser to return to the workbook.

h. Enter your name in the center section of the worksheet footer, save the workbook, then preview and print the worksheet in landscape orientation on one page.

i. Close the Stock Analysis workbook, saving your changes, then exit Excel.

▼ VISUAL WORKSHOP

Start Excel, create a new workbook, then save it as **Thymes.xlsx** in the drive and folder where you store your Data Files. Open the file EX N-20.htm in your browser from the drive and folder where you store your Data Files. Create the Web page shown in Figure N-29 by pasting the information from the Web page into your Thymes.xlsx file, formatting it, adding the fourth quarter information, then saving it as an HTML file named **thymes.htm.** Add your name to the footer of Sheet1 of the Thymes.xlsx workbook, and print the worksheet. Print the thymes.htm Web page from your browser. (*Hint*: The colors are in the Office theme.)

FIGURE N-29

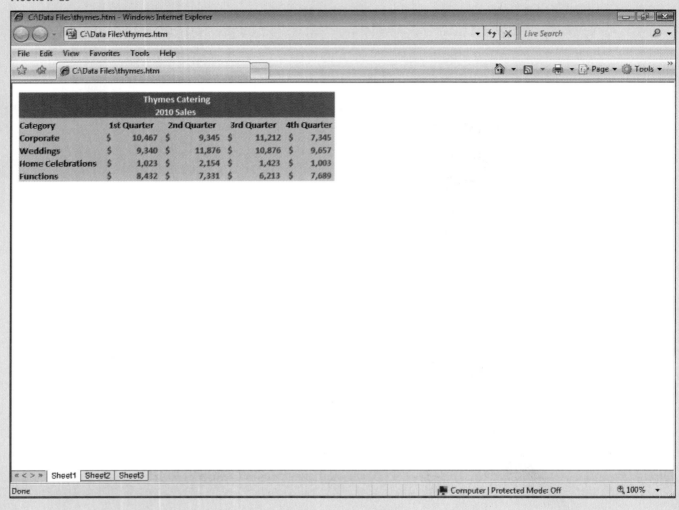

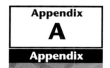
Restoring Defaults in Windows Vista and Disabling and Enabling Windows Aero

Files You Will Need:

No files needed.

Windows Vista is the most recent version of the Windows operating system. An operating system controls the way you work with your computer, supervises running programs, and provides tools for completing your computing tasks. After surveying millions of computer users, Microsoft incorporated their suggestions to make Windows Vista secure, reliable, and easy to use. In fact, Windows Vista is considered the most secure version of Windows yet. Other improvements include a powerful new search feature that lets you quickly search for files and programs from the Start menu and most windows, tools that simplify accessing the Internet, especially with a wireless connection, and multimedia programs that let you enjoy, share, and organize music, photos, and recorded TV. Finally, Windows Vista offers lots of visual appeal with its transparent, three-dimensional design in the Aero experience. This appendix explains how to make sure you are using the Windows Vista default settings for appearance, personalization, security, hardware, and sound and to enable and disable Windows Aero. For more information on Windows Aero, go to *www.microsoft.com/windowsvista/experiences/aero.mspx*.

OBJECTIVES

Restore the defaults in the Appearance and Personalization section

Restore the defaults in the Security section

Restore the defaults in the Hardware and Sound section

Disable Windows Aero

Enable Windows Aero

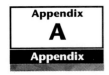

Appendix
A
Appendix

Restoring the Defaults in the Appearance and Personalization Section

The following instructions require a default Windows Vista Ultimate installation and the student logged in with an Administrator account. All of the following settings can be changed by accessing the Control Panel.

STEPS

- To restore the defaults in the Personalization section

  1. Click Start, and then click Control Panel. Click Appearance and Personalization, click Personalization, and then compare your screen to Figure A-1

  2. In the Personalization window, click Windows Color and Appearance, select the Default color, and then click OK

  3. In the Personalization window, click Mouse Pointers. In the Mouse Properties dialog box, on the Pointers tab, select Windows Aero (system scheme) in the Scheme drop-down list, and then click OK

  4. In the Personalization window, click Theme. Select Windows Vista from the Theme drop-down list, and then click OK

  5. In the Personalization window, click Display Settings. In the Display Settings dialog box, drag the Resolution bar to 1024 by 768 pixels, and then click OK

FIGURE A-1

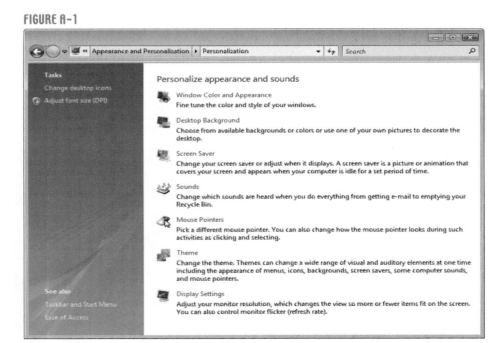

- To restore the defaults in the Taskbar and Start Menu section
  1. Click Start, and then click Control Panel. Click Appearance and Personalization, click Taskbar and Start Menu, and then compare your screen to Figure A-2
  2. In the Taskbar and Start Menu Properties dialog box, on the Taskbar tab, click to select all checkboxes except for "Auto-hide the taskbar"
  3. On the Start Menu tab, click to select the Start menu radio button and check all items in the Privacy section
  4. In the System icons section on the Notification Area tab, click to select all of the checkboxes except for "Power"
  5. On the Toolbars tab, click to select Quick Launch, none of the other items should be checked
  6. Click OK to close the Taskbar and Start Menu Properties dialog box

- To restore the defaults in the Folder Options section
  1. Click Start, and then click Control Panel. Click Appearance and Personalization, click Folder Options, and then compare your screen to Figure A-3
  2. In the Folder Options dialog box, on the General tab, click to select Show preview and filters in the Tasks section, click to select Open each folder in the same window in the Browse folders section, and click to select Double-click to open an item (single-click to select) in the Click items as follows section
  3. On the View tab, click the Reset Folders button, and then click Yes in the Folder views dialog box. Then click the Restore Defaults button
  4. On the Search tab, click the Restore Defaults button
  5. Click OK to close the Folder Options dialog box

- To restore the defaults in the Windows Sidebar Properties section
  1. Click Start, and then click Control Panel. Click Appearance and Personalization, click Windows Sidebar Properties, and then compare your screen to Figure A-4
  2. In the Windows Sidebar Properties dialog box, on the Sidebar tab, click to select Start Sidebar when Windows starts. In the Arrangement section, click to select Right, and then click to select 1 in the Display Sidebar on monitor drop-down list
  3. Click OK to close the Windows Sidebar Properties dialog box

FIGURE A-2

FIGURE A-3

FIGURE A-4

Restoring the Defaults in the Security Section

The following instructions require a default Windows Vista Ultimate installation and the student logged in with an Administrator account. All of the following settings can be changed by accessing the Control Panel.

STEPS

- To restore the defaults in the Windows Firewall section
    1. Click Start, and then click Control Panel. Click Security, click Windows Firewall, and then compare your screen to Figure A-5
    2. In the Windows Firewall dialog box, click Change settings. If the User Account Control dialog box appears, click Continue
    3. In the Windows Firewall Settings dialog box, click the Advanced tab. Click Restore Defaults, then click Yes in the Restore Defaults Confirmation dialog box
    4. Click OK to close the Windows Firewall Settings dialog box, and then close the Windows Firewall window

- To restore the defaults in the Internet Options section
    1. Click Start, and then click Control Panel. Click Security, click Internet Options, and then compare your screen to Figure A-6
    2. In the Internet Properties dialog box, on the General tab, click the Use default button. Click the Settings button in the Tabs section, and then click the Restore defaults button in the Tabbed Browsing Settings dialog box. Click OK to close the Tabbed Browsing Settings dialog box
    3. On the Security tab of the Internet Properties dialog box, click to uncheck the Enable Protected Mode checkbox, if necessary. Click the Default level button in the Security level for this zone section. If possible, click the Reset all zones to default level button
    4. On the Programs tab, click the Make default button in the Default web browser button for Internet Explorer, if possible. If Office is installed, Microsoft Office Word should be selected in the HTML editor drop-down list
    5. On the Advanced tab, click the Restore advanced settings button in the Settings section. Click the Reset button in the Reset Internet Explorer settings section, and then click Reset in the Reset Internet Explorer Settings dialog box
    6. Click Close to close the Reset Internet Explorer Settings dialog box, and then click OK to close the Internet Properties dialog box

FIGURE A-5

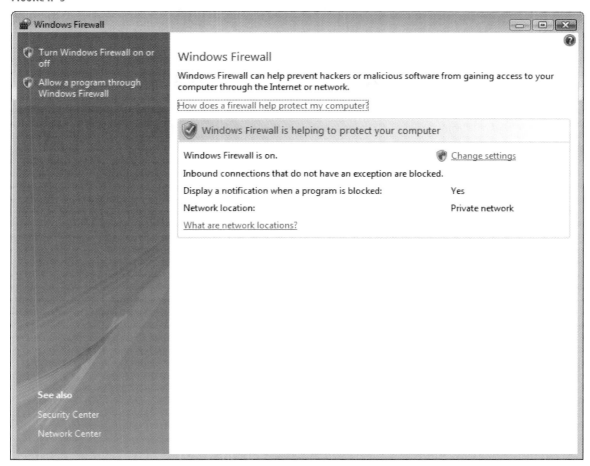

FIGURE A-6

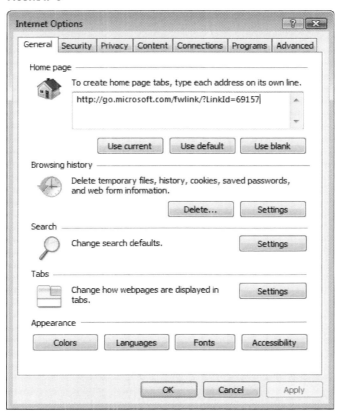

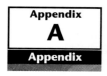

Restoring the Defaults in the Hardware and Sound Section

The following instructions require a default Windows Vista Ultimate installation and the student logged in with an Administrator account. All of the following settings can be changed by accessing the Control Panel.

STEPS

- To restore the defaults in the Autoplay section

    1. Click Start, and then click Control Panel. Click Hardware and Sound, click Autoplay, and then compare your screen to Figure A-7. Scroll down and click the Reset all defaults button in the Devices section at the bottom of the window, and then click Save

- To restore the defaults in the Sound section

    1. Click Start, and then click Control Panel. Click Hardware and Sound, click Sound, and then compare your screen to Figure A-8

    2. In the Sound dialog box, on the Sounds tab, select Windows Default from the Sound Scheme drop-down list, and then click OK

- To restore the defaults in the Mouse section

    1. Click Start, and then click Control Panel. Click Hardware and Sound, click Mouse, and then compare your screen to Figure A-9

    2. In the Mouse Properties dialog box, on the Pointers tab, select Windows Aero (system scheme) from the Scheme drop-down list

    3. Click OK to close the Mouse Properties dialog box

FIGURE A-7

FIGURE A-8

FIGURE A-9

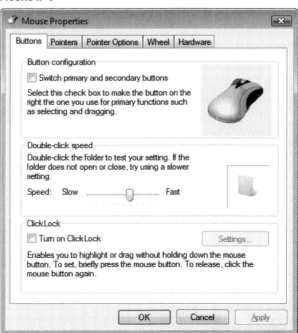

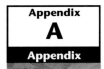
Disabling and Enabling Windows Aero

Unlike prior versions of Windows, Windows Vista provides two distinct user interface experiences: a "basic" experience for entry-level systems and more visually dynamic experience called Windows Aero. Both offer a new and intuitive navigation experience that helps you more easily find and organize your applications and files, but Aero goes further by delivering a truly next-generation desktop experience.

Windows Aero builds on the basic Windows Vista user experience and offers Microsoft's best-designed, highest-performing desktop experience. Using Aero requires a PC with compatible graphics adapter and running a Premium or Business edition of Windows Vista.

The following instructions require a computer capable of running Windows Aero, with a default Windows Vista Ultimate installation and student logged in with an Administrator account.

STEPS

- **To Disable Windows Aero**

We recommend that students using this book disable Windows Aero and restore their operating systems default settings (instructions to follow).

1. **Right-click the desktop, select** Personalize, **and then compare your screen in Figure A-10. Select** Window Color and Appearance, **and then select** Open classic appeareance properties for more color options. **In Appearance Settings dialog box, on the Appearance tab, select any non-Aero scheme (such as** Windows Vista Basic **or** Windows Vista Standard) **in the Color Scheme list, and then click OK. Figure A-11 compares Windows Aero to other color schemes. Note that this book uses Windows Vista Basic as the color scheme**

- **To Enable Windows Aero**

1. **Right-click the desktop, and then select** Personalize. **Select** Window Color and Appearance, **then select** Windows Aero **in the Color scheme list, and then click OK in the Appearance Settings dialog box**

FIGURE A-10

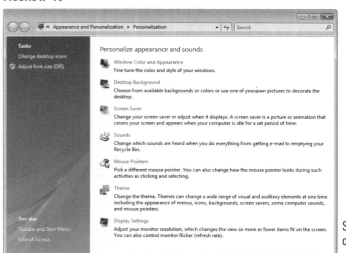

FIGURE A-11

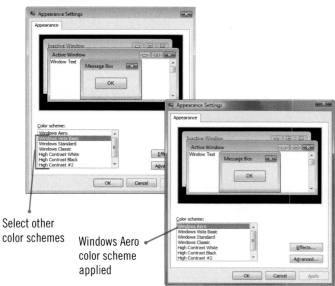

Select other color schemes

Windows Aero color scheme applied

Glossary

3-D reference A reference that uses values on other sheets or workbooks, effectively creating another dimension to a workbook.

Absolute cell reference In a formula, type of cell address that does not change when you copy the formula; indicated by a dollar sign before the column letter and/or row number. *See also* Relative cell reference.

Accessories Simple programs to perform specific tasks that come with Windows Vista, such as the Calculator for performing calculations.

Active The currently available document, program, or object; on the taskbar, the button of the active document appears in a darker shade while the buttons of other open documents are dimmed.

Active cell The cell in which you are currently working.

Active window The window you are currently using.

Add-in A supplementary program that provides additional program features; for example, the Solver add-in enables you to find a solution to a calculation that has several inputs; the Analysis ToolPak provides optional Excel features. To activate an add-in, click the Office button, click Excel options, click Add-Ins, then click Go. Select or deselect add-ins from the list.

Address Bar A horizontal box near the top of a window that shows your current location in the computer's file hierarchy as a series of links separated by arrows; used to navigate to other locations on your computer.

Alignment The placement of cell contents; for example, left, center, or right.

AND condition A filtering feature that searches for records by specifying that all entered criteria must be matched.

Apply (a template) To open a document based on an Excel template.

Argument In the Visual Basic for Applications (VBA) programming language, variable used in procedures that a main procedure might run. *See also* Main procedure.

Arithmetic operators In a formula, symbols that perform mathematical calculations, such as plus (+), minus (–), multiplication (*), division (/), or exponentiation (^).

Ascending order In sorting worksheet records, the lowest value (the beginning of the alphabet, or the earliest date) appears at the beginning of the sorted data.

ASCII file A text file that contains data but no formatting; instead of being divided into columns, ASCII file data are separated, or delimited, by tabs or commas.

Attributes Styling characteristics such as bold, italic, and underlining that you can apply to change the way text and numbers look in a worksheet or chart. In XML, the components that provides information about the document's elements.

Auditing An Excel feature that helps track errors and check worksheet logic.

AutoComplete In the Visual Basic for Applications (VBA) programming language, a list of words that appears as you enter code; helps you automatically enter elements with the correct syntax.

AutoFill Options button Feature that lets you fill cells with specific elements (such as formatting) of the copied cell.

AutoFilter A table feature that lets you click a list arrow and select criteria by which to display certain types of records; *also called* filter.

AutoFilter list arrows List arrows that appear next to field names in an Excel table; used to display portions of your data. *Also called* filter list arrows.

AutoFit A feature that automatically adjusts the width of a column or the height of a row to accommodate its widest or tallest entry.

Backsolving A problem-solving method in which you specify a solution and then find the input value that produces the answer you want; sometimes described as a what-if analysis in reverse. In Excel, the Goal Seek feature performs backsolving.

Backup A duplicate copy of a file that is stored in another location.

Backward-compatible Software feature that enables documents saved in an older version of a program to be opened in a newer version of the program.

Banding Worksheet formatting in which adjacent rows and columns are formatted differently.

Boolean filter A word or symbol for locating programs, folders, and files by specifying one or more criteria so that you have a greater chance of finding what you need.

Booting A process that Windows steps through to get the computer up and running.

Bug In programming, an error that causes a procedure to run incorrectly.

Byte One character of storage space on disk or in RAM.

Calculated columns In a table, a column that uses one formula that automatically adjusts to accommodate additional rows.

Calculation operators Symbols that indicate what type of calculation to perform on the cells, ranges or values.

Category axis Horizontal axis of a chart, usually containing the names of data groups; in a 2-dimensional chart, also known as the x-axis.

Cell The intersection of a column and a row in a worksheet, datasheet, or table.

Cell address The location of a cell, expressed by cell coordinates; for example, the cell address of the cell in column A, row 1 is A1.

Cell comments Notes you've written about a workbook that appear when you place the pointer over a cell.

Cell pointer A dark rectangle that outlines the active cell.

Cell styles Predesigned combinations of formatting attributes that can be applied to selected cells, to enhance the look of a worksheet.

Change history A worksheet containing a list of changes made to a shared workbook.

Changing cells In what-if analysis, cells that contain the values that change in order to produce multiple sets of results.

Chart sheet A separate sheet in a workbook that contains only a chart, which is linked to the workbook data.

Charts Pictorial representations of worksheet data that make it easier to see patterns, trends, and relationships; *also called* graphs.

Check box A box that turns an option on when checked or off when unchecked.

Click To quickly press and release the left button on the pointing device; also called single-click.

Clip A media file, such as art, sound, animation, or a movie.

Clip art A graphic image, such as a corporate logo, a picture, or a photo, that can be inserted into a document.

Clipboard Temporary storage area in Windows.

Code *See* Program code.

Code window In the Visual Basic Editor, the window that displays the selected module's procedures, written in the Visual Basic programming language.

Collapse button A button that shrinks a portion of a dialog box to hide some settings.

Color scale In conditional formatting, a formatting scheme that uses a set of two, three, or four fill colors to convey relative values of data.

Column heading Identifies the column letter, such as A, B, etc.; located above each column in a worksheet.

Command An instruction to perform a task.

Command button A button that completes or cancels an operation.

Comments In a Visual Basic procedure, notes that explain the purpose of the macro or procedure; they are preceded by a single apostrophe and appear in green. *See also* Cell comments.

Comparison operators In a calculation, symbols that compare values for the purpose of true/false results.

Compatible The capability of different programs to work together and exchange data.

Complex formula A formula that uses more than one arithmetic operator.

Compress To reduce the size of file so that it takes up less storage space on a disk.

Computer window The window shows the drives on your computer as well as other installed hardware components.

Conditional format A type of cell formatting that changes based on the cell's value or the outcome of a formula.

Consolidate To combine data on multiple worksheets and display the result on another worksheet.

Constraints Limitations or restrictions on input data in what-if analysis.

Contextual tab Tab on the Ribbon that appears when needed to complete a specific task; for example, if you select a chart in an Excel workbook, three contextual Chart Tool tabs (Design, Layout, and Format) appear.

Copy To make a duplicate copy of a file that is stored in another location.

Criteria range In advanced filtering, a cell range containing one row of labels (usually a copy of column labels) and at least one additional row underneath it that contains the criteria you want to match.

Custom chart type A specially formatted Excel chart.

Data entry area The unlocked portion of a worksheet where users are able to enter and change data.

Data label Descriptive text that appears above a data marker in a chart.

Data marker A graphical representation of a data point, such as a bar or column.

Data point Individual piece of data plotted in a chart.

Data series A column or row in a datasheet. Also, the selected range in a worksheet that Excel converts into a chart.

Data source Worksheet data used to create a chart or a PivotTable.

Data table A range of cells that shows the resulting values when one or more input values are varied in a formula; when one input value is changed, the table is called a one-input data table, and when two input values are changed, it is called a two-input data table. In a chart, it is a grid containing the chart data.

Data validation A feature that allows you to specify what data is allowable (valid) for a range of cells.

Database An organized collection of related information. In Excel, a database is called a table.

Debug In programming, to find and correct an error in code.

Declare In the Visual Basic programming language, to assign a type, such as numeric or text, to a variable.

Default A setting that is built into a program that is used by that program until you change the setting.

Delete To remove a folder or file.

Delimiter A separator such as a space, comma, or semicolon between elements in imported data.

Dependent cell A cell, usually containing a formula, whose value changes depending on the values in the input cells. For example, a payment formula or function that depends on an input cell containing changing interest rates is a dependent cell.

Descending order In sorting an Excel table, the order that begins with the letter Z or the highest number in a table.

Desktop The graphical user interface (GUI) displayed on your screen after you start Windows that you use to interact with Windows and other software on your computer.

Destination program In a data exchange, the program that will receive the data.

Details Pane A pane located at the bottom of a window that displays information about the selected disk, drive, folder, or file.

Device A hardware component in your computer system.

Dialog box A type of window in which you specify how you want to complete an operation.

Dialog box launcher An icon available in many groups on the Ribbon that you can click to open a dialog box or task pane, offering an alternative way to choose commands.

Document To make notes about basic worksheet assumptions, complex formulas, or questionable data. In a macro, to insert comments that explain the Visual Basic code.

Document window The portion of a program window that displays all or part of an open document.

Documents folder The folder on your hard drive used to store most of the files you create or receive from others.

Double-click To quickly click the left button on the pointing device twice.

Drag To point to an object, press and hold the left button on the pointing device, move the object to a new location, and then release the left button.

Drag and drop To use a pointing device to move or copy a file or folder to a new location.

Drive A physical location on your computer where you can store files.

Drive name A name for a drive that consists of a letter followed by a colon, such as C: for the hard disk drive.

Drop-down list button A button that opens a list with one or more options from which you can choose.

Dynamic page breaks In a larger workbook, horizontal or vertical dashed lines that represent the place where pages print separately. They also adjust automatically when you insert or delete rows or columns, or change column widths or row heights.

Edit (Excel) To make a change to the contents of an active cell. (Windows) To make changes to a file.

Electronic spreadsheet A computer program that performs calculations and presents numeric data.

Element An XML component that defines the document content.

Embed To insert a copy of data into a destination document; you can double-click the embedded object to modify it using the tools of the source program.

Embedded chart A chart displayed as an object in a worksheet.

Expand button A button that extends a dialog box to display additional settings.

Exploding pie slice A slice of a pie chart that has been pulled away from the whole pie, in order to add emphasis.

Extensible Markup Language (XML) A system for defining languages using tags to structure data.

External reference indicator The exclamation point (!) used in a formula to indicate that a referenced cell is outside the active sheet.

Extract To place a copy of a filtered table in a range you specify in the Advanced Filter dialog box.

Field In a table (an Excel database), a column that describes a characteristic about records, such as first name or city.

Field name A column label that describes a field.

File A collection of stored electronic data, such as text, pictures, video, music, and programs.

File extension Additional characters assigned by a program added to the end of a filename to identify the type of file.

File hierarchy The structure for organizing folders and files; describes the logic and layout of the folder structure on a disk.

File management A strategy for organizing folders and files.

Filename A unique, descriptive name for a file that identifies the file's content. A filename can be no more than 255 characters, including spaces, and can include letters, numbers, and certain symbols.

Filter To display data in an Excel table that meet specified criteria. *See also* AutoFilter.

Filter arrows *See* AutoFilter list arrows.

Folder A container for a group of related files. A folder may contain subfolders for organizing files into smaller groups.

Folder name A unique, descriptive name for a folder that identifies what you store in that folder.

Font The typeface or design of a set of characters (letters, numerals, symbols, and punctuation marks).

Font size The size of characters, measured in units called points (pts).

Format (n.) The appearance of text and numbers, including color, font, attributes, borders, and shading. *See also* Number format. (v.) To enhance or improve the appearance of a document.

Format bar A toolbar in the WordPad window that displays buttons for formatting, or enhancing, the appearance of a document.

Formula bar The area above the worksheet grid where you enter or edit data in the active cell.

Formula A set of instructions used to perform one or more numeric calculations, such as adding, multiplying, or averaging, on values or cells.

Formula prefix An arithmetic symbol, such as the equal sign (=), used to start a formula.

Freeze To hold in place selected columns or rows when scrolling in a worksheet that is divided in panes. *See also* Panes.

Function (Excel)A built-in formula that includes the information necessary to calculate an answer; for example, SUM (for calculating a sum) or FV (for calculating the future value of an investment) (Visual Basic) In the Visual Basic for Applications (VBA) programming language, a predefined procedure that returns a value, such as the InputBox function that prompts the user to enter information.

Gadget A mini-program on the Windows Sidebar for performing an every day task, such as the Clock gadget for viewing the current time.

Gallery A collection of choices you can browse through to make a selection. Often available with Live Preview.

Gigabyte (GB or G) One billion bytes (or one thousand megabytes).

Goal cell In backsolving, a cell containing a formula in which you can substitute values to find a specific value, or goal.

Goal Seek A problem-solving method in which you specify a solution and then find the input value that produces the answer you want; sometimes described as a what-if analysis in reverse; also called backsolving.

Gridlines Evenly spaced horizontal and/or vertical lines used in a worksheet or chart to make it easier to read.

Group On the Ribbon, a set of related commands on a tab.

Hard copy A paper copy of a file.

Hard disk A built-in, high-capacity, high-speed storage medium for all the software, folders, and files on a computer.

Header row In a table, the first row that contains the field names.

Hotspot An object that, when clicked, will run a macro or open a file.

HTML Hypertext Markup Language, the format of pages that a Web browser can read.

Hyperlink An object (a filename, a word, a phrase, or a graphic) in a worksheet that, when you click it, displays another worksheet or a Web page called the target. *See also* Target.

Icon A small image on the desktop or in a window that represents a tool, resource, folder, or file you can open and use.

Icon sets In conditional formatting, groups of images that are used to visually communicate relative cell values based on the values they contain.

If...Then...Else statement In the Visual Basic programming language, a conditional statement that directs Excel to perform specified actions under certain conditions; its syntax is "If *condition* Then *statements* Else [*elsestatements*].

Inactive window An open window you are not currently using.

Input Information that produces desired results, or output, in a worksheet.

Input cells Spreadsheet cells that contain data instead of formulas and that act as input to a what-if analysis; input values often change to produce different results. Examples include interest rates, prices, or other data.

Input values In a data table, the variable values that are substituted in the table's formula to obtain varying results, such as interest rates.

Insertion point A blinking vertical line that appears when you click in the formula bar; indicates where new text will be inserted.

Instance A worksheet in its own workbook window.

Instant Search A Windows tool you use to quickly find a folder or file on your computer.

Integrate To incorporate a document and parts of a document created in one program into another program; for example, to incorporate an Excel chart into a PowerPoint slide, or an Access table into a Word document.

Integration A process in which data is exchanged among Excel and other Windows programs; can include pasting, importing, exporting, embedding, and linking.

Interface The look and feel of a program; for example, the appearance of commands and the way they are organized in the program window.

Intranet An internal network site used by a group of people who work together.

Keyboard shortcut A key or a combination of keys that you press to perform a command.

Keyword (Excel) Terms added to a workbook's Document Properties that help locate the file in a search. (Macros) In a macro procedure, a word that is recognized as part of the Visual Basic programming language. (Windows) A descriptive word or phrase you enter to obtain a list of results that include that word or phrase.

Kilobyte (KB or K) One thousand bytes.

Labels Descriptive text or other information that identifies rows, columns, or chart data, but is not included in calculations.

Landscape orientation Print setting that positions a document so it spans the widest margins of the page, making the page wider than it is tall.

Launch To open or start a program on your computer.

Legend In a chart, information that explains how data is represented by colors or patterns.

Linear trendline In an Excel chart, a straight line representing an overall trend in a data series.

Link (Windows) A shortcut for opening a Help topic or a Web site. (Office) To insert an object into a destination program; the information you insert will be updated automatically when the data in the source document changes.

Linking The dynamic referencing of data in other workbooks, so that when data in the other workbooks is changed, the references in the current workbook are automatically updated.

List arrows *See* AutoFilter list arrows.

List box A box that displays a list of options from which you can choose (you may need to scroll and adjust your view to see additional options in the list).

Live Preview A feature that lets you point to a choice in a gallery or palette and see the results in the document without actually clicking the choice.

Live taskbar thumbnails A Windows Aero feature that displays a small image of the content within open, but not visible windows, including live content such as video.

Live view A file icon that displays the actual content in a file on the icon.

Lock (Windows) To lock your user account, then display the Welcome screen. (Excel) To secure a row, column, or sheet so that data in that location cannot be changed.

Lock button A Start menu option that locks your computer.

Lock menu button A Start menu option that displays a list of shut-down options.

Log Off To close all windows, programs, and documents, then display the Welcome screen.

Logical conditions Using the operators And and Or to narrow a custom filter criteria.

Logical formula A formula with calculations that are based on stated conditions.

Logical test The first part of an IF function; if the logical test is true, then the second part of the function is applied, and if it is false, then the third part of the function is applied.

Macro A set of instructions recorded or written in the Visual Basic programming language; used to automate worksheet tasks.

Main procedure A macro procedure containing several macros that run sequentially.

Manual calculation option An option that turns off automatic calculation of worksheet formulas, allowing you to selectively determine if and when you want Excel to perform calculations.

Map An XML schema that is attached to a workbook.

Map an XML element A process in which XML element names are placed on an Excel worksheet in specific locations.

Maximized window A window that fills the desktop.

Megabyte (MB or M) One million bytes (or one thousand kilobytes).

Menu A list of related commands.

Menu bar A horizontal bar in a window that displays menu names that represent categories of related commands.

Metadata Information that describes data and is used in Microsoft Windows document searches.

Microsoft Windows Vista An operating system.

Minimized window A window that shrinks to a button on the taskbar.

Mixed reference Cell reference that combines both absolute and relative addressing.

Mode In dialog boxes, a state that offers a limited set of possible choices.

Mode indicator An area in the lower-left corner of the status bar that informs you of a program's status. For example, when you are entering or changing the contents of a cell, the word 'Edit' appears.

Model A worksheet used to produce a what-if analysis that acts as the basis for multiple outcomes.

Modeless Describes dialog boxes that, when opened, allow you to select other elements on a chart or worksheet to change the dialog box options and format, or otherwise alter the selected elements.

Module In Visual Basic, a module is stored in a workbook and contains macro procedures.

Move To change the location of a file by physically placing it in another location.

Multilevel sort A reordering of table data using more than one column at a time.

Multitask To perform several tasks at the same time.

Name box Left-most area of the formula bar that shows the cell reference or name of the active cell.

Named range A contiguous group of cells given a meaningful name such as "July Sales"; it retains its name when moved and can be referenced in a formula.

Navigate To move around in a worksheet; for example, you can use the arrow keys on the keyboard to navigate from cell to cell, or press [Page Up] or [Page Down] to move a screen at a time.

Navigation Pane A pane on the left side of a window that contains links to your personal folders, including the Documents, Pictures, and Music folders.

Normal view Default worksheet view that shows the worksheet without features such as headers and footers; ideal for creating and editing a worksheet, but may not be detailed enough when formatting a document.

Notification area An area on the right side of the taskbar that displays the current time as well as icons for open programs, connecting to the Internet, and checking problems identified by Windows Vista.

Number format A format applied to values to express numeric concepts, such as currency, date, and percentage.

Object A chart or graphic image that can be moved and resized and contains handles when selected. In object linking and embedding (OLE), the data to be exchanged between another document or program. In Visual Basic, every Excel element, including ranges.

Object Linking and Embedding (OLE) A Microsoft Windows technology that allows you to transfer data from one document and program to another using embedding or linking.

OLE *See* Object Linking and Embedding.

One-input data table A range of cells that shows resulting values when one input value in a formula is changed.

Online collaboration The ability to incorporate feedback or share information across the Internet or a company network or intranet.

Operating system Software that manages the complete operation of your computer.

Option button A small circle you click to select only one of two or more related options.

Or condition The records in a search must match only one of the criterion.

Outline symbols In outline view, the buttons that, when clicked, change the amount of detail in the outlined worksheet.

Output The end result of a worksheet.

Output values In a data table, the calculated results that appear in the body of the table.

Page Break Preview A worksheet view that displays page break indicators which you can drag to include more or less information on each page in a worksheet.

Page Layout View Provides an accurate view of how a worksheet will look when printed, including headers and footers.

Panes Sections into which you can divide a worksheet when you want to work on separate parts of the worksheet at the same time;

one pane freezes, or remains in place, while you scroll in another pane until you see the desired information.

Paste Options button   Allows you to paste only specific elements of the copied selection, such as the formatting or values.

Personal macro workbook   A workbook that can contain macros that are available to any open workbook. By default, the personal macro workbook is hidden.

PivotChart report   An Excel feature that lets you summarize worksheet data in the form of a chart in which you can rearrange, or "pivot," parts of the chart structure to explore new data relationships.

PivotTable   Interactive table format that lets you summarize worksheet data.

PivotTable Field List   A window containing fields that can be used to create or modify a PivotTable.

PivotTable report   An Excel feature that allows you to summarize worksheet data in the form of a table in which you can rearrange, or "pivot," parts of the table structure to explore new data relationships; also called a PivotTable.

Plot   The Excel process that converts numerical information into data points on a chart.

Plot area   In a chart, the area inside the horizontal and vertical axes.

Point   (n.) A unit of measure used for fonts and row height. One inch equals 72 points, or a point is equal to $1/72^{nd}$ of an inch. (v.) To position the tip of the pointer over an object, option, or item.

Pointer   A small arrow or other symbol on the screen that moves in the same direction as the pointing device.

Pointing device   A hardware device, such as a mouse, trackball, touch pad, or pointing stick, or an onscreen object for interacting with your computer and the software you are using.

Populate a worksheet with XML data   The process of importing an XML file and filling the mapped elements on the worksheet with data from the XML file.

Portrait orientation   A print setting that positions the document on the page so the page is taller than it is wide.

Post   To place an interactive workbook in a shared location.

Power button   A Start menu option that puts your computer to sleep (your computer appears off and uses very little power).

Precedents   In formula auditing, the cells that are used in the formula to calculate the value of a given cell.

Presentation graphics program   A program such as Microsoft PowerPoint that you can use to create slide show presentations.

Preview Pane   A pane on the right side of a window that shows the actual contents of a selected file without opening a program. Preview may not work for some types of files.

Previewing   Prior to printing, to see onscreen exactly how the printed document will look.

Primary Key   The field in a database that contains unique information for each record.

Print area   A portion of a worksheet that you can define using the Print Area button on the Page Layout tab; after you select and define a print area, the Quick Print feature prints only that worksheet area.

Print Preview   A full-page view of a document that you can use to check its layout before you print.

Print title   In a table that spans more than one page, the field names that print at the top of every printed page.**Procedure**   A sequence of Visual Basic statements contained in a macro that accomplishes a specific task.

Procedure footer   In Visual Basic, the last line of a Sub procedure.

Procedure header   The first line in a Visual Basic procedure, it defines the procedure type, name, and arguments.

Program code   Macro instructions, written in the Visual Basic for Applications (VBA) programming language.

Program tab   Single tab on the Ribbon specific to a particular view, such as Print Preview.

Project   In the Visual Basic Editor, the equivalent of a workbook; a project contains Visual Basic modules.

Project Explorer   In the Visual Basic Editor, a window that lists all open projects (or workbooks) and the worksheets and modules they contain.

Properties   1) Characteristics or settings of a component of the graphical user interface; 2) File characteristics, such as the author's name, keywords, or the title, that help others understand, identify, and locate the file.

Properties window   In the Visual Basic Editor, the window that displays a list of characteristics, or properties, associated with a module.

Property In Visual Basic, an attribute of an object that describes its character or behavior.

Publish To place an Excel workbook or worksheet on a Web site or an intranet in HTML format so that others can access it using their Web browsers.

Quick Access toolbar Customizable toolbar that includes buttons for common Office commands, such as saving a file and undoing an action.

Quick Launch toolbar A toolbar on the left side of the taskbar; includes buttons for showing the desktop when it is not currently visible, switching between windows, and starting the Internet Explorer Web browser.

RAM (Random Access Memory) The physical location used to temporarily store open programs and documents.

Range A selection of two or more cells, such as B5:B14.

Range object In Visual Basic, an object that represents a cell or a range of cells.

Read-only format Data that users can view but not change.

Record In a table (an Excel database), data about an object or a person.

Recycle Bin A desktop object that stores folders and files you delete from your hard drive(s) and that enables you to restore them.

Reference operators Mathematical calculations which enable you to use ranges in calculations.

Refresh To update a PivotTable so it reflects changes to the underlying data.

Regression analysis A way of representing data with a mathematically-calculated trendline showing the overall trend represented by the data.

Relative cell reference In a formula, type of cell addressing that automatically changes when the formula is copied or moved, to reflect the new location; default type of referencing used in Excel worksheets. *See also* Absolute cell referencing.

Removable storage Storage media that you can easily transfer from one computer to another, such as DVDs, CDs, or flash drives.

Report filter A feature that allows you to specify the ranges you want summarized in a PivotTable.

Resizing button A button that you use to adjust the size of a window, such as Maximize, Restore Down, and Minimize.

Restart To shut down your computer, then start it again.

Return In a function, to display.

Ribbon Area that displays commands for the current Office program, organized into tabs and groups.

Right-click To quickly press and release the right button on the pointing device.

Ruler A horizontal bar in the WordPad window that marks a document's width in 1/8ths of an inch (also shows one-inch marks).

Run To play, as a macro.

Scenario A set of values you use to forecast results; the Excel Scenario Manager lets you store and manage different scenarios.

Scenario summary An Excel table that compiles data from various scenarios so that you can view the scenario results next to each other for easy comparison.

Schema In an XML document, a list of the fields, called elements or attributes, and their characteristics.

Scope In a named cell or range, the worksheets where the name can be used.

Screen capture A snapshot of your screen, as if you took a picture of it with a camera, which you can paste into a document.

Scroll To adjust your view in a window.

Scroll arrow button A button at each end of a scroll bar for adjusting your view in small increments in that direction.

Scroll bar A vertical or horizontal bar that appears along the right or bottom side of a window when there is more content than can be displayed within the window so that you can adjust your view.

Scroll box A box in a scroll bar that you can drag to display a different part of a window.

Search criteria (Windows) One or more pieces of information that helps Windows identify the program, folder, or file you want to locate. (Excel) In a workbook or table search, the text you are searching for.

Share *See* Shared workbook.

Shared workbook An Excel workbook that several users can open and modify at the same time.

Sheet tab Identifies sheets in a workbook and lets you switch between sheets; sheet tabs are located below the worksheet grid.

Shortcut A link that gives you quick access to a particular folder, file, or Web site.

Shortcut menu A menu of common commands for an object that opens when you right-click that object.

Shut Down To completely shut down your computer.

Sidebar A Windows Vista desktop component that displays gadgets.

Single-click *See* Click.

Single-file Web page A Web page that integrates all of the worksheets and graphical elements from a workbook into a single file in the MHTML file format, making it easier to publish to the Web.

Sizing handles Small dots at the corners and edges of a chart, indicating that the chart is selected.

Sleep To save your work, turn off the monitor, then reduce power consumption to all the hardware components in your computer so it appears off; press any key to use your computer again.

Slider A shape you drag to select a setting that falls within a range, such as between Slow and Fast.

SmartArt Predesigned diagram types for the following types of data: List, Process, Cycle, Hierarchy, Relationship, Matrix, and Pyramid.

Sort To change the order of records in a table according to one or more fields, such as Last Name.

Sort keys Criteria on which a sort, or a reordering of data, is based.

Source program In a data exchange, the program used to create the data you are embedding or linking.

Spin box A text box with up and down arrows; you can type a setting in the text box or click the arrows to increase or a decrease the setting.

Start button The button on the left side of the taskbar that opens the Start menu to start programs, find and open files, access Windows Help and Support, and more.

Stated conditions In a logical formula, criteria you create.

Statement In Visual Basic, a line of code.

Status bar (Windows) A horizontal bar at the bottom of a window that displays simple Help information and tips. (Excel) Bar at the bottom of the Excel window that provides information about various keys, commands, and processes.

Structured reference Allows table formulas to refer to table columns by names that are automatically generated when the table is created.

Sub procedure A series of Visual Basic statements that performs an action but does not return a value.

Subfolder A folder within another folder for organizing sets of related files into smaller groups.

Suite A group of programs that are bundled together and share a similar interface, making it easy to transfer skills and program content among them.

Summary function In a PivotTable, a function that determines the type of calculation applied to the PivotTable data, such as SUM or COUNT.

Switch User To lock your user account and display the Welcome screen so another user can log on.

Syntax In the Visual Basic programming language, the formatting rules that must be followed so that the macro will run correctly.

Tab 1) A set of commands on the Ribbon related to a common set of tasks or features. Tabs are further organized into groups of related commands. 2) A sheet within a dialog box that contains a group of related settings.

Table An organized collection of rows and columns of similarly structured data on a worksheet.

Table styles Preset formatting combinations for a table.

Table total row The area at the bottom of a table used for calculations with the data in the table columns.

Tag A word or phrase assigned to a file that reminds you of a file's content.

Target The location that a hyperlink displays after you click it.

Target cell In what-if analysis (specifically, in Excel Solver), the cell containing the formula.

Taskbar The horizontal bar at the bottom of the desktop; displays the Start button, the Quick Launch toolbar, and the Notification area.

Template A file whose content or formatting serves as the basis for a new workbook; Excel template files have the file extension .xltx.

Terabyte (TB or T) One trillion bytes (or one thousand gigabytes).

Text annotations Labels added to a chart to draw attention to a particular area.

Text box A box in which you type text.

Text concatenation operators Mathematical calculations that join strings of text in different cells.

Themes Predesigned combinations of colors, fonts, and formatting attributes you can apply to a document in any Office program.

Thumbnail A smaller image of the actual contents of a file.

Tick marks Notations of a scale of measure on a chart axis.

Tiled Repeated, like a graphic in a worksheet background.

Title bar Area at the top of every program window that displays the document and program name.

Title bar The top border of a window that displays the name of the window, folder, or file and the program name.

Toggle A button with two settings, on and off.

Toolbar A set of buttons you can click to open menus or select common commands that are also available from a menu bar, such as saving and printing.

ToolTip A label that appears and identifies the purpose of an object when you point to it.

Touch pointer A pointer on the screen for performing pointing operations with a finger if touch input is available on your computer.

Tracers In Excel worksheet auditing, arrows that point from cells that might have caused an error to the active cell containing an error.

Track To identify and keep a record of who makes which changes to a workbook.

Translucency The transparency feature of Windows Aero that enable you to locate content by seeing through one window to the next window.

Trendline A series of data points on a line that shows data values that represent the general direction in a series of data.

Two-input data table A range of cells that shows resulting values when two input values in a formula are changed.

USB flash drive (also called a pen drive, jump drive, keychain drive, and thumb drive) A popular, removable storage device for folders and files that provides ease of use and portability.

User interface A collective term for all the ways you interact with a software program.

Validate A process in which an xml schema makes sure the xml data follows the rules outlined in the schema.

Validation *See* Data Validation.

Value axis In a chart, vertical axis that contains numerical values; in a 2-dimensional chart, also known as the y-axis.

Values Numbers, formulas, and functions used in calculations.

Variable In the Visual Basic programming language, an area in memory in which you can temporarily store an item of information; variables are often declared in Dim statements such as *DimNameAsString*. In an Excel scenario or what-if analysis, a changing input value, such as price or interest rate, that affects a calculated result.

View A set of display or print settings that you can name and save for access at another time. You can save multiple views of a worksheet.

Views Display settings that show or hide selected elements of a document in the document window, to make it easier to focus on a certain task, such as formatting or reading text.

Virus Destructive software that can damage your computer files.

Visual Basic Editor A program that lets you display and edit macro code.

Visual Basic for Applications (VBA) A programming language used to create macros in Excel.

Wallpaper The image that fills the desktop background.

Watermark A translucent background design on a worksheet that is displayed when the worksheet is printed. Watermarks are graphic files that are inserted into the document header. Worksheet backgrounds created with the Background button on the Page Layout tab do not print.

Web query An Excel feature that lets you obtain data from a Web, Internet, or intranet site and places it in an Excel workbook for analysis.

Welcome screen An initial startup screen that displays icons for each user account on the computer.

What-if analysis A decision-making tool in which data is changed and formulas are recalculated in order to predict various possible outcomes.

Wildcard A special symbol that substitutes for unknown characters in defining search criteria in the Find and Replace dialog box. The most common types of wildcards are the question mark (?), which stands for any single character, and the asterisk (*), which represents any group of characters.

Window A rectangular-shaped work area that displays a program or file, folders and files, or Windows tools.

Windows *See* Microsoft Windows Vista.

Windows 3-D Flip A Windows Aero feature that allows you to display stacked windows at a three-dimensional angle to see even more of the content of all open windows and select the window you want to use.

Windows Aero A Windows Vista feature supported in some editions (or versions) of Windows Vista that enhances the transparency (or translucency) of the Start menu, taskbar, windows, and dialog boxes; enables live taskbar thumbnails, Windows Flip, and Windows 3-D Flip.

Windows Flip A Windows Aero feature that allows you to display a set of thumbnails, or miniature images, of all open windows so that you can select and switch to another window.

WordArt Specially formatted text, created using the WordArt button on the Drawing toolbar.

Workbook A collection of related worksheets contained within a single file.

Worksheet A single sheet within a workbook file; also, the entire area within an electronic spreadsheet that contains a grid of columns and rows.

Worksheet window An area of the program window that displays part of the current worksheet; the worksheet window displays only a small fraction of the worksheet, which can contain a total of 1,048,576 rows and 16,384 columns.

Workspace An Excel file with an .xlw extension containing information about the identity, view, and placement of a set of open workbooks. Instead of opening each workbook individually, you can open the workspace file instead.

X-axis The horizontal axis in a chart; because it often shows data categories, such as months, it is also called the category axis.

XML (Extensible Markup Language) A system for defining languages using tags to structure data.

Y-axis The vertical axis in a chart; because it often shows numerical values in a 2-dimensional chart, it is also called the value axis.

Z-axis The third axis in a true 3-D chart, lets you compare data points across both categories and values.

Zooming in A feature that makes a document appear bigger but shows less of it on screen at once; does not affect actual document size.

Zooming out A feature that shows more of a document on screen at once but at a reduced size; does not affect actual document size.

Index